T0306329

Zanskar to Ziro

No Stilettos in the Himalayas

Zanskar to Ziro

No Stilettos in the Himalayas

SOHINI SEN

NIYOGI
BOOKS

Published by
NIYOGI BOOKS
Block D, Building No. 77,
Okhla Industrial Area, Phase-I,
New Delhi-110 020, INDIA
Tel: 91-11-26816301, 26818960
Email: niyogibooks@gmail.com
Website: www.niyogibooksindia.com

Text © Sohini Sen
Photographs © Sohini Sen

Editor: Gita Rajan
Design: Sohini Sen, Shashi Bhushan Prasad

ISBN: 978-93-85285-86-8
Publication: 2017

All rights are reserved. No part of this publication may be reproduced or transmitted in any form or by any means, electronic or mechanical, including photocopying, recording or by any information storage and retrieval system without prior written permission and consent of the Publisher.

Printed at: Niyogi Offset Pvt. Ltd., New Delhi, India

For kindred souls, and our own failing memories

CONTENTS

ACKNOWLEDGEMENTS

My most favourite line in one of my most favourite books is this: 'Piglet noticed that even though he had a Very Small Heart, it could hold a rather large amount of Gratitude.'

It is not often I get to express my gratitude for all you beautiful people in my life: you hardly pause to listen. Now that I finally have your attention, here goes:

Thank you, Rima Dhillon of Chandigarh, even if you did not accept my Facebook request. Without your oxygen cylinder, this book would not be written.

Thank you, Shankar Prajapati of Bhaktapur, Nepal. I regret not saving your mobile number, and I pray you emerged from the earthquake untouched.

Thank you, Ugyen Drukpa (UD, 'as he likes to be called') of Bhutan, for all the religious narratives you tried to transfer to my minuscule headpiece. Thank you, Tashi Wangmo and Ugyen Wangdi, for patiently, painstakingly, balancing that overload with names of all the flowers and trees and birds that UD could not remember.

Thank you, Hamid, Pawan, Dinesh, Omkar, Jeet, Nandu, Tsarap and Tandin, for not dropping us off a cliff: opportunities, you had in plenty, but you chose to be super-efficient drivers and fine gentlemen.

Thank you, Tultul and Bikash Niyogi, for electing to continue your relationship with this author, Mohua Mitra, both for creating and for sustaining my bond with the Niyogis, and Nirmal Kanti Bhattacharjee, for finding the manuscript of this book 'compelling'.

Thank you, Gita Rajan, for your attention to detail and editing finesse.

Thank you, Swati Dasgupta, for all the home food and clean towels every time we halted at New Delhi, your bedroom that we took over, and all the 'chauffeuring'. It pays to have capable and caring cousins, despite the early bedtime.

Thank you, dad—how I wish you could read this—for walking a toddler gently, yet persuasively, into the world of books. Thank you, Professor Rajeshwari C. Patel, for expanding that world with your library and love.

And thank you, Sumita Rakshit, for being you.

Pp 6-7: 'Life is like a blanket of snow. Be careful how you step on it. Every step will show': Peaks of Suru Valley

Pg 8: 'To see a world in a grain of sand and heaven in a wild flower': At Landour

PROLOGUE

We could always go back. At least that is what we tell ourselves. Do the places we have not done yet. Walk around Mount Kailash, Manasarovar. Pause a while on Kala Patthar to gaze at Mount Everest, the highest peak in the world.

If the cash does not last—I am most certain it will not—we could go back to stay forever. At the cold yet sunny Dar Kot village maybe, its deserted 100-year-old houses still proudly bearing exquisite wood carvings on their door frames. Rent ourselves a small cottage. Grow our own vegetables. Take turns about going uphill every day to the small grocery shop for bread. Take turns, for the winding steps past the Ram Leela grounds and the little temple complex are steep and many, and our knees rusted.

While waiting at the grocer's, one could sit on the rickety bench by the road to look at the snow-blown Panchachuli Range against the blue sky. Have a cup of tea, its local infusions causing a sharp sting in the throat and then clearing the inevitable phlegm. Return then to the cottage, to a comfortable routine of shared household chores. There would be an afternoon of reading together, an evening filled with a magical sunset, finally an early night under a star-spangled sky. Watched over by our love.

For that is what it has been: A late-in-life love affair with a ruggedly handsome, temperamental young man. It helped that my friend Sumita and I fell in love with the same man. In the last 10 years or more, we have trailed him doggedly. Not on Facebook or

'I saw the sunset forty-four times': The mantle of dusk falls over Tawang

Twitter, but in the open, in and out of the northern edges of this country. From the Zanskar Valley in Ladakh through Himachal Pradesh, Uttarakhand, Nepal, Sikkim, Bengal and Bhutan to Ziro in Arunachal Pradesh.

He has been indifferent, unaware of our existence even. Born of the tumultuous union of two vast land masses, and one of the youngest of his kind in the world, he is violent at times, unpredictable always.

He is the Himalayas.

As a two-women team, travelling to remote towns and villages for a glimpse of his vastness has come with some difficulties:

> The tremendous online and offline research on a place so that its real essence would be revealed to us.
>
> The searches for women-friendly accommodations—clean bed sheet and clean washroom being the only keywords. We did not always get both.

Chauvinism and sexual harassment—issues we either ignored, or dealt with very firmly. To blend in, we always wore androgynous attire, both for convenience as well as not to draw attention to our femininity. It was sometimes the only option. A search among the online retail stores for women's high-altitude apparel would lend substance to my statement. Wearing unisex clothes once led to the theft—and thankfully, subsequent recovery—of one of Sumita's new polo-neck T-shirts. More of that in the right place.

The inability to get off the car and mark our territory just about anywhere on the long, winding mountain trails. It did not help to watch male tourists get off together from the shared taxi driving just ahead of us and line the road; especially when we had ourselves been in our car for seven hours or more. There is some truth in 'auto suggestion', after all.

Illness—one of us falling ill made the other feel completely helpless and vulnerable. Our first aid kit grew bulkier with the experience from every trip. Altitude issues? Pack Diamox next time. Breathlessness? Decdan. It helps when your doctors themselves love travelling. Anecdotes are shared with the prescriptions, and my favourite is the one where the eminent cardiologist in a team of travelling physicians was the first one down with Acute Mountain Sickness. But I digress.

Ironically, just the one time we did not carry a portable oxygen cylinder I had a desperate need for it. Almost paid with my life there.

We needed, of course, to ensure safety. For mountaineers, Sherpas are a lifeline. For us, our rented cars and their drivers had to play that role. Two ladies on an unknown, solitary road with one unknown male driver, which is what most of our journeys to the mountains have been. Any of the drivers—locals—could have picked up a friend on the way, and we would have lost the 2:1 advantage and God knew what else with it. This is

> where we have been extremely lucky to have gentlemen in the driving seat.
>
> Barring one.
>
> Ever since we read the news about the staff of a five-star resort prising a room latch loose during the day and returning to rape its inmate in the dead of night, we checked every screw fastening every latch on our hotel windows and doors. With diligence. Every night before retiring. No matter if it were the same room we had slept in the previous night. Together, Sumita and I have pushed the heaviest chair or sofa available against the door, and if it was not heavy enough, placed one of our loaded duffel bags on it. As a final measure, we would unpack my sturdy tripod—fondly named Tipu—and place it beside the bed.
>
> I harbour serious doubts whether Sumita would, given the situation, have the reflexes to pick the tripod up, let alone wield it against the intruder. She has the same, if more serious, doubts. But intruders there have been none.

Over 10 years and a minimum of 10,000 kilometres across the Himalayas alone, we have not tried to achieve any greatness, set records. Like the many insignificant, gurgling rivulets on our way, we have merely gone where the heart led us. Our journeys did not join all the high-altitude dots on the Himalayas. Nevertheless, they offered us the big picture.

Here's the thing: since we have survived, we just might be reckoned carefree, adventurous souls. If anything happened to us—there was no dearth of possibilities—we would be summarily dismissed in social conversations as foolhardy women who had it coming.

Sobering thought, that.

I remember a line from Du Maurier's *Monte Verità:* '...in the mountains we come closest to whatever Being it is that rules our destiny.' For people who live among the Himalayan ranges, religion is not a dogma but an urge to define, to limit, and perhaps only thus understand, the overwhelming powers of nature. Faced with the same impassable might of the elements and often the absolute uncertainty of their expression, we found it easy to be credulous, to accept that Guru Padmasambhava and Shiva—both, interestingly, trident-bearing and clad in tiger skin—had walked on the Himalayas; that the sunset-red peaks of the Panchachuli Range were the clay ovens the Pandavas had cooked their last meal on; or that numerous gods of Animism surrounded us in the garb of trees or boulders.

As the ranges revealed themselves and their people, we were often brought down to our knees by the sheer, almost painful beauty and simplicity of it all.

To be honest, by exhaustion, too.

Our souls loved the ascent, but the bodies fought hard to keep up. We have been frightfully cold, seriously unwell, or just plain, awfully dehydrated and hungry. But every time we retired to the plains to lick our wounds, we realised how happy we had been up there.

As Ibn Battutah said, travelling leaves you speechless, then turns you into a storyteller. Thus, this story: our story, now inexorably intertwined with the fine, silken threads of all that we have read, and the coarse, yak hair strands of a colourful oral narrative that has always belonged to the mountains, and is—like the mountains—growing, changing, alive.

JAMMU AND KASHMIR

SURU VALLEY

Looking up along the sheer, barren cliff faces, the traveller may find nothing.

On a mist-laden dawn, grey clouds loom over the towering crests and then gently dissolve in the crude, rocky chalices between them, softening the rugged contours with light, glacial snow. But for the call of *chungkas*—the red-billed choughs circling over the peaks—and the gushing Suru River flowing thousands of feet below, the ranges are silent, inviolate.

It is only when the late morning sunlight falls directly on the peaks, turning them to coral, that a keen eye may discover the few specks of white canvas on almost every summit, and the occasional orange-green flutter of a flag. There is no road embracing those ranges, yet something labours up the steep rock face: a caravan of packhorses with provisions from the war-ridden Indian villages of Hunderman and Brok.

For they stay up there—*'Hearts with one purpose alone/Through summer and winter'*—young men in fatigues living out of hidden bunkers and tents in often sub-zero temperatures and rarefied air, to protect an invisible line between two restive nations: India, Pakistan.

This is the Line of Control: LoC, Kargil.

Pp 16-17: 'Forget not that the earth delights to feel your bare feet and the winds long to play with your hair': Suru Valley spreads out before the Thungos Massif

Facing page: 'Let there be no purpose in friendship save the deepening of the spirit': By the shores of Tso Moriri

Here, in Kargil and Drass, Operation Vijay, the Indo-Pak war of 1999, has defined the forbidding Himalayan peaks not by their altitude, but by the battles fought over their recapture, the blood shed. Rhino Horn, Batra Top, Tiger Hill, Tololing: the names had rolled off proudly, dramatically, from the lips of young Kuber Singh of the Kumaon Regiment at the Kargil War Memorial, Drass, even as he pointed at the peaks behind him with a stiff, outstretched arm.

'Almost no one had heard of Kargil before the war,' says Gulzar, our local driver from Kumbuthang village. 'During the recapture, villagers helped the Indian soldiers find their way up the hills. My father was one of them. The Army has done a lot for us in return.' There are border allowances for people who live close to the LoC, special privileges for those who helped the Indian Army, free education for their children at the Army schools.

It is not a happy place, the LoC, though the Pakistani villages on the other mountain range are identical to Hunderman or Brok—down to the tall, light green poplars that surround the deep green-and-silver domes of mosques—and on good days, Pakistani soldiers may even be spotted at an impromptu game of cricket. A signboard on the road to Hunderman warns the visitor of landmines on its neighbouring slopes. Among the mud-brick village houses nestling below the road, there are the desolate remains of bunkers, and the rock face bears the marks of heavy shelling.

'India did not give up its claim on just this one mountain range, and the separatists are demanding all of Kashmir... what stupidity,' remarks Gulzar.

Large stretches of the state have been under curfew for more than two months now. The butchering of Indian soldiers in the Pakistan-orchestrated attack at Uri, near Srinagar, is just days away.

Rivers do not respect lines of control. We watch the green Suru River cross the LoC with ease and flow into Pakistan. Tomorrow, driving down the Kargil-Zanskar road that cuts through the Great Himalayan and the Zanskar ranges, we will trace Suru to its origin, the Penzella glacier.

It is a smooth drive at first, on a tar road that runs parallel to: the bubbling Suru River; rows of tall green poplars that stand not in one another's shadow; stunted, yellow-leaved willows punctuated by sweet briar hedges loaded with red fruit; the lush, almost luminescent, green fields of model village Trespone; and the ancient rock etchings of Buddha and his female attendants lying forgotten by the roadside at Lankarchey.

It has snowed just before this visit to Ladakh, our second in four Ladakhi summers, and there is an abundance of white peaks and glaciers in the cornflower-blue horizon. The Tip-top glacier shows up first, its snow melting into slender, silver threads of water that satiate Kumbuthang and its Army cantonment. An hour later, snow-covered twin peaks Nun (23,410 ft) and Kun (23,250 ft)—separated by a four-kilometre-long white plateau—and the Pinnacle Peak (22,810 ft) present themselves, towering over a widening river where men fish with light blue nets.

The road has now turned into a boulder-laden track, slowing our pace. Atop the hills, wild horses silhouetted against the azure sky raise their noses from the grass with an elegant turn of their cream and brown necks. They look down at our car: incurious, unafraid.

We halt near Parkachik village, just where the Suru separates the road from the Shafat glacier: a large yet disappointing, frothy coal-grey mass with just a hint of ice-blue at the edges. The sun is directly overhead. Gulzar suggests a lunch break.

'Is there a washroom somewhere?' I ask.

'No, Madam*ji*. No washrooms.'

A white wagtail hops ahead of us as we walk off the dirt road and over small boulders to one of the couple of tea-shacks for lunch. Gulzar lays a palm on Sumita's back for some seconds. It seems a casual touch: probably to caution her about the boulders. So we think.

The signboard on the shack reads:

'Jaffaria
Hotel & T. Stall
Available Dall Chawal, Sabzi Chawal, Omlate
Rooti, Maggi, Nimkeen & Laptain Tea'

A short, bearded man, presumably Jaffaria himself, offers a meal of black beans 'dall', rice and 'omlate'. We drag the faded red plastic chairs and the equally faded table into a narrow patch of shade outside the dingy, one-room shack and wait for lunch, even as a brood of white hens speedily peck at theirs behind the mud walls.

Our fare is simple, edible. While we eat, a magpie watches us a while, then glides down to the river, its cerulean wings gleaming in the sun.

One of the hens suddenly lets out a screech. Gulzar has the hen by the neck, which he is about to wring.

'Hey, why are you doing that?' I exclaim.

'He has asked me to kill it,' he replies, pointing to the shack-owner. 'They want it for their lunch.'

'Can't the killing wait until after we have eaten?' I try to keep my voice reasonably normal.

'*Kyun*?' Gulzar expresses genuine surprise.

'Let us finish lunch first,' I insist. He puts the hen down, his face falling.

The Suru leads us along its valley, to majestic views of snow-loaded peaks often prosaically named after their altitude. A jagged Peak 5780m jostles the taller Peak 6495m and its Rungofarka glacier. Lingsarmo right next to them—wider, and despite its softer contour the tallest at 6955 m or 22,818 ft—has its own glacier, too.

Rungofarka and Lingsarmo were two of the 104 peaks along the Line of Actual Control (LAC) and Line of Control (LoC) that the Indian government had opened up for expeditions in 2010, as part of a confidence-building measure that would spell normalcy in Jammu and Kashmir.

A faded-white chorten at a turn marks our transition from the Muslim to the Buddhist segment of Kargil district. Among the boulders by the roadside, black redstarts fly in short laps—too many to count, and too swift to photograph—their fist-sized, orange-black bodies blending perfectly with the low, wild bushes that cover the valley floor in autumn shades of deep orange and scarlet.

Autumn has preceded us here in the valley with a palette of sunset hues: while the mountain peaks are laden with fresh snow, the Aconogonum tortuosum streaks the lower slopes with a bright, powdery orange, the meadow bistort is sending up tiny spikes that are a deep shade of maroon, and among the riotous orange and red bushes walks a lone, ebony-black horse. The Suru is blue, taking its colour from the clear blue sky, and sheep grazing by it are a pale brown, just the colour of the boulders.

This is the Gulmatungo region. Or, a painting by Monet.

Startled by our car, a *phia,* the long-tailed marmot, jumps into a hollow on our left. To our right, and some distance away, a couple more marmots snuggle close to each other in the tall grass, then together raise their heads to watch the road.

Gulzar hits the brake suddenly. Shaken by the jolt, we look ahead. A rivulet is rushing across the road to join the Suru.

We are close to Rangdum village, at an altitude of 12,000 ft.

Rangdum Monastery, founded in 1783, sits on a knoll overlooking an amphitheatre-shaped valley enclosed by tall, striated ranges. Rushing into the valley through the gaps between the peaks, a strong wind eddies over four thin rivulets, throwing the white wagtails and the black redstarts off balance every time they take wing. Guided by the shepherd's tuneless, staccato whistle that travels across the plains, straggling sheep leap and stumble over the moraines to join the flock. Donkeys graze among ordered rows of short, gold-leaved willow trees. But for the willows, the grey, moraine-covered land is as barren as the mountains.

The Nun Kun Deluxe Camp is a cluster of 20 tents squatting at the base of the Rangdum Monastery. But we need to go through an Indian Army check post first.

The jawans halt our car.

'Who are these foreigners?' they ask Gulzar.

'They are Indians,' he replies.

One of the soldiers peers into the car, stares at me a while. 'Passport,' he demands curtly.

'The Eskimo has fifty names for snow because it is important to them':
Peak 5780m, Peak 6495m with its Rungofarka Glacier, and Lingsarmo, Suru Valley

'We are from Kolkata, bhai!' I reply in Hindi. He is convinced by the vernacular. We are allowed to pass.

'Somewhere among these ranges is a shortcut trek route to Srinagar,' Gulzar tells us. 'A few years ago, terrorists had come in by one such route, and butchered three lamas at the Rangdum Monastery. The check post was set up after that.'

I would later read the *Frontline*'s online report of the incident. On a summer night in July 2000, monks of Rangdum Monastery were woken by the urgent honking of a truck. Young lamas Tashi Motup, Zoolpa Stanzin, Lama Kunchok and Stanzin Tsering thought that the truck driver could be lost, or unwell. When they stepped out to check, Motup, Stanzin and Kunchok were shredded by over 30 rounds fired from an automatic rifle. Tsering managed to dive into a stream, and hid in it to save his life.

Nazir Ahmed, the driver of the hijacked truck, was a resident of Srinagar. He would later inform the police, and report that the killers spoke in a language that sounded like the Gujjar dialect, with a strong Punjabi intonation. After the massacre, they forced Ahmed to drive them close to Panikhar village, and disappeared in a sheep farm.

We are the first to arrive at the Nun Kun Deluxe Camp this evening, and get to select our tent. The sun goes down, and with the twilight, the mountains turn dull, forbidding. The wind is freezing. The walk to the dining tent for a hot cup of tea is only slightly uphill, and I find myself straining hard to breathe. It is not normal.

As we near the dining tent, a lady wishes us a good evening. Mrs Rima Dhillon from Chandigarh is with a bird-watchers' group that has just driven in, and will spend the night in the tents.

We introduce ourselves.

'My friend is a little unwell,' Sumita shares with Mrs Dhillon, 'she has a shortness of breath.'

'Please let us know if you need anything,' Mrs Dhillon says instantly, 'we have medicines, blood pressure measuring equipment, oxygen cylinders, the works.'

'Thank you, I will,' Sumita replies.

We walk back to our tent. There are no lights yet. The generator will be turned on at 7:00 pm, just for three hours.

When the lone CFL comes on in the tent post seven, I trudge uphill again to the staff annexe—the only concrete building, one-storeyed and with a green sloping roof—to charge my camera battery. I find a multi-plug electrical outlet, and push in the charger.

The battery has been overworked all day. Recharge will take hours.

Dinner is served at 7:30 pm, and we climb back to the dining tent. I have no appetite. As I tinker with my bowl of soup, the birdwatchers keep up a merry conversation. They are joined by Stephen, a young Information Technology (IT) professional from Germany.

'I had asked for six months of leave,' says Stephen, busy spooning up the Indian food he loves so much. 'I was given two. But I am okay with that.'

'I have never understood much about Information Technology,' says Rima.

'It is a profession where you would want a six-month sabbatical every six months,' I say. 'Trust me, we've been there.' She laughs.

There are cherries for dessert. 'Cherries are good for acclimatisation at high altitudes,' says one of the gentlemen, 'but freshly picked, not like these they have just poured out of a can.' I have some, anyway.

Mobile phones are dead, and there is, of course, no intercom. For everything, we walk. Need warm water for drinking? Carry the steel jug to the staff annexe. Wish to visit the washroom? Walk in the opposite direction, down the entire row of tents to the cluster of outdoor toilets. Has the battery been recharged fully? Walk uphill to the staff annexe, check and collect.

By 9:00 pm—despite the regular prophylactic dose of Diamox we have been taking for three days now—I have extreme difficulty breathing. I am nauseous, irritable. Talking is an immense effort. The normally snug woollen cap on my head feels tight as a noose.

I know this to be an attack of cerebral oedema, a manifestation of Acute Mountain Sickness, or AMS.

'Autumn is a second spring when every leaf is a flower': Suru Valley

To confirm, I try to walk on an imagined straight line: right heel before my left big toe, then left heel before the right big toe. Each foot should point forward while I walk.

It is a fairly simple task, but one that I find immensely difficult to achieve this night. Sumita watches me from the flapping door of our tent, anxious. For her sake, I keep my face straight.

I have, as the 'tandem gait' test has just shown, seriously impaired coordination. I need to travel down to a lower altitude.

We are seven hours away from Kargil, and the road we have just travelled is so bad that a return journey is quite impossible tonight.

It is a beautiful night. A brilliant moon and numerous rings of large, glistening stars hang low in the cloudless sky. The valley below is bathed with radiance, rivulets shine like silver yarn. It is a night of time-lapse photography, of sitting outside the tent on the low, folding canvas seats in silence and harmony.

I sit huddled inside the tent instead. 'Your eyes seemed larger,' Sumita would tell me later, 'and shining. You spoke and behaved differently. I did not know you then.'

Sumita goes in search of Rima Dhillon. Rima walks up to our tent door with an oxygen cylinder, which we accept. 'Do you wish to check your friend's BP?' the gentleman with Rima asks Sumita. 'I could give you the blood pressure measuring instrument right now.'

'I don't think I will need that yet,' I call out to him.

'Could you please show me your tents?' Sumita requests Rima. 'Just in case there's an emergency in the night...'

'Sure,' the birdwatchers say, 'don't hesitate to call us.'

It is past 10:00 pm, and the lone light in the tent goes off with the generator. The moon has gone behind the mountain. There is not even a pinhead of light in the entire valley. Sumita and I lie on wooden cots not two feet away from each other, yet we cannot see a thing.

'I think I will use the oxygen,' I tell her after a while.

In the light of her head torch, I prise open the seal of the portable oxygen cylinder with a key. Inhale. It is meant to contain 10 litres of the life-saving gas, but finishes with as many deep breaths.

We go back to bed. I can talk only in laboured monosyllables, and Sumita fights the urge to keep asking me if I feel better.

My head still hurts. The rock-hard pillow makes it worse. I sleep a little, fitfully. Sumita stays awake all night, thinking, 'Will I get up in the morning, and find her dead? Is this how it ends?'

It is our longest night.

The first light of dawn has never been so welcome. I feel almost normal. Braving the intense cold, Sumita begins a vigil outside our tent: the birdwatchers would leave at 6:00 am, and she would like to buy a second oxygen cylinder from them before that.

Rima Dhillon unhesitatingly hands her a second cylinder, but would not hear of payment.

'How are you?' she asks me.

'Alive and kicking, thanks to you,' I smile.

'God works in mysterious ways,' is all she says.

I am able to eat some breakfast. While we wait for Gulzar to arrive with the car, I perch on a low seat outside the tent. The sun on my face feels good. White wagtails and black redstarts flitter around the cream canvas tents, at times trotting close to my feet.

Sumita watches me watching the birds. 'Don't you wish to take photographs?'

It seems an effort to go into the tent, get my camera. 'I think I will just look at them,' I reply.

'Zanskar Valley is more remote than Suru Valley,' Sumita says, 'do you feel up to the journey?'

It is a tough decision, and probably a reckless one.

It's a go.

ZANSKAR VALLEY

This is no road, this dull grey, moraine-strewn, undulating track that at regular intervals is interrupted by narrow, gushing rivulets born of glacial melt.

This is the only road into Zanskar River Valley.

Gulzar straightens his stiff back, then leans forward and places his skinny elbows on the steering wheel. '*Shukar karo,* weather *toh achchha hain,*' he says, '*Khuda na khasta baarish aa jaati toh sab patthar raaste ke upar hotey.*'

He is a driver who knows this road, and we do believe that a sudden shower would wash down more moraines and mud onto the road, render even this slow, noisy, shuddering progress impossible. What with the merciless, nose-clogging, camera-ruining sheets of red dust rising on either side of us and rushing in through every infinitesimal gap in the Xylo, a few drops of rain could have been welcome, though.

Then there is the scorching heat, making it quite hard to believe that we are at an altitude higher than 10,000 ft, that this is September, and that the pass we just crossed, the prayer-flag draped Pensi La (14,436 ft), would soon be covered in snow and closed for eight odd months. Sumita, sitting behind Gulzar, has her right arm and right cheek turning red. I have the same glorious yet painful complexion on my left side, and Gulzar, bearing the full frontal brunt of the sun, is a gangly red lobster in dark glasses and a green, printed bandana tied over its head.

Gulzar appears concerned about my illness at Rangdum last night. 'Your lips are dry,' he says, staring at them. I appreciate the concern, not the stare.

'I am not well, either,' he continues, 'I have a headache.'

'We have medicines for that,' I tell him. 'Remind me to give you some when we reach Pibiting.'

When the Drang Drung glacier (15,680 ft) from the Zanskar Range on our right travels almost down to the road, it is a welcome distraction and a photo break. A 23-km trail of ice and snow, Drang Drung is probably the largest glacier in Ladakh after the Siachen on the Karakoram Range. Peak 5835m (21,490 ft) seems to rise from it, and the Doda or Stod River, a tributary of the Zanskar River, flows down towards the Zanskar Valley.

'Zanskar River is itself a tributary of the Indus, right?' Sumita asks.

'Yes, and it has two main tributaries,' I tell her. 'The Doda is one. The other is actually formed by two rivers: the Kargyag River, rising near Shingo La, and the Tsarap River, from near Baralacha La.'

On any normal road, these 130-odd kilometres from Rangdum in Suru Valley to Pibiting village in Zanskar Valley should not take us seven hours. On any normal road that takes seven hours to cover, one should find a washroom and a tea-shack. Yes, even on the hills.

The road to Zanskar has nothing.

'Madam*ji*, washroom *jayenge*?' Gulzar asks.

He is not joking. He has spotted some large boulders by the road, and this is his way of asking whether we wish to make use of the privacy they offer.

Soon, there are no boulders, the land on either side of the road almost as barren as the mountains beyond, except for flat, round patches of red buffalo-berry bushes and the occasional fat, long-tailed marmot snoozing among them.

We pass little green and white signboards that mark out the villages—five to seven single-storey mud house clusters that dot the mountain slopes way beyond the road—Akshow, and Chibra; then the sudden verdure of Abran where the only restaurant on this stretch

'I move, therefore I am': The 23-km long Drang Drung Glacier in Suru Valley

used to be, with a white yak ambling off the road and a village toddler waving at our car; Kushul, with a dog standing guard on a shoulder-high boundary wall, and a cow wading with her bleating calf through the rivulet over the road; desolate looking Hamiling and Bakarsey; Skyagam with its Chomo Gompa and the police check post; Remala, Manda, Phey, Rantaksha, Stara, Ubarak and suddenly, the clear blue waters of a lake with a bright-hued statue of Padmasambhava and a white wagtail perching on a smooth rock by its shore.

The sprawling compound of Sani Kani Khar—the Sani Monastery—is close by, with an assortment of chortens and a two-storeyed building that date anywhere between the second and the 17th centuries. The oldest chorten on the grounds is the Kanika Stupa, built by the Kushan Emperor Kanishka in the 2nd century. One of the holiest Buddhist sites of that era, the 20-ft reliquary stands behind the main building, but no markers highlight its significance in the passage of Buddhism.

Warblers play hide-and-seek among wild olive or oleaster trees heavy with pink fruit. It is a job to find the old couple that keeps the keys to the sanctum, and the lady is irritable at this unannounced visit. 'Seems like we interrupted her cooking,' Sumita says in an aside. It is either that or the warm poncho-like shawl she has on in this unbearable heat. It seems a practice with the locals, this wearing of warm clothes like a second skin, no matter how high the day temperatures might be. Gulzar, too, never takes off his full-sleeved pullover.

The famous Indian Buddhist saint Naropa (966-1041 AD) from the Vikramshila University of Bihar is said to have meditated near the Kanika Stupa, and the monastery has witnessed the presence of Guru Padmasambhava for five years. But the very realistic red wooden phallus suspended from the rafters above the main door of the sanctum makes me wonder how the Divine Madman of Bhutan is connected with this ancient monastery.

Time to drive on. An immensely dusty road—made dustier by the iron claws of a hydraulic excavator picking up loads of dry mud from both sides of the path and dumping it onto a truck—leads to the congested village of Padum. I am glad we drive two kilometres further,

'Just as a solid rock is not shaken by the storm, even so the wise are not affected by praise or blame': Buddha rock sculpture, Kargil

through the rows of Padum's nondescript houses to the quieter village of Pibiting, with its traditional houses and the tiny monastery perched on a hillock.

Omasila Hotel is still under construction. Our bathroom door is too big for its frame, the glass panes on the room windows have many secret passages for insects to scurry in after dusk. With golden birches full of warblers outside the said windows and snow-capped peaks rising beyond them, the infrastructure shortcomings are easily ignored.

Zanskar Valley has seen a lot of progress. At dinner, hotel-owner Norbu's father regales visitors with old tales. 'Local people did not even know what a pressure cooker was. Someone had got hold of a cooker, and he put it on the stove. When the cooker started letting off steam, a villager thought there was a spirit inside it. So he took a long pole, stood at a safe distance, and *whack*—smashed the top of the lid!'

These days, most of the children go to school, he says. 'Education is important. Do you know why the people of south Kashmir are doing whatever the separatist leaders are telling them to do? They are uneducated. If I try telling the people of Zanskar to throw stones at vehicles, will they do it? *Never*.'

Zanskar has had its own leaders: kings, really. At 12,879 feet, the village of Zangla, some 37 kilometres from Pibiting, has not one, but two royal palaces. Sonam Tundup Namgyal, the last titular ruler of probably one of the tiniest kingdoms among the Himalayas, died in 1987. His son, Nima Norbu Namgyal, now holds a government position in Leh.

An unpretentious house with a large, tiled courtyard just beyond a row of chortens is where we arrive first, the only tourists this September morning. This is the current residence of the 'royals'.

Gulzar calls out to the women working outside the house, asking for someone to show us around. There is a lot of laughter from the women—we suspect at Gulzar's flawed use of the local language—and after we have waited on the first floor terrace of the house for a while, a young girl comes to take us in to the family sanctum.

She is Stanzin, the grand-daughter of the last ruler. We are fortunate to find her at Zangla, for she is doing her graduation in Arts at Leh. Stanzin shows us a photograph of her father and grandfather, a golden Buddha statue with blue curls and serene, blue eyes—'His Holiness the Dalai Lama gave it to my father'—and a rare photograph of Pandit Jawaharlal Nehru with Kushok Bakula Rinpoche. Lama Rinpoche was considered the reincarnation of Arhat Bakula, one of the 16 Great Arhats who were the direct disciples of the Buddha.

During a visit to Ladakh in the summer of 1949, Nehru had requested the young lama to join politics. In 50 years of public life, Kushok Bakula Rinpoche worked towards the welfare of Ladakhis and strove to bring Ladakh closer to the rest of India despite the complex political environment. It is said that through traders and pilgrims, Lama Rinpoche had come to know about the massive build-up of Chinese troops in Western Tibet in the April of 1962, and he was the one who informed Nehru of the impending attack on Ladakh.

'Why do you have two palaces?' I ask Stanzin.

'This small one is where they would bring my grandfather during an attack, for his safety,' she says. 'The one you see there on the hill top was the actual palace.'

She hands out three small steel keys knotted to a grimy piece of cloth: 'the keys to a palace'. Gulzar takes them from her and passes them on to me. His fingers brush mine. I am not sure the touch is accidental.

A hot and tiring climb up some 200 steps from the valley floor takes us to the palace ruins. The keys open the main door, and a small sanctum.

Ancient *thangka*s stiff with age and crumbling like parchment hang from the mud walls of the sanctum. Several flat stones propped in a corner bear intricately etched and painted images of the Buddha, and Goddess Tara: the colours are faded, the figures barely distinguishable. At the base of three wooden chortens almost completely bereft of their carvings are some exotic flowers sculpted out of peach-hued, fist-sized chunks of semi-precious stone.

In one of the rooms in this mud-brick building that offers fascinating views of the Zanskar River and its entire valley far below, Hungarian scholar Alexander (Sándor) Csoma de Kőrös had compiled the first Western dictionary of the Tibetan language in 1823. A framed pencilled sketch of the scholar sits in a corner of the low-ceilinged room, the single square window lighting up an austere face.

Here, on the most barren reaches of the Himalayas, austerity and hardships are a part of life. Some times, a sip of rice wine might see one through.

Stongde Monastery, founded by Tibetan lama Marpa Lotsava in 1052 AD, is the second largest monastic establishment of the Zanskar

'Sow seeds with tenderness and reap the harvest with joy': Fields of Stongde village

Valley. When we huff and puff up the stairs of the red-white building, the sanctum is locked. Gulzar, the one-member search party, ferrets out the lama with the keys from a nook.

The lama smells strongly of rice wine, but is quite sober. He takes us patiently through the Gon-khang, a temple dedicated to the guardian deities of Buddhism. Points out paintings of the deities on the dimly-lit walls. 'These were done with gold dust blended in water,' he says. Intricate outlines shine through the grime of centuries.

Outside the monastery gates, slender white birches sway in the wind, and the afternoon sun shimmers through their golden leaves. A translucent half moon kisses the top of the stark promontory towering over Stongde.

Stark is often spectacular. The Bardan Monastery we drive to the next day is a 17th century structure atop a gigantic outcrop that rises from the Zanskar River's shores 11 kilometres from Padum. The first, and the best, view of the monastery is from the dirt road where the only other traffic is a batch of packhorses.

The young lama we meet inside is surprisingly well-conversant in English. He shows us ancient wall paintings of the Circle of Life, 'the best-preserved ones in the entire valley'; the sombrero-like hat used for the religious dances, and offers us a flask of butter tea before disappearing into a recess to complete his morning prayers.

We sit a while on the courtyard, near a large prayer wheel and a niche full of ancient etchings on stone. Steam rises in slow loops from our mugs of golden, creamy-textured butter tea. Rhythmic drumbeats roll out from the recess. Brightly coloured prayer flags flutter above the sunny patio.

It feels good to live in this moment. It feels good to be alive.

A cluster of lively young monks in red robes throng the large, central courtyard of Karsha Monastery. The youngest of them, in a traditional hat with turned-up corners that is too big for his four-year-old head, runs along the very low white courtyard wall, dragging the red plastic car clutched in his little fist over its flat, wide surface.

With white-washed buildings scrambling half-way up a rust-coloured rock face in an intricate labyrinth of monks' quarters and prayer halls, Karsha is Zanskar's largest monastery, and one of its most ancient. Even though it dates back to the 10th century, the monastery came into prominence only around the 15th.

The concrete staircase to the monastery's prayer hall is long and winding. A senior lama hurries down the steps.

'Are the sanctums open?' we ask him.

'Climb slowly,' he says, 'I will send someone up with the key.'

The sunny terrace leading to the prayer hall offers: a bird's eye view of Karsha village; barley fields forming a green and yellow pattern of squircles on the valley floor; the winding Zanskar River; an unbroken range of snow-topped mountains in the far horizon.

The lama who joins us soon opens the locked prayer hall with its golden statues of the Buddha, Tsong-kha-pa and Padmasambhava, silver chortens, and numerous wooden shelves stashed with holy scripts wrapped in bright silken cloth.

Some of the shelves have awkward empty spaces.

'When the Pakistanis attacked,' the lama tells us, tracing our glance, 'they burnt some of our holy scripts.'

He points to a large silver-plated chorten decorated with semi-precious stones. 'They broke this chorten, too, and took away the stones and the silver. But the body was undamaged.'

'Body? Whose body?'

The chorten has a small glass front with an ornate copper frame. The lama switches on the torch of his mobile phone and throws light on the glass. We now notice the profile of a man seated inside the chorten.

'It is the remains of the founding lama of this monastery,' the lama says. 'When he died, his body was covered in salt and preserved in the seated position. After it was dry, mud was applied on his chest and stomach, further drying it.' He shows us a framed photograph of the corpse. It has the emaciated lama seated in the lotus position: his palms on his lap, his eyes open.

I would read later that this was the mummy of Rinchen Zangpo (958-1055 AD), the 'Great Translator' of tantric texts into Tibetan.

'When the chorten was renovated after the Pakistani attack, the body was taken out,' the lama continues, 'the fingernails were still growing.'

It is long past lunch time, and growing pangs of hunger lead us to Uttarakhand Dhaba in Padum, close to the helipad. The owner is from Kalsi, Uttarakhand, but has lived in Padum for the last two decades.

'Is it true that the helipad has the remains of an Indian Army helicopter?' I ask him.

'Yes, of course,' he says. 'I saw it crash. The blades just came off before landing. No one died. For a week after that, Army pilots flew in every day and took away bits and pieces from it. Just the body stands there now.'

A broken helicopter on a helipad edged by snow-topped mountains: sounds like a good photo opportunity. We walk down to take a look.

The silver shell of the helicopter shines in the dying light of day, 'Indian Air Force' written on it in large black letters. Planning to sit in the cockpit for a photo, I step in.

'Medicine is a science of uncertainty and an art of probability':
Amchi or Tibetan doctor at Padum, Zanskar

Rush out the same instant.

At least a hundred primitive Ladakhis have been there before me. Done *that*. The stink is intense, unsettling.

Primitive is at times interesting. I am curious to know about ancient Tibetan medicine. An *amchi*, a practising Tibetan doctor, lives at the base of the Pibiting Monastery. 'Let's consult him about your headache,' I tell Gulzar.

Under a traditional Tibetan blue silk-and-black wool hat, the *amchi* has a genial face criss-crossed by a thousand wrinkles. He hunkers down on his doorstep, frail knees drawn up close to his chin. We sit around him on flat stones. I make Gulzar act the interpreter.

'Do you make the medicines yourself?'

'I make some from the local herbs and other ingredients. I cannot divulge the names. I also order medicines from Dharamshala, in

Himachal.' He shows me drawstring pouches made of sheepskin, with tiny wooden name tags for the powders they contain. 'These come with a book of instructions.'

The *amchi* feels Gulzar's left wrist for his pulse, listens to his symptoms and wraps two powders in little paper packets. 'Take one spoon of this in the morning, and of that, at 6:00 pm, both with warm water,' he says. His hand shakes a little.

'How old are you?' I ask him.

Gulzar interprets the answer, a little incredulous: 'A hundred years old.'

'Is your son an *amchi*, too? Will he take up the profession after you?'

'No.'

The son arrives right then. He looks sceptically at this impromptu doctor's chamber.

'Check my pulse, too,' I tell the old man on an impulse. I extend my left arm.

'No, not that hand. Show me your right hand,' the *amchi* says.

'He believes men have their heart on the left side of the body, and women have theirs on the right,' the son pipes up in Hindi now. He looks at me for a reaction.

I smile at him in silence, and extend my right wrist to the *amchi*. He feels my pulse, and then says, 'Your pressure is low. You are feeling dizzy, and you have a headache.'

He is right.

The wind howls all night among the birches of Omasila Hotel. Morning dawns cloudy. It is the morning of our return.

A common kestrel sits with its matte pink back to the road as we approach the Drang Drung glacier again. I would like a photograph of Sumita and me with the river of snow.

Sumita sits down on a boulder facing the glacier while I set up the tripod a little behind her, raise the head three feet from the ground. Even as I kneel and fix the camera on it, Gulzar comes to sit precariously on his haunches right next to the tripod, pretending to look through the camera. His face is disturbingly close to mine. There can now be no doubt of his intentions.

I spring up. 'Move away this instant,' I tell him sternly. 'You are in the way.'

He moves away with a look of total incomprehension and hurt. He does the act well.

When the shot is taken and we return to the Xylo, I remember a passage from *Almost Somewhere: Twenty-Eight Days on the John Muir Trail* by Suzanne Roberts:

> *'Women don't enter the wilderness in the same way men do; we constantly return to our physical bodies and the ways in which they could be threatened, not by bears or bugs but by men. Our bodies become a filter between us and the landscape, preventing us from enjoying both.'*

It is time to release the car.

LEH

'Con·flu·ence | noun |: a coming or flowing together, meeting, or gathering at one point.'

On our first visit to Ladakh, we are at Nimmu about 35 kilometres outside of Leh this July morning, resting our elbows on the railing by the smooth tar road. Far below us, blue rafts lie in waiting even as a row of would-be sailors execute their mandatory loosening-up exercises. Bend, touch toes, straighten. Bend again. In their red life-jackets and matching helmets, they look like a regiment of red ants at a food gathering. Beyond them, at the base of huge and barren mountain ranges, the grey-green waters of the Indus meet with the grey Zanskar. Mighty forces converge and flow on together towards the striking blue horizon.

That is what life is too, I reflect. A confluence: of people, possibilities, and timing. Convergences that might bring subtle or forceful changes: in a land, an era, a race. A person.

Leh is a study in such convergence. Of religions: Islam, Buddhism, Hinduism, Christianity, Bon. Of races: Tibetan, Monpa, Dard, Balti. The blending has not always been voluntary; some have been flung together in the cauldron of war.

The mud walls of Zorawar Fort, constructed in 1836, hold the relics of the battles that led to the merger of Ladakh, Baltistan and western parts of Tibet with the Dogra Kingdom of Jammu. Some of the present-day Ladakhis call this merger 'an accident of history'.

It was the regime of Maharajah Ranjit Singh (1780–1839) in Punjab. The Treaty of Amritsar (1809) signed between him and the British—

then occupying the rest of India east of the Sutlej River—meant that the British could not advance into Punjab and the Maharajah could not expand his territory east of the Sutlej. The only direction the Sikh kingdom could be expanded was north of Kashmir and into Ladakh.

Maharajah Ranjit Singh was helped in his conquest of Kashmir by one of his vassal princes: Gulab Singh, the Dogra King of Jammu. In a landmark achievement in Indian military history, General Zorawar Singh, the Wazir of Kishtwar, led Gulab Singh's army into harsh, high-altitude terrains to conquer Ladakh (1834), Baltistan (1840) and parts of western Tibet (1841).

Not all battles are as violent. Gurudwara Shri Pathar Sahib has its own legend of a conquest. Sikh Guru, Nanak Dev, had travelled along Nepal, Sikkim, Tibet and Yarkand to arrive in Leh in 1517. Around this time, a demon was said to live on a mountain some distance from Leh. He used to kill and devour the inhabitants. When Guru Nanak—fondly called Nanak Lama by the locals—heard about the demon, he sat down by a river near the mountain and began to meditate.

From his mountain perch, the demon saw Guru Nanak and rolled down a huge boulder to crush him. But the boulder touched the Guru's body and turned to soft wax.

The demon came down the mountain convinced that the Guru had died. He found Nanak Dev deep in meditation. In his anger, the demon kicked the boulder. His foot sank into the wax. He finally realised the Guru's powers and begged him for forgiveness.

The stone boulder with which the demon is believed to have attacked Guru Nanak occupies the shrine at Gurudwara Shri Pathar Sahib. It has a deep imprint at its centre, said to be that of the Guru's body.

It is no longer wax.

The bustling town of Leh and its outskirts alternately offers us relics of war and peace. The sparkling-white Shanti Stupa built in 1991 by Japanese monks to promote world peace sits on a rocky ridge at Changspa.

It is a steep climb. On the first level of the stupa is a golden Buddha statue with blue curls. The second level holds brightly coloured reliefs that narrate the story of his life. The restaurant adjacent to the stupa offers a hot cup of honey, ginger and lemon tea and a balcony with panoramic views of Leh and beyond. The tea costs 50 rupees a cup, the view is free.

Our stay in Leh is punctuated by trips to Phyang, Nubra Valley, Pangong Tso and Tso Moriri. The day we return to Leh from Phyang, there is bad news on television. Nine explosions have rocked the Bodh Gaya temple complex, a UNESCO World Heritage Site in Bihar. Lord Buddha is said to have attained enlightenment there, under the Mahabodhi tree on the temple premises.

The terrorist attack targeted international Buddhist tourists, a retaliation for the killings of Rohingya Muslims in Myanmar. But it has immediate implications for us: Buddhists in Leh have declared a strike. With its considerable population of Muslims, all of Leh is fraught with tension.

'Don't worry, Ma'am,' assures our travel agent Zakir over the phone. 'Things will be okay tomorrow.'

'Be melting snow. Wash yourself of yourself': Ladakh from the air

We have arrived at our guest house and released the car. We are tired, hungry. The guest house does not serve any food except breakfast. This has not been an issue so far: just as Darjeeling has its Glenary's and Keventer's, Leh boasts of its German Bakery. It has been our favourite food joint until now.

All shops and eateries at the market must be closed this evening. German Bakery might still be open: after all, it caters to international tourists.

Night falls meanwhile, and what we have come to tolerate as a daily nuisance occurs with unfailing punctuality: there is a power cut. All across Leh.

'Oh, great,' I exclaim. 'Now we can't even go out to check if anything at all is open!'

We do have powerful torches, and have regularly gone out to dinner—a 20-minute walk to the market—in pitch darkness. But this night is different.

Hunger always shuts my brain down. Sumita's has a wave.

'Let's ask Dev. I am sure he has at least a pack of noodles.'

Dev, from Himachal Pradesh, is the all-purpose 'boy' at the guest house. During one of our day outings in Leh, he had entered our room with the pretext of cleaning and nicked Sumita's new polo-neck tee.

People living on the hills are remarkably honest as a rule. So Dev had us surprised. We knew he had stolen the T-shirt. Yet we kept telling him to look for it: 'It may have fallen somewhere, gone under the wardrobe (rooted to the floor) or the bed (the 'box' kind, so close to the floor that even a sheet of paper would not go under it).'

We knew he knew that we knew he had it. The nagging helped. Two days later, we did find the tee neatly folded and placed back in the wardrobe. Right where we had seen it last. Nothing more was said.

But tonight, Dev does have noodles. There is just a single pack of Maggi, though. He is willing to cook it for us, even add some volume with chopped coriander leaves.

He serves it hot. Being Librans, Sumita and I separate the 70 gms worth of noodle strands absolutely equally.

I have never loved coriander flavour more.

We go to bed early. It is a cold, dark night, and will seem darker and endless once the noodles are digested. Best be asleep.

Things are back to normal the next morning. At regular intervals through the day, Indian Army helicopters fly over the immaculate snow-wrapped Stok Kangri Range, circling against the deep azure sky with their customary drone. That is normal. Ladakh's proximity to India's muscle-flexing neighbours ensures a heavy presence of the Indian Army all through the year.

The Hall of Fame, set up by the Indian Army XIV Corps serves both as a museum showcasing local culture and a war memorial. The walls are filled with photo frames: the faces frozen in time are young. Like at the war memorial of Drass, large boards highlight the recapturing of strategic, high-altitude posts during the Kargil war.

One board stands out. It has a copy of Captain Vijyant Thapar's last letter home. Written on a blue inland letter form, and addressed simply 'To my family', it reads:

> *'Dearest Papa, Mama, Birdie and Granny,*
>
> *'1. By the time you get this letter, I'll be observing you all from the sky enjoying the hospitality of the Apsaras.*
>
> *'2. I have no regrets, in fact even if I become a human again, I'll join the Army and fight for my nation.*
>
> *'3. If you can, please come and see where the Indian Army fought for your tomorrow.... '*
>
> *'5. Whatever organ can be taken, should be done.... Papa you should feel proud, Mama so should you, meet* <name erased> *(I loved her)...*
>
> *'OK then it's time for me to join my clan of the Dirty Dozen. My aslt party has 12 chaps.*
>
> *'Best of Luck to you all.*
>
> *'Live Life King Size.*
>
> *'Yours*
>
> *'Robin.'*

Captain Thapar received the Vir Chakra. Posthumously. The Vir Chakra citation describes his act of valour:

> *'On 28 June 1999 Captain Vijyant Thapar was commanding the leading platoon of Alfa Company, which was tasked to assault area Knoll in Drass Sector from the north during Operation Vijay... he was grievously injured in the hand and stomach but continued to advance ordering his men to follow him. Roused by the actions of their young Platoon Commander barely out of the Academy, the platoon charged up the hill against the dominating enemy position. This audacious action unnerved and forced the enemy to abandon a tactically superior position. The officer, however, succumbed to his injuries.... '*

A balding man in Army uniform meditates in the Palden Lamo temple of Spituk Monastery. The interiors of the temple are dark and menacing. A huge, black statue of Vajra Bhairava with a striking likeness to Goddess Kali stands surrounded by *dakini*s. The faces are all hidden behind shrouds, except that of the demon at Vajra Bhairava's feet. The shrouds and the silent presence of the soldier in a corner make it all seem like a scene from an Alistair MacLean novel.

Once outside, we squint in the bright sunlight. A hundred multi-coloured prayer flags hang from loosely tied strings. Bending low to go past them, we sit down on a bench to put on our shoes. The soldier comes out of the temple, and sits down next to us. We exchange a greeting. He was an officer of Operation Vijay too, and fought at Kargil.

'We have just visited the Hall of Fame,' Sumita tells him. 'It made us feel so low. What a loss of young lives... heart-wrenching.'

'It happens in a war. All of us follow orders, unquestioning,' he says. 'It is also natural for every soldier to expect that his needs, his family's needs, will be met. That does not always happen, you know. So these days, everyone wants to be a leader. But all of us cannot be kings, right? At the end of the day, it is most important to be a good human being.'

In the 17th century, Leh became the capital of the Himalayan Kingdom of Ladakh, which then extended to most of western Tibet. King Senge Namgyal built Leh Palace, also known as Lachen Palkar Palace, around this time.

Leh Palace—a nine-storey structure of mud bricks and poplar wood—towers over the old town, designed in the Tibetan style later more famous in the Potala Palace of Lhasa. The Lachen Palkar Palace was abandoned in the mid-19th century after the Dogra invasion.

Not just invaders, good human beings with a mission have also arrived in Ladakh. August Herman Francke, a Moravian Missionary, visited Ladakh at the end of the 19th century. An avid scholar, he wrote about the history of Ladakh, its religious practices and archaeological findings. Li Gotami, an artist and a photographer from a Parsi family of Mumbai, and her husband Lama Govinda travelled to western Tibet as early as the 1940s.

At the Leh Palace, we come across an exhibition titled *First Frames – In the Footsteps of Early Explorers.* It showcases the photographs taken by Francke, Li Gotami and Lama Govinda. I am drawn to the photograph of a rock inscription. It shows a herd of animals with large, curling horns surrounding a small group of stick-like human figures. The figures seem armed. The boulder was discovered near the ruins of a castle called Alchi-mkhar-gog, at Alchi, a short ride from Leh.

A narrow village lane curling around packed curio shops leads to the Alchi Chos-kor Complex, a UNESCO World Heritage Site in the Indus River Valley. The murals and stucco images date between the 11th and the 13th century AD.

Alchi, with its dark and mystic Sumstek or the three-storey shrine, the Manjushri Temple, and the sunny courtyard with rustling trees and fluttering prayer flags is an oasis of serenity.

The image of peace does not last. Back to the village crossroads, we are caught in a traffic jam. Settling down for a long wait, we notice little schoolboys clustering around something, bug-eyed with admiration.

It is a pair of army-green Royal Enfield Bullets. Their owners—strapping soldiers in uniform—have just got off to have some tea.

PHYANG

A monastery named after a blue mountain. An appliquéd scroll that drapes five floors of a building. A 2,000-strong population who have probably never heard of novelist, playwright and composer Anthony Burgess, but seem to believe and follow what he said: 'It's always good to remember where you come from and celebrate it. To remember where you come from is part of where you're going.'

Phyang, 20 kilometres west of Leh, is all this and more.

If one can take a bit of jostling occasionally, it is good to include a local festival as part of a trip. It gives an insider's view of the local culture; the inhabitants are turned out in the best traditional attire, and are at their happiest. Dr Bera, my ophthalmologist-turned-friend, is our 'go-to' man when it comes to all matters Ladakhi. He has been to Ladakh innumerable times.

'Don't go to the bigger festivals. Too touristy,' Dr Bera said, 'If you are including Tso Moriri, you could do the Korzok Gushtor. Then again, that is a very small affair. Try the one at Phyang.'

And that is how we are at Phyang village, with its 500 houses but one tourist accommodation: the Hidden North Guest House run by Tashi Lonchey and his Italian wife, Cristina Martinelli.

Our drive to Phyang from Leh has a halt at the Likir Monastery. A 75-ft high gilded statue of Maitreya Buddha welcomes us. Likir's tiny museum is a treasure house of Tibetan currency, old *thangkas*, tapestries with dragons woven in silken thread, portable temples similar to Rajasthan's *kavads*, and Tibetan weapons.

When we arrive at Phyang, Gang Ngonpo, the blue mountain, and the snow-covered Stok Kangri (in Ladakhi, *kangri* means a mountain of snow) Peak beyond it are bathed in a soft twilight. The roughly 600-year-old Gangon Tashi Chodzong monastery perches on a hilltop. The village sprawls at its base: one and two-storeyed houses and the occasional white chorten amid waves of green and yellow fields separated by zigzagging stacks of oval boulders. A nameless *tokpo*, or river, gurgles past the fields.

At first sight, Phyang is an Eden in the rugged, ruthless terrain that defines most of Ladakh. But a conversation with our hostess Cristina reveals the fragility of this Eden. The tremendous cloudburst that hit Ladakh in 2010 had caused massive landslides in Phyang, too. Nature's fury had torn through the original Hidden North Guest House like it was a pack of cards.

Cristina recounts the traumatic incident, 'The cloudburst happened just after midnight on August 6. Among our guests that night was a Spanish family with children. We woke all of them up.'

Just as they were fleeing from the guest house, the hillside crumbled down and broke in through their back door. 'Most of us were in pyjamas, and had no shoes on.' Soaked to the skin, the motley group walked through the rain, mud and rocks to reach a neighbour's house atop a hill. 'When we returned home the next morning, we found all the animals dead. We lost our uncle Angdu, too.'

A devastated Cristina thought she had also lost the fragile life pulsating in her womb. But her son survived, and is called Tashi Namgyal: the victorious one. The guest house was rebuilt, this time at a higher spot.

It is no wonder then, that people who face such hardship would place their faith in the gods for peace and happiness. So, as in other monasteries in Ladakh, the lamas of Phyang Monastery too perform an annual, week-long puja, and *chaam* (masked) dances.

A statue in the inner sanctum of the monastery catches our eye the next day. It is of Atish Dipankar Srigyan, or Atiśa Dīpamkara Śrījñāna. A master in Mahayana and Vajrayana Buddhism from

Bengal, Srigyan had travelled across the Himalayas as a preacher and arrived at Phyang in the 10th century. The prayer room walls are rich with frescoes and behind its glass cases are idols with many hands.

This is the first day of the festival, but there is hardly a soul in the sanctum. The courtyard of the monastery on the other hand is teeming with locals and foreign tourists. Senior lamas sit on a raised podium in traditional red-and-gold attire and large red hats that look like Japanese fans. They play drums and cymbals and chant from scripts. There is a separate band of musicians as well, young boys and men with long brass clarinets. With red-and-gold robes and red, beak-shaped hats, they look like a crackle of exotic cockatoos.

'Look,' Sumita tugs at my sleeve, even as a murmur travels through the crowd.

Some 20 men in dull grey attire have just brought out a huge roll of cloth onto the courtyard, struggling under its weight. With great physical effort, coordination and instructions from lamas, the roll is pulled up to the top of the five-storey building adjacent to the monastery, and unfurled.

It is a huge and beautiful *thangka,* or a scroll, depicting Skyabje Jigten Gombo, the founder of the Dringungpa monastic order.

The *thangka*—exhibited once in three years, in the years of the pig, the snake and the monkey of the Tibetan calendar—creates a wave of great religious fervour among locals, and frenzied excitement among foreigners. The devout raise folded palms in prayer. Almost like a gun salute, 50 or more zoom lenses are simultaneously raised towards the *thangka*. It needs several announcements from the podium to calm the mob of photographers and move them towards the sides of the courtyard, where most of the locals are already squatting.

Soon, in twos and threes, strange figures pour out of the monastery wearing multi-hued silk robes and green, brown, red, white, yellow and orange masks. Some of the masks have skull-crowns, large spherical eyes, large canines and a fearsome expression. Armed with little swords or a bow and an arrow, the figures slowly begin to gyrate to the beat of the drums. Children seated on the ground around the periphery of the courtyard cringe at their approach.

The dance steps are simple, repetitive. So is the drum beat. Only the masks and robes change with each dance. It is a mystic, layered narrative, the significance of which seems lost on most of the local and foreign audience. '*Tsedup, tsedup*', is all the locals can tell us, eagerly repeating the word for emphasis. *Tsedup*, we gather, means 'festival'.

The midday sun glares down, and the courtyard gets uncomfortably hot. Retreating to the guest house for lunch, we meet a gentleman at the dining table. Tsewang Namgyal is Tashi Lonchey's brother. He is an IFS officer who has completed his term at Singapore and will soon proceed to Canada.

'I grew up here,' Tsewang Namgyal says. 'Phyang was a lot greener before the floods. We had an uncle who lived at Leh. As a boy, I often rode a horse over the hills carrying supplies for him.'

I have often wondered why small boys are sent to the monastery to become lamas. 'Why shouldn't they be allowed to grow up and make up their minds as to what they want to be?' I ask him.

'Primarily financial reasons,' Namgyal replies. 'Earlier, one child from each family would be sent to the monastery where, apart from becoming a lama, he was sure to be clothed and fed. The monastery occupied a significant part in the lives of people, so they would even build their houses around it. These days the local boys join the Indian Army.'

'Would that be the Ladakh Scouts? We saw their logo at the Hall of Fame in Leh.'

'Yes, absolutely. Some also work as permanent labour in the Army storehouses.'

'Why is it that the local people we met at the monastery could not tell us anything about the festival?' I blurt out my frustration.

'Life is very hard in these parts,' the government official says with sympathy, 'so folks have no time to dwell on the significance of religion.' Then, with a little twinkle in his eyes, he adds, 'We have outsourced all religious activities to the lamas. They instruct, and we follow.'

'I used to know the significance of the different coloured masks,' Tashi Lonchey tells us later. 'But I don't remember them very well. Let me talk to Lama Rigzin, and see if he can give you an audience tomorrow. He will be able to explain it all.'

At Tashi's request, our driver Nazir helps us look for Lama Rigzin the next day. We follow Nazir into the dark hall from which we had seen the dancers emerge. It turns out to be the dressing room where young lamas are rehearsing their steps. They do not have their masks on, and are definitely not used to ladies barging into their private quarters. While they turn into statues that blush and stare, we find Lama Rigzin. He is too busy to give us an audience. So he lends us Lama Namgyal, one of the monastery seniors, for our enlightenment.

Lama Namgyal takes us to a small room on the first floor of the monastery. The walls are mud-plastered. Several red plastic chairs form the only furniture. A couple of child lamas are peering out through the lone window that offers an exclusive view of the festivities.

Lama Namgyal is a genial, patient man who speaks Hindi and a bit of English as well.

'So, what do you want to know?' he asks.

'Everything you can tell us about the festival.'

'This monastery was built by Denma Kunga Drakpa,' he begins. 'When Denma came to Phyang, he set up a tent on a field and looked at the beautiful surroundings. He saw a hill that looked like three animal shapes. Denma Kunga Drakpa sat in meditation, and had a vision of the protectress Achi astride her blue horse. He thought this an auspicious sign and decided to build the monastery on top of the hill.'

Meanwhile in the courtyard, four masked men are causing a commotion. Unlike the rest of the dancers, they wear masks with long grey hair and grey beards. The features are almost human, with dark, wrinkled skins, long noses and slits for the eyes and mouth.

The 'old' men are carrying a small boy in a red robe and a conical red cap. They take a lap of the courtyard, and then put the boy gently down at its centre. The men prostrate before the child with great ceremony, and proceed to feed him mango juice from a tetrapak carton.

The locals are in splits.

We cannot help interrupting Lama Namgyal: 'Why is everyone laughing? Who is that boy?'

Lama Namgyal laughs, too. 'Those men are the religious teachers. They are quite well-versed in scriptures. Everyone is not allowed to approach us lamas, but people are free to go to these teachers and clarify their doubts. The teachers may do some clowning at times to retain the attention of the audience. Today, they are pretending that the boy is His Holiness the Dalai Lama.'

The dancers have come in again, and we finally get to ask the revered lama about the significance of the mask colours.

'In Vajrayana or Tantric Buddhism, which is what we practise here, Mahakala and Mahakali are symbolic of the Yin and the Yang,' Lama Namgyal says. 'We represent Mahakala with the green or brown mask and Mahakali with the red. If you have noticed, they always come out together.'

The white masked dancer, he says, symbolises a *dakini*—once a female evil spirit, now considered a protecting deity—and the ones in orange and yellow masks are her assistants.

'After death,' Lama Namgyal says, 'it is believed that our souls go to *par lok*, the other world. Gods may visit that world to rescue our souls. If we do not know what they look like, we might run away from them in fright. How will they rescue us, then? So, we hold this annual dance-drama so that the villagers get to recognise the gods they would meet in the afterlife.'

Placed this way, enlightenment is easy and deliverance easier. But for now, the rainbow-burst of twirling dancers sure is a photographer's *nirvana*.

Time to get clicking.

NUBRA VALLEY

Driving steadily uphill from Leh, we have left the Shanti Stupa behind, the hilltop it perches on now not much more than a mere anthill in the green valley below. The stupa seems like a white crane delicately balancing on the hill, poised for flight.

The change in altitude and hence the change in perspective are enhanced when the Stok Kangri Peak, at a height of slightly over 22,000 ft, seems at eye level. But we know that this is an illusion, for we have not reached Khardung La yet, and even that is only at 18,380 feet.

We have spent three days in Leh and two at Phyang village before venturing to drive over the Khardung La, or Khardung Pass—until recent times the highest motorable road in the world—to Nubra Valley. Five days well spent in knowing the 'Leh' of the land, and in acclimatising to the altitude.

The air gets colder to teeth-rattling as we cross the South Pullu Army Camp. The road gets progressively worse until it is just a dirt track between snow-covered scree slopes of corrugated mountains with numerous pencil-sharp peaks and a deep gorge. At every sudden, sharp turn, the road seems to take a perverse pleasure in twisting our transverse abdominal muscle out of shape.

Our car follows a rickety, puny blue milk van until a string of prayer flags comes into view. We are at Khardung La. This is the Ladakh Range: a section of the Trans-Himalayas that merge with the Kailash Range in Tibet.

What seems at first a cluster of small buildings with tin roofs turn out to be:

'The highest cafeteria in the world'.

A Shiva temple.

A souvenir shop.

A board inside the souvenir shop offers a list of Ladakhi words along with what they mean. Karakoram, we now know, stands for a 'place of black gravel', Khardung La is a 'pass of lower castle' and Siachen—a witness to high-altitude trench warfare between India and Pakistan—the 'rose place' (*sia*: rose, *chen*: place).

Suddenly, I have a vision of blood drops blooming on pristine glacial snow. Rose place, indeed.

A pileup of rough boulders pretending to be steps leads up to a Buddhist monastery on an adjacent hill.

'On our way back from Nubra, I am going to climb up to the monastery,' Sumita says. Now is not a good idea, she knows. There isn't enough oxygen at this height. We are both somewhat blue around the lips and gasping a little with every movement. But a photograph of us with the altitude signpost has to be taken.

Sumita positions herself before the signpost, while I move away to the other side of the road to set up the tripod and the camera timer. What with cars driving down the road every other minute, the setup takes a while. Hamid, our driver is impatient. '*Zyada der yahan rukhna nahin chahiye,* Madam,' he fusses.

Groups of tourists have watched our elaborate photo session. After our shot is done, they approach me with their cameras, requesting for some family shots. They know that this will be a once-in-a-lifetime photograph. Much to Hamid's irritation, I cannot help but oblige them before moving on.

Unfortunately, there is a bottleneck soon after the pass. We are stuck behind a row of SUVs. A foreign cyclist tries to wriggle between our car and the outer edge of the road. He takes a look at the massive drop to his right, wobbles, and desists. Underneath his green helmet, I catch a glimpse of fear on his sunscreen-white face.

The ranges rising to our left are covered with a thick layer of snow. Grey-brown from continuous exposure to car exhausts, the snow has spilled on to parts of the road, and will start melting as the day progresses, making all rides slippery and dangerous.

Tension-prone Hamid cannot bear this delay. '*Ab bhukto*,' he says, and bangs his head down on the steering wheel. He stays that way for a while, his arms hanging limp from knobbly shoulder joints. We let him be. Thankfully, we do not have to suffer his little tantrum or the bottleneck for too long.

North Pullu Army Camp (16,000 ft) on the other side of Khardung La is a sunny place cradled by purple-green ranges. Food shacks do brisk business by the road, and it is time for a tea-and-aloo-paratha break.

Hamid's mood improves. We eat at one of the white plastic tables placed outside the shack. Two Alpine or yellow-billed choughs sit on the roof of the shack and gaze at the distant snow-covered peaks. Their coal-black feathers glisten in the sun.

The Nubra Valley, though named after the Nubra River, actually has the Shyok River ('river of sorrow', the board at the souvenir shop had said) flowing through it. Its mud-coloured waters lead the way to Diskit (10,430 ft), Nubra's headquarters.

The 105-feet statue of Maitreya or the Future Buddha on a hillock is visible for miles around. From his vantage point, the Buddha watches Pakistan. Diskit Monastery, the largest and oldest surviving monastery of Nubra Valley, is a cluster of buildings arranged higgledy-piggledy over an adjacent peak. It was established in the 14th century by Changzem Tserab Zangpo, a disciple of Tsong-Kha-Pa, the founder of the Gelugpa or Yellow Hat sect of Tibetan Buddhism.

Several hairpin bends and steep stairs take us to the monastery. Breathtaking, both: the climb and then the bird's eye view. Acres of verdant green fields stretch towards a silver streak of sand at the base of grey-blue mountains. These are the villages of Diskit and Hunder.

The main prayer hall of Diskit Monastery has *thangka*s painted in a Chinese style. In a separate temple stands a huge Vajra Bhairava statue, unveiled only during festivals. Statues of the arhats, 16 direct disciples of the Buddha, have a room to themselves.

Leaving the monastery and the huge Buddha behind, we drive past yellow fields of mustard where women work with hoes. A donkey sits by the roadside wearing an ear-drop made of multi-coloured strands of wool. He looks mournful.

Soon, shifting sand dunes and oases mark our entry into the desert zone of Nubra Valley. But this desert has snow-tipped mountains bordering it.

It is late afternoon when we check into the guest house at Hunder (9,900 ft). The trellis of Chinese roses by the tall glass windows is a harbinger of the flowers, fruit-laden trees and birds that colour this desert village. Out on a walk later, we would see the plumpest rose-finch that ever sang from a tree.

Hamid drives us to the desert the next day. Double-humped Bactrian camels saunter on the sands. Some sit around lazily, only to flop down on their sides at our approach. The hint cannot get broader: Off-duty.

We do not take a ride together. Sumita has a go first, so I can take some photographs. We have chosen the camel with the largest humps. While this ensures a high and warm backrest, it is quite impossible to grip the camel's wide back with a leg-clasp. But the camels are gentle, and the danger of falling off, minimal.

It is a 20-minute amble towards the snowy peaks of the Karakoram and back. The Karakoram Range is home to K2, the second highest peak of the world with an elevation of 28,251 feet, and the world's second longest glacier, the Siachen. Sumita and her camel are now but specks against the towering ranges. Their snow-covered peaks are mist-hidden this morning.

When it is my turn, I strike up a conversation with the camel handler.

'Do you have a name for your camel?'

'Yes, I call him Namjot. Actually, it is Navjyot, but we Ladakhis pronounce the word softly,' he says. 'We had Malinga and Yusuf Pathan, too,' he adds a second later, 'they have now retired.'

He means camels, of course, not cricketers.

When my ride is over, Namjot squats to let me down. I run a palm over his head: it is smooth and downy. He half closes his eyes with pleasure.

Not all visitors to the dunes ride a camel, though. Local teenagers ride cycles. Families gather for a picnic. Young girls run against the wind, their colourful dupattas a stark contrast to the white sands.

Hamid settles down by a rivulet to wash his car mats. We find a dune to stretch our legs slightly sore from the ride. Amid this picture of peace, the camels are shorn of their colourful cloth saddles and stirrups and released into a seabuckthorn jungle. It is their lunch break.

PANGONG TSO

Journeys are often as vibrant as the destination.

In the five-hour and 154-km drive from Leh to Pangong Tso, we pack in a stop at the Hemis Monastery, the wealthiest of its kind in India.

As expected, there are huge statues of Guru Padmasambhava and the Buddha. Both are striking, though definitely not at par with the 49-feet Maitreya Buddha we have seen at Thiksey Monastery.

The prayer rooms in Hemis have colourful—if quite graphic—paintings of gods and their consorts on the walls.

I am most impressed and disappointed by the monastery museum. Impressed, by its rich collection of statues from the Pala Dynasty, its Gandhara sculptures, ancient bows made of ibex horns, and blue-and-white Chinese ornamental vases that look very much like Ming Dynasty pottery to my untrained eyes.

Disappointed, for we are asked to leave my camera and our mobile phones in a locker before entering the museum.

When we drive on again, past the village of Zingral, a convoy of intimidating Army trucks approaches us from the opposite direction. They do not slow down, nor move to the left.

Our car is on the valley side of the uneven dirt track. I cannot help looking out of my window. All that prevents us from going over the steep drop and landing unceremoniously on Zingral's tin-roofed village homes is a single, haphazard row of boulders. These rocks have at some point rolled down from the high slopes on our right, and now perch precariously by the edge of the road.

'Watch out, Hamid bhai!' I exclaim.

Hamid manages to retain control over his nerves and his steering wheel. We wobble past the trucks now thundering down the road behind us.

Still shaken, we find ourselves at Chang La, or the Chang Pass. At 17,586 ft, it is one of the highest motorable passes in the world, close behind the heels of Khardung La (18,380 ft).

We have crossed Khardung La twice already on our journey from Leh to Nubra Valley and back, so the altitude or the icy winds of Chang La do not generate as much shiver down our spines as they should normally have. But since the same spines have undergone a considerable threat of dislocation on the 20-km stretch of dirt road leading to Chang La, we take a recuperative tea break at the pass.

A couple of hours later, we notice four fat and furry beings watching us from the long stretch of green grasslands to the left of the road. Beady-eyed and buck-toothed, they look like giant squirrels. These are marmots, too, though not long-tailed like their cousins in Suru and Zanskar River valleys.

'Tourists had started feeding biscuits to the marmots,' Hamid says. 'So these animals began to sit in the middle of the road and beg for food. Many got run over. The government has now banned feeding of wild animals.'

We soon discover that the man-marmot interactions have made these furballs quite aware of their popularity. At a U-turn of the dirt road, Sumita spots a marmot sitting on its haunches. 'I just saw another marmot,' she says. 'I think it has died from the cold. It looked quite frozen to me.'

The marmot was on her side of the road, and I wait for the car to complete the U-turn so I can see it for myself. It is still seated in the same posture, head cocked, the long nails of its forepaws clasped together.

'Does not look dead to me,' I say. But it is true the marmot has not moved at all.

'It is dead, right, Hamid bhai?' Sumita asks.

Hamid does not bother to look: 'Yes Ma'am, it is dead.'

I am not convinced, somehow. 'Please stop the car. I want to take a photo anyway,' I tell him.

Sumita lowers her window pane. I crouch over her shoulder, aim and shoot. There is a loud click of the shutter. The marmot dives into its hole.

'Told you it wasn't dead,' I declare triumphantly.

'Come to think of it, when I saw the marmot first, it was facing me,' Sumita recollects. 'Then we took that U-turn, and it was still facing us.'

'That proves it,' I say. 'It was actually posing for a portrait photo!'

Not all encounters are this happy. On yet another stretch of green, skinny auburn horses with thick black manes sit and doze. Some lie on their sides. They barely move.

'Why do they seem so listless?' Sumita asks. I am afraid I know the answer. It is a common practice around these parts to release old and infirm work-horses into the open, where they graze while they still have the strength to, and wait to die.

Huge and barren mountain ranges in all shades of beige, ochre, brown—purple, even—part suddenly like stage curtains to reveal the molten jewel of a lake.

This is the Pangong Tso, *tso* being the Ladakhi word for 'lake'. The Tibetans call it Banggong Co, or the 'long, narrow, enchanted lake'.

What lies before us is just about a third of the 134-km long lake, the rest of which lies in China-occupied Tibet. It is a magical expanse of water that looks like a huge sapphire set in a ring of mountain ranges. Even as we watch, the water changes colour. It is now ultramarine blue in the distance, reflecting the burnt sienna of the barren mountain ranges.

Nearer the shore, where the hues change to a luminous blend of teal and cerulean blue, a screech of brown-headed gulls holds a conference. I am sure if I look closely, I should be able to find a Jonathan Livingston and a Fletcher among them.

I think to myself: the inhabitants of Lukung and Spangmik villages by the shores of Pangong Tso are the luckiest on earth. But even if they do know it, they keep this secret very close to their heart. Poker-faced, they go about the serious business of preparing momos,

'A perfect idea of freedom and flight, limited by nothing at all':
Brown-headed gull with its catch from Pangong Tso

making tea, or organising night stays for folks who turn up at their villages every tourist season planning to stay an hour, yet ending up staying a night. Or two.

At Spangmik, we first check out the homestays. All rooms are small, with low ceilings, and practically all of their floor space occupied by beds. The bed sheets are old but washed. The blanket rolls are thick, and look capable of handling the cold nights at 13,900 feet.

The rooms give off a smell of sun-dried cowpat. The narrow windows have glass panes but they are dusty and splattered with paint. So not ideal.

The late afternoon light throws the dozen or more cream canvas tents by the shore into sharp relief against the cobalt waters. We veer towards a tent for our stay. The tents are far more expensive than the homestays, but come with an attached toilet, and are much closer to the lake than the mud-brick houses.

Night falls, and the mountains take on an eerie silhouette in the faint light of a quarter moon. The sound of a lone guitar strummed casually by one of the boys in the nearby kitchen tent competes with the generator's steady hum. Tonight, we are the only guests.

Dinner is being cooked. Our short walk to the dining tent turns into a trot: the wind blowing in from the now ink-black lake is freezing.

I do not know then that the enthusiastic young chef cooking momos for us has never made a momo in his life, and that he has taken up the task solely to impress his lady guests. When the steamed momos arrive, I find the flour coating half-cooked. I still eat some, for there is nothing else to eat.

Through the night, the momos keep me awake and writhing with stomach ache. Thankfully, Sumita's stomach has accommodated them well, and she is none the worse the next morning.

At first light, the tougher tourists—a couple of bikers who arrived late in the night and pitched their own tents, and I—are out by the lake. Humans are not the only species, however. On a boulder near the tent, a cream-and-brown bird with a black sash and a tiny pair of black horns watches us with sharp, swift head movements.

This is a horned lark.

After breakfast, Sumita and I collect a pile of stones and set about building a *lha tse*, or a chorten by the lake. A brown-headed gull swoops down to touch the rippling lake waters with its claws, and when it rises up again, a silver fish wriggles in its grip. Hundreds of little waves break on the shore, and the warm sunlight splinters into a million diamonds that dance on the water. I am tempted to quote Emperor Jehangir:

'Agar Firdaus ba-ru-i-zamin ast, hamin ast u hamin ast, u hamin ast.'

If there is a heaven on earth, it is here.

Just under the crystal-clear water, the smooth stones are delightfully multi-coloured. I dip my hand into the waves and pick up a marble pebble.

It is heart shaped.

TSO MORIRI

This is no country for old men.

For millions of years, the pink and the purple, the yellow and the burnt sienna mountains have claimed the azure sky as their own. For miles, River Indus has carved its own glorious route, and the road that meekly runs by it is the one less travelled. Villages by this road have esoteric names: Kiari and Hemya and Chumathang and Sumdo. Lush yellow fields speak of a human presence, but no villagers walk the road. There are short, smart, metal bridges over little streams, but no cars trundle over these bridges.

Except ours.

It is a lonely, long and beautiful route, lined by the occasional row of trees from behind the safety of which woolly deer or Tibetan blue sheep look up at us with a fearless, soft gaze.

At Chumathang, Hamid halts for our lunch at one of the two roadside restaurants near a nameless lake. It is the usual fare of black beans curry and rice. Our little waitress, too, has a gentle fawn's gaze. Post lunch, she arrives at the table with a mop, but instead of clearing up, drapes her elbows around the back of a plastic chair and looks up at us with a smile.

'*Photu*?' she asks shyly.

'Yes, of course. I would love to take your photo,' I reply, and focus. With the shutter going off, her day is made.

Before we drive on, we scramble up the hill behind the restaurant to reach the toilets. The Ladakhi toilet deserves a mention. In a small

'A lake carries you into recesses of feeling otherwise impenetrable': Tso Moriri

enclosure that often lacks a door, two rectangular stones are placed on either side of a small but deep hole in the ground. There is at times a pile of dry mud and a small shovel kept nearby. After the job is done, the user is expected to shovel some dry mud into the hole. To hide the evidence, as well as to ensure it gets absorbed that much faster into the soil and helps fertilise the fields.

Shovelling is an act often eschewed.

The first time I paid a visit to a Ladakhi toilet, I made the mistake of looking down the hole. It revealed to me the entire history of the Ladakhi biology. With so much reference material lying all around, I am not surprised how easily the experts could match the bacteria *Helicobacter pylori* found in Ötzi the Iceman—the 5,300-year-old European mummy—with that in the present-day Ladakhi gut.

We skip the hot spring at Chumathang, pausing instead to marvel at Tso Kiagar. It is a small lake that does not draw tourist attention, but today holds the reflection of a snow-covered mountain.

Quite a while afterwards, a cerulean blue streak appears between mountain wedges. We are at the Tso Moriri Wetland Conservation Reserve, in south-eastern Ladakh.

At an altitude of 15,075 ft, Tso Moriri or Lake Moriri stretches for 28 kilometres from north to south, and is about 4-6 kilometres wide. This is the largest high-altitude lake in the Trans-Himalayan region, and, unlike Pangong Tso, entirely within India.

Our proximity to the Indo-Tibetan border is emphasised by the sentry post at the entrance to Korzok, a village by the lake. We show our IDs to the Indian soldier, and sign in a register, which is also meant to record our exit.

It is quite another matter, however, that while leaving two days later, I would find that someone else had already placed an exit time and his signature next to my name.

And we blame only the Chinese soldiers for all their incursions.

Tourist presence is insignificant in this land. The lake and its adjoining marshland are crowded with brown-headed gulls, bar-headed geese, brahminy shelducks. The green, flowering meadow stretching to the lake is alive too, with hordes of mouse hare. They live underground, in labyrinthine colonies given away by neat round holes peppering the grass. With bright, sparkling eyes, they are a constant tease for the photographer as they scamper in and out of these holes before one can say Jack Robinson.

Above ground, living facilities for travellers are almost as basic as the hare's. We put up at one of several batches of tents: half a kilometre away from and in full glorious view of the waters of Tso Moriri. The toilets, though thankfully western and not Ladakhi, are shared by all travellers, and 20 steps away from the tents.

At night, these 20 steps would seem the equivalent of 20 miles, for the freezing cold wind would try to slice one's nose—the only exposed appendage—off one's face.

With the bright orange dusk, there pops up another existential question: do we have electricity?

'We usually do have power, Ma'am,' says the Man Friday. 'None tonight, though. This morning, a driver rammed his car into an electric pole several kilometres away, uprooting it.'

The lines will be repaired, of course. No one knows when. And no, there are no generators. On a normal day, we could have shifted to another set of tents, run by another villager. That man has a generator. But 'the road to Lukung and Spangmik has had a landslide, Ma'am. Totally blocked,' says Man Friday. 'So, most of the tourists who were going to Pangong Tso have come here, to Korzok. All other tents are full.'

If the landslide happened two days earlier, we would be stuck by the shores of Pangong. Indefinitely.

Or worse, permanently: under the rockfall.

'Should we then spend two nights at Korzok like we meant to?' I ask Sumita. I am cold, and the prospect of walking to the dining tent and to the toilets in pitch darkness, uninviting.

'We may never come this far again,' Sumita says. She is as tired as I am, but has the quiet resilience I often lack. 'Let's stay on and make the best of what we have.'

In any case—I console myself—the electricity would have just meant a lone bulb inside our tent, instead of the candle that now bravely fights the wind causing a ruckus with the tent flap. There are no charging points to feed my camera battery. Mobile phone batteries are not an issue: our mobile phones have fallen silent many hours ago.

The wind howls all night, crying to be let in through the tent corners. Right behind our tent a donkey brays, insistent. Between the wind and the donkey, it is sleep I miss. In my tightly clutched fist, the camera battery absorbs heat from my body and manages to retain some charge.

Morning brings a magical sunrise and a queue for the toilet. A tall and lanky foreign lady comes out of one. She smiles at us and we smile back.

'It is hard to sit on that,' she says, pointing to the WC planted crookedly into an uneven mud floor with the frank camaraderie only fellow travellers on difficult journeys share. 'My knees were coming up to my chin almost!' We laugh together.

'Where are you from?' she asks.

'Oh, we've come from very far,' Sumita says. 'From Kolkata. Where are you from?'

'Switzerland.'

'Gosh, that's definitely farther than Kolkata,' Sumita exclaims. 'Switzerland is a picturesque country. What brings you here?'

'I have been to India several times earlier,' the lady says. 'When I visit such remote places, where it is hard to get even the basic facilities, I tell my husband that it teaches me to be thankful for the simple comforts we have at home, say, a hot shower. But I find India very beautiful.'

It is indeed a fresh, beautiful day. On the slopes of the mountain behind our tent, a Changpa nomad boy herds a large flock of disobedient sheep. In Tibetan, *changpa* means 'northerners'.

Pack horses arrive at the Korzok village with more nomadic men. We do not see any of their *rebos*, or yak-hair tents, though. These are usually woven from the hair of mature, black yaks. The weaving starts with the blessings of an astrologer, and even a single strand of white hair left in the weave is said to be unlucky.

Once upon a time, these nomadic people would extract salt from the brackish lakes near the Tibetan border, load bags of it on their yaks, and travel far to exchange the salt for grain. The Changpa women were said to wear headgear dotted with turquoise, gold and amber. With China taking over Tibet, the borders closed and so did the trade. The nomads are now largely high-altitude pastoralists.

In the dim interiors of the 400-year-old Korzok Monastery, lamas punctuate their rhythmic chants with sips of butter tea. The statue of Shakyamuni Buddha catches a sliver of the morning light and gleams. Strange masks on the walls look at us with stern, questioning eyes. They are old, but they have been dusted well. Korzok Gushtor, the annual festival, was held just two days ago.

We seize the day to walk through the winding village paths that exude the smell of sun-dried dung, watch a toddler squatting unsupervised in the driver's seat of a stationary tractor, and huff-n-puff our way up to the view point atop a hill that reveals the entire lake, the snow-topped range cradling it and the village houses and tents by the shore.

Hamid suggests a drive to the remote, uninhabited side of the lake. Long unbroken mountain ranges—a row of matte pink inverted ice-cream cones thwacked on the ground with the ice popping out from the wrong end—line the far horizon. Large yet slender shards of stone stacked just anyhow form natural chortens on our side. We are perched on a hillock, and the lake lies way below, a sheet of molten lapis lazuli under the midday sun.

Multi-coloured prayer flags flutter from a solitary pole. I ask the reed-thin Hamid to pose next to it, so I can take his photograph. He is eager, happy to oblige. Driving us over several days has made him realise we are not risk-loving maniacs. He has learned to relax. Photograph taken, he goes down to Tso Moriri's shore. For the next quarter of an hour, he is a boy again, jillicking stones over the placid waters.

Enthused, we go down to the lake, too. The water lapping at our bare feet is refreshingly cold, but not freezing. From where we are, Korzok is a distant stack of dun-coloured dolls' houses, punctuated by ordered rows of cream canvas tents.

We return to the tents only for lunch, which holds a pleasant surprise: watermelons for dessert. They have been brought all the way from Leh.

Outside, the sparkling lake continues to beckon. Thousands of nameless flowers on the meadow nod their bright little white, yellow, blue and purple heads. It is impossible not to crush some of them on our way to the lakeside, and in return, they smear our sneakers with a heady fragrance.

A village lady working on her field puts her shovel aside and sits down on the grass with a friend. They sit a couple of feet apart, both facing the endless blue lake and the snow-touched mountains, and share a companionable silence. We follow their example, and sit down too.

This is no country for old men. But here, by the gull-crowded shores and the fragrant field of flowers, we hear our tired urban souls clap their hands and sing.

Returning to Leh, we do not follow the River Indus but plan to drive past Tso Kar at 15,280 feet and 50 kilometres from Tso Moriri. The route goes through Taglang La (17,582 ft) and should allow more wildlife sightings.

The shores of the nameless river leading us to the lake are covered with a white, fine grain. 'Those are salt deposits, Ma'am,' Hamid explains. 'In Ladakhi, *karra* means salt. That is why we call the lake Tso Kar, or White Lake.'

We are in the Changthang Plateau, and the area around Tso Kar, known as More Plains, is a haven for birdwatchers. Ibex, snow foxes and snow leopards live on the surrounding hills. Today, though, there is just a herd of kiang—Tibetan wild ass with shiny brown coats—strolling loose-limbed on a stretch of green.

I suddenly spot movement in a rough patch of land by the roadside, dotted with pebbles and a smattering of wild, scruffy, ankle-high bushes. A superbly camouflaged pair of Tibetan sand grouse is waddling away from the road.

Hamid eases the car to a stop, shuts the engine down. I get off on tiptoes.

Looking only through my camera with a finger on the shutter button, I follow them in silence, involuntarily mimicking their gait. I sense, not hear, the noiseless laughter of Sumita and Hamid behind my back. Manage a good photograph before the birds fly away, disgusted with my intrusion.

A tea stall by Tso Kar has bunches of yak hair hanging from its stone walls. The skull of a sheep with huge arching horns hangs from a post. From the flowering, fragrant shores of Tso Moriri so much like the Lake Districts, we have transitioned to a Wild West ambience. Suddenly, it is clear why the Changpa nomads were also called Chinese cowboys. But on this sunny morning, their horses do not throw up a dust storm. Instead, one of their clan now approaches us with a smile, and cups of over-sweetened black tea.

HIMACHAL PRADESH

RAMPUR

'This is where the Hindustan-Tibet Road overlaps with National Highway 5,' I tell Sumita, even as we approach Rampur, on our way from Shimla to Sarahan.

'Hindustan-Tibet Road? Wasn't that built during the British rule?' Sumita asks.

'Yes, in the mid-19th century,' I reply. 'Lord Dalhousie, the British Governor-General of India, had initially selected Shimla as the summer capital of the East India Company. But he preferred to work from Chini, or Kalpa as we know it now, in Kinnaur. Kalpa was then four marching days away from Shimla, and had a good location: just off the ancient Silk Route travelled by traders from Central Asia and China. Soon, Lord Dalhousie would order the laying of the Hindustan-Tibet Road from Kalka to Shipki La, a pass on the Tibet border.'

He would write about the road later:

> *'I returned to Simla by the new road, which I commenced one year ago, and which, when it shall be finished, will not be surpassed, I flatter myself, by any mountain road in the world.'*

Pp 78-79: 'It is better in prayer to have a heart without words than words without a heart': Bheema Kali Temple, Sarahan

Facing page: 'I'd like to go by climbing a birch tree': At Tabo

In reality, though, the East India Company's Board of Control in London, burdened by the expenses from the conquest of Punjab, could not be convinced about the low cost of construction. The road remained a bridle path, seven to eight feet wide and passing through Theog, Narkanda, and Kotgarh to Rampur, to end at Kalpa.

Do visit the Padam Palace while you pass through Rampur, a cousin had said. Padam Palace belongs to the Rampur-Bushahr kings, and is known for its exquisite wood carvings.

The state of Bushahr was one of the oldest hill states after Kashmir. Legend says it was founded by Pradyuman, the son of Lord Krishna. History credits Rana Danbar Singh, an immigrant Rajput from the Deccan, as the founder.

Rampur, our pit stop on the drive from Shimla to Sarahan, is crowded and chaotic this October noon. An election rally is on, and Padam Palace is the chosen venue.

The sprawling grounds of the palace are covered with tarpaulin sheets. As tourists, we stand out like a couple of sore thumbs amid the sea of political festoons and the famous *thepangs*—the traditional green and grey Kinnaur caps that most attendees wear. While no one bars our entry to the grounds, the blank stares make us uncomfortable. In any case, the palace at this moment is a photographer's nightmare.

We beat a hasty retreat down some 20 steps off the road and into HPTDC's Hotel Sutlej View, hoping to grab a quick lunch. The hotel, too, is flooded with rally attendees. They spill over the bar and into the dining hall. The waiters, and they are few, look totally fuddled and incapable of handling our order, any order.

It is a long wait for food.

Batches of rallyists stride in and take over adjacent tables. Proceed to stare at us until we are forced to look away and then stare some more. Just when we decide to leave, our simple lunch of rice and kidney beans curry arrives. We gulp down the food and are soon on our way to Sarahan.

'I have lived a great deal among grown-ups. I have seen them intimately, close at hand. And that hasn't much improved my opinion of them': Election rally, Rampur Palace, Sarahan

As far as I am concerned, this visit to Padam Palace does not count. We would have to stop here again on our return journey.

Some 20 days later, we do get a closer look at Padam Palace. There are no rallies, and the sunny palace grounds seem deserted.

Started in 1919 by Raja Padam Dev Singh and completed in 1925, the two-storeyed Padam Palace looks colonial; its turrets topped with red inverted cone roofs so that the snows may glide off them. The upper floor has intricate wood and stained glass work, deep chocolate floral lattices, and white eaves. The lower floor is embraced by stone arches. It is said that instead of cement, a paste of black gram was used to glue the stone slabs together. The blue-grey front door with the royal emblem has exquisite carvings and Belgian glasswork.

A hexagonal open wooden structure held up by pillars painted in blue and white occupies a side of the lawn. The eaves of its double-tiered slate-layered roof have rainbow-hued floral designs. This is the Machhkandi, the venue where the king would meet his subjects.

I take my fill of photographs, and then we climb the small flight of stairs onto the veranda that encircles the front rooms of the palace.

A couple of tall, beautiful wooden dressers lie neglected on the veranda. Through the glass on the closed doors, we get a glimpse of the stained glass work inside. It makes us long to get in.

As we hang around, a couple of men approach the stairs. One of them is in a traditional cap and cream kurta pyjamas. The other wears a navy-blue suit.

Sumita asks Mr Blue Suit in Hindi, '*Bhaisaab*, palace *ke andar jaa sakte hain*?'

A security guard walks up. 'Please *aap nichhey chaley jaaiye,'* he says firmly. *'Raja sahib aaye hain, aur koi bhi yahan pe* allow (sic) *nahi hain.'*

That is disappointing. We turn towards the stairs, when Mr Blue Suit says in impeccable English, 'So, you want to see my palace? Come on in.'

We follow him and the three or four men now accompanying him into a drawing room. The men leave us and walk into an adjoining chamber to the right, busy in discussions.

It is a well-kept drawing room, done up in style:

Plush sofas, a fireplace.

The life sized painting of an erstwhile king above the fireplace.

More works of art created with semi-precious stones on the warmly-lit walls.

Polished wood side-tables with black-and-white photographs of the royal family.

A photo of a young man with a striking resemblance to Mr Blue Suit.

'There are more rooms to our left,' Sumita says in a low tone. It is a question.

'I don't know how safe it is to go further in,' I say in an equally low tone.

I have noted the number of men. In such situations, my gut tends to swerve towards caution. 'We should not stretch our luck.'

We stay put. Soon, Mr Blue Suit returns to the drawing room. With entourage.

'Where are you from?' he asks, and we answer.

'Kolkata? I was there for a month recently, because of the elections. How is Mamata*ji*?'

He has a twinkle in his eye and a smile. His men laugh.

'She must be fine,' I reply. 'We were travelling all this while and haven't really been keeping track of the news back home.'

'So, where did you go in Himachal?'

'Sarahan, Kalpa, Nako, Tabo, Kaza and Langza,' I say.

'The Spiti Valley,' one of the aides says to Mr Blue Suit. Deferentially.

'I see.'

We walk out together.

Mr Blue Suit points to the camera around my neck, 'Since you do take photographs, maybe you can take a photo with my phone? Could you please take a photograph of me with this gentleman here? He flies my helicopter for the election rally.'

The man in the kurta pyjamas is the pilot.

Mr Blue Suit hands me his phone and the two men pose together against the ornate palace door. I take a couple of photos, and hand the phone back to him. After a mutual 'Thank you', he gets into a red Santro Xing and the car drives off.

We take the security guard aside: 'Who was that gentleman in the blue suit?'

'That was Raja Virbhadra Singh,' says the now-polite guard.

It suddenly falls into place. Until that moment, he has just been a name on various inaugural plaques across the state, and the potential candidate from the Congress party for the post of Chief Minister.

He would in fact go on to be the Chief Minister of Himachal Pradesh that year. Completely indifferent to political landscapes, what Sumita and I will both remember is his gracious gesture towards two ladies schoolgirl-eager for a glimpse into the life of the royals.

SARAHAN

Stately pines and oaks dominate the route from Shimla to Sarahan, at an altitude of 7,103 feet. As we step onto the unkempt lawn of our small resort at Sarahan, a little ball of black fur resembling a bear cub looks up from his intense pursuit of nothing in particular. At my call, the month-old pup comes bounding towards me and pulls up sharply at my sneakers. I bend down to pluck off a couple of nettles stuck to his very dusty coat, and realise why he looks like a miniature bear: someone has hacked off his tail.

Whether from the lack of that significant appendage, or the extreme climate, our baby bear—we discover—has a streak of forgetfulness. Given a biscuit, he treats it like a bone and settles down on a hotel mat with the treasure between his paws, ready to gnaw it to powder. But the very next second, he completely disregards the biscuit, twirls around, and begins a frenzied chewing of my shoe laces. Or fingers.

For he is a 'Bear of Very Little Brain'.

In the soft pink light that often marks dusk on the mountains, we take in Sarahan's other high points: the snow-clad Shrikhand Peak (20,430 ft), and the 800-year-old Bheema Kali temple with its slanted slate roofs, golden towers, and carved silver doors. This is one of the 51 Shakti Peethas, places where, according to legend, the body parts of Shiva's consort Sati had fallen.

A recap: While Brahma was creating the universe, he needed help from Shiva. Goddess Shakti was born from Shiva's powers and she helped Brahma create the universe. Once this was done, Brahma had to reunite Shakti with Shiva. To achieve this, Brahma's son King Daksha performed yagnas, and Shakti was born as Sati, Daksha's daughter. She, it was understood, would get married to Shiva.

Things do not always go according to plan. Shiva had meanwhile cursed Brahma for a lie, and had cut off Brahma's fifth head. Daksha, understandably, started hating Shiva and did not want him to get married to Sati. She, however, fell in love with Shiva and married him.

A furious Daksha arranged for a yagna to which he invited just about everyone except Shiva and Sati. Despite Shiva's efforts to dissuade her, Sati went to the yagna, where Daksha spoke insultingly about Shiva. Sati was unable to take this humiliation, so she committed suicide.

Enraged and inconsolable, Shiva destroyed Daksha's yagna, and cut off Daksha's head. He lifted Sati's body on his shoulders and began the *tandava,* the celestial dance of destruction across all creation.

To free him from his attachment to Sati, Vishnu cut Sati's corpse into bits with his Sudarshan Chakra. The body parts fell at several spots across India and these sites are known as the sacred Shakti Peethas.

The next morning, which happens to be my birthday, we wish to offer a traditional worship at the Bheema Kali temple.

Shops selling appropriate offerings abound around the temple. For ₹ 101, I buy a plateful of goods for the goddess. It has:

A whole coconut.

A red ribbon.

A small sheet of velvet stick-on bindis.

Half a dozen red glass bangles.

A small mirror.

Joss sticks.

'Give the plate to the priest,' says the gentle shopkeeper. 'He will keep some of the offerings and return the rest. Then come back to me with the plate, and I will pack the prasad for you.'

With its Indo-Tibetan architecture, the temple built by the Bushahr kings has intricate wood carvings. The open porch shimmers with multi-coloured zari streamers. Dusshera festivities are near.

We take off our shoes and prepare to enter.

'No socks,' says a guard, 'no phones, no cameras.'

My camera and our mobile phones go into one of the lockers next to the gate, and I am handed the key.

'What's wrong with socks?' I ask the guard. Even through my socks, the slabs of the temple compound are stone cold. Stone, and cold.

'No socks,' the poker-faced man repeats. I am tempted to ask him his name. He would probably say it is Nozox.

A covering on the head is a must, and there are pink and yellow silken skull caps available at the gate for temporary use. They look and smell used. It is just as well that we have our woollen caps on.

Thus, shivering and barefoot, into the temple.

Once inside, the narrow and winding staircases are carpeted, warm. I bang my head against a couple of low ceilings and doorways. After what seems an unending maze of stairs and passages, we reach the altar.

The fair idol of Bheema Kali, the presiding deity of the Bushahr rulers, wears a pleasant expression. She does not inspire the awe that the name Kali usually does for us Bengalis.

I hand the steel plate to the priest, tell him it is my birthday. He chants some hymns over the plate, keeps some of the offerings at the altar, and returns the rest, along with a handful of puffed rice and laddoo pieces from the large brass thali before him. Then takes a red thread and ties it around my wrist.

I point to Sumita. 'Please tie one on her wrist too.'

The priest frowns.

'It is *your* birthday, so I have tied the thread around your wrist,' he says. 'If I tie one for her, the other visitors will also ask me to tie threads for them. I cannot be doing this all day.'

I insist. I am not sure about the protective powers of a thread, but I do believe in sharing. Probably not accustomed to stubbornness from a woman, the dour man keeps my wish.

Puja done, we walk up to the lawns of Shanti Kunj, the royal palace with its ornate balcony and stained glass windows. Not a patch on Rampur Palace, I note.

The Hanuman temple close by has a unique, four-headed idol of the monkey god. And an irascible old, unkempt priest very forthcoming about his views of big cities as thieving havens as opposed to the innately honest Himachali villages.

'In Kolkata, if you leave a 10-rupee note on a pavement, it will disappear in five minutes,' he says. Wags his dark, long finger with bulging blue veins—probably the most exercised part of his knobbly body from all the daily wagging—at my DSLR: 'Leave your expensive camera on this temple step, and come back tomorrow. It will still be here.'

I do not wish to contest his views, nor take him up on his challenge.

A short drive up the side of a mountain takes us to Rangori village: a cluster of wooden houses with fruit-laden apricot trees and golden corn drying on porches. A ledge just off the road has a tiny Shiva temple, light orange marigolds in bloom, and deep orange butterflies hovering over them.

At a view point very literally named Hawa Mahal, the wind rustles among tall chir pines. Fresh green pine needles catch the sunlight, and turn silver. While we gaze at the mountain ranges lining the horizon and all of Sarahan below us, a huge, red-faced rhesus macaque sizes us up from its perch on a tree.

Our aimless wanderings take us past the Naloti stadium, where local boys are enjoying a good game of football. The Sarahan Pheasantry, said to be the world's first ever captive breeding centre for the satyr tragopan pheasant, is next to the stadium.

A steep, 1,448 feet hike among towering trees with their unseen population of extremely vocal birds leads to the Pheasantry. A pair of Himalayan monals—the state bird—and a few tragopans walk about in their cages.

An eventful day rolls into a lazy evening. Out strolling among the busy market lanes near our resort, we find a tea-shack. It is a little after

6:30 pm, but the shop-owner is ready to down his shutters and call it a night.

Not wishing to disappoint us, he makes us some black tea. Tells us about the approaching snowfall—'sometimes a pile this high in front of my shop'—and his two little sons studying in an Army school at Dehradun.

'So you served in the Indian Army?'

'No, but my friend does. He has no children, so I had my sons admitted in his quota.'

Suddenly, there is some commotion on the unlit street outside. A man shouts something, a reversing sedan screeches to a halt. All of us rush out to check.

Our little black Bear scurries out from under the car. He blends with the night, and the driver has had no inkling of his presence on the street; but for the pedestrian's keen eyes, Bear would be paste.

The incident does not bother the 'Bear of Very Little Brain': he is too young to be afraid. It is a relief to watch him bounding back to the resort. My pockets bulging with glucose biscuits for the pup, we thank the shopkeeper, and follow.

KALPA

At Jeori, the road from Sarahan meets National Highway 5. Turning right from Jeori towards Kalpa, we are on a highway that lopes through tunnels gouged out of mountain ranges.

Huge, elongated boulders still hang precariously from tunnel roofs, and signposts warn drivers which way the road ahead would curve. The curves are sharp, and come upon us suddenly, but they come with giant, mushroom-shaped remnants of the range left standing on the edge of the precipice—to serve as natural fences.

Pawan takes the curves well even as we climb, his bespectacled eyes focused on the road. He does not take the truck drivers as well, and there are many hurtling down from Kalpa or beyond. At almost every turn, the trucks approach us, belligerent and unwilling to yield an inch of space on the switchback. Pawan cowers every single time, steering the Tavera under an overhang, or perching it delicately on the edge of the curve until the current Goliath has passed.

'We are the ones travelling uphill, Pawan. We should be allowed to go first,' I tell him. 'Why are you so afraid?'

'They are local vehicles, Ma'am,' he replies. 'They can see the number-plate and realise instantly that I am not one of their own. Why get into a tiff?'

Pawan, like the Tavera, comes from Chandigarh. He has none of the heft and boisterousness we tend to associate with people from the north of India, his thick handlebar moustache a striking contrast to his tall but wiry frame.

Slowly, he starts to talk about himself. 'I was very hot-tempered in my youth. There was a boy from our neighbouring village who used to bother a girl in mine. So, one day, I went to teach him a lesson. We fought, and I hit him with the edge of a sword. Almost cut off his neck.'

The boy survived, but Pawan was jailed. 'My father had to meet someone important, pay a lot of money to get me freed.' His term behind the bars has cured him of his aggression.

He does keep a thick cudgel under his seat, though. Somehow, it helps him keep his cool.

In its wide valley far below, Sutlej gushes on aggressively, the clear green waters a reminder of River Teesta in North Bengal. On the far side of the Sutlej, the mountains harbour entire government offices within them. Painted cement arches lead into tunnels at the base of the range.

If I were to work in those offices, I would definitely want to know about the emergency exit.

About 10 kilometres ahead of Kalpa lies the small and bustling town of Reckong Peo, just Peo to Himachalis. Its busy chowk, reminiscent of the maw of a shark, is ringed in by immense snow-laden ranges rising sharply into the sky like a row of jagged teeth.

Pawan says we should grab some lunch, and drops us at the chowk before finding a spot to park the Tavera.

We pick on a hotel-cum-restaurant, and climb up the stairs to its open terrace, both sunny and cold, and with a marvellous view of the ranges. Perfect place for a lunch break.

Or so we think.

'Can't take orders,' a waiter tells us. The cretin has waited for us to pull up two chairs and plonk down. 'Cook absent today.'

'Well, this is lunch time, and you must be feeding something to your resident guests? Just give us whatever's ready. '

'Nothing is ready,' he insists. 'Minimum two hours to make.'

At a soot-blackened but well frequented sweet shop we wolf down a couple of samosas and hot jalebis, and wash them down with excessively sweet—'*cheeni kum*' would become our refrain on this trip—black tea.

'Let's buy apples,' Sumita says.

I walk into Peo's version of a departmental store; choose some bright red freshly gathered apples from a basket.

'How do you charge these?' I ask the store keeper.

'₹ 40 per kg,' he says.

Just 10 days ago, in Kolkata, I bought the fruit for ₹ 120 a kg. With great delight, I pile up his measuring scale.

'You are a tourist? Where are you going?' he asks.

While he listens to my answer, I notice him adding an extra 130 gms for the price of a kilogram of the juiciest apples we have had to date.

For a long while afterwards, the silence in the Tavera is broken only by the sound of crunching. In the back seat, Huck Finn and Tom Sawyer wipe the thick, ruby-red juice rolling down their chins with the backs of their palms. His share of apples rolling gently in the hollow of the passenger seat next to him, Pawan taps his fingers on the steering: he has a tune in his head.

We troop into Kalpa at 9,711 feet, with very grubby fingers and happy hearts.

Before us in the cloudless horizon rise the majestic Kinnaur Kailash and Jorkanden ranges.

Kinnaur Kailash is barren.

Jorkanden, snow-laden.

The quaint, sleepy village of Kalpa with its ancient little monastery and equally or more ancient temple, rests at their feet.

Dusk lights up the massifs in a surreal volcanic glow. Orange clouds rise like smoke.

The sun sets.

Around eight the next morning, it is back as a sparkling diamond atop Kinnaur Kailash, turning the Shivling Peak into a silhouette. Shivling gets its name from the 79 ft-high phallic boulder that stands on its crest and often looks rainbow-hued in the sunlight. Climbing enthusiasts trek an impressive 19,000 ft to offer puja at the boulder.

Hotel Kinnaur Kailash offers us an extremely comfortable stay. It is just as well, considering what we would have to plod through later on this trip. Our ground floor room has walls the shade of butter, polished wooden furniture, warm lighting and a rusty but functional room heater. The large glass windows open out to a view of the mountains, and with the curtains pulled aside, we may lap up the sight from under the thick blankets on the double bed.

The only catch: with the curtains parted, we are quite visible to the enthusiastic shutterbugs on the lawn.

It is a day to explore the countryside, and we set out for Roghi village, 5 kilometres away. Having met up with his driver buddies at Kalpa, Pawan is in a cheerful, chatty mood.

'A tourist had asked his driver to take him to Suicide Point. When the driver took a look at the steep drop, his head started reeling. He felt so ill, he had difficulty driving any further,' Pawan narrates.

We are not remotely suicidal this fine morning. We have no urge to visit Suicide Point, and tell Pawan as much.

'But we will anyway drive past Suicide Point on our way to Roghi,' he says with schoolboy excitement.

Suicide Point, it turns out, is a small ledge that protrudes from a turn in the road to Roghi. A fall from it would be sharp, swift, and into a yawning, serrated crevasse. Unless one is extremely unlucky, death should be equally swift.

Pawan positions himself with one foot firmly on the road and another on the ledge. 'Please take my photo,' he says. 'I will show it to my missis (sic) and frighten her.'

I oblige, but intending to spare the poor woman—who must anyway be worrying about him whenever he is away—decide never to send him a print.

Roghi is a cluster of narrow passages and staircases between village houses that seem too quiet to be inhabited, except for the solitary hen fluttering out of a nook at the sound of our footsteps.

The courtyard of the lone temple with its quaint wood-and-stone structure is deserted. Wood carvings on the temple doors are crude, as if the work of children. We discover:

A procession of instrument players.

A king offering worship.

An attendant fanning the king.

Tigers painted in yellow and black.

The sanctum is locked, dark. A deity sits in a palanquin, swathed in shining cloth and a strange headgear: it could be made of black yak hair.

A village girl runs by. 'Who is the god worshipped here?' we manage to call out to her.

'Narayan,' she replies, and runs away before we can ask about the priest. Or a key.

Back at Hotel Kinnaur Kailash, we laze over lunch at the dining hall. It is a sunny, warm space done up in wood, with large glass windows on all sides, and offers an uninterrupted 360-degree view. With shining glassware, chequered table cloths and uniformed waiters, the feel is quite colonial.

So is the roasted chicken. Lord Dalhousie would have loved it.

A lady visitor comes up to us. She is part of a two-couple team. 'Are you from Delhi?' she asks.

'Kolkata,' Sumita replies.

'And there's just the two of you travelling? Going further up?'

'Yes, to both.'

'Wow,' the lady says, 'I used to think only girls from Delhi were so brave!'

At sunset, the entire Kinnaur Kailash Range is on fire again. It is a day to Lakshmi Purnima or Sharad Purnima, and the almost perfect orb of the moon rises from behind the orange peaks. As we watch, strains of haunting music from local drums and clarinets waft to us from the monastery below.

The next day, we are at the crossroads of Kalpa village where calf-sized mountain dogs snooze in the sun. An alley with small shops selling plastic goods, stationery items, and golden apples in large cardboard trays leads straight to the Lochawa La-Khang or Samdub Choeling, or the Hu-Bu-Lan-Kar monastery. Founded by Rinchen Zangpo.

Sunny and warm, the monastery porch comes with a white chorten in the centre, rows of prayer wheels all around, and an uninterrupted view of the entire mountain range that nestles our hotel.

The goddess in the monastery sanctum has a fair, feminine face and a calm, though unsmiling, expression. She wears a garland of alternating ₹ 10 and ₹ 5 notes around her neck.

From the monastery, the road continues past the Army green local post office with its red signage, to end at the village temple.

Ornate wooden dragons coil around the temple's pillars. A thick brass door etched with Indian gods opens out to the sunny, central courtyard. On the temple wall hangs a faded photo of the precincts, taken by one William Simpson during a local festival in 1864. In the photo, the incumbent deity is being carried out on a *doli* (palanquin). It is the only view of the deity that we get, for the door to the sanctum is padlocked.

State-wide Kinnaur festivities—cultural programmes and a fair—are on at Reckong Peo. We pay a visit.

Makeshift stalls are chockfull of woollens, plastic goods, amulets and charms, dry fruits, sickles, knives and all manner of household goods. Locals have turned out in their early winter wear, with most men and women donning the traditional Kinnauri cap. Shopkeepers and buyers bargain with gusto and good humour.

Tourists are few, though.

Probably not welcome, either.

Aggressive porters try to offload huge bundles over our heads; a local bus screeches to a halt just inches away, covering us with dust. The driver grins.

Undaunted, we buy hand-knit woollen socks in flamboyant patterns for ourselves—primarily for their warmth factor, I should clarify—and a Kinnauri cap for Pawan.

For the rest of our trip, Pawan wears his cap like it is stitched to his scalp: it does wonders to his position among the locals.

RAKCHAM-CHITKUL

Paul Theroux has said, 'Tourists don't know where they've been, travelers don't know where they're going.'

We begin this journey across Himachal as tourists: every single stopover on our route plotted carefully, all accommodation booked in advance. Even those in the remote, cold corners of Nako, Tabo, and Kaza.

We know where we are going.

And then, we change quite a bit of it.

A lazy afternoon in Kalpa finds Sumita snuggling under a soft blanket while I browse through my morning's photo collection. 'Do you think we should have done Sangla and Chitkul?' I ask her suddenly.

'You said they would be crowded, touristy places, didn't you?' she says, surprised.

'I know. But maybe we could cover Chitkul in a day trip from here? We do have a spare day, right?'

It is an idea I want to follow up. The hotel staff discourages it: It would be an inordinately long journey over mountain roads, and we could not hope to return before nightfall. Pawan discourages it strongly: he has his driver's seat pushed back, his feet up on the dashboard. He is looking forward to an off-day.

I call up a few of the well-travelled men I know. One of them suggests a night halt midway between Sangla and Chitkul. 'Why don't you drive straight to Chitkul, roam around, and then spend a night at Rakcham? Return to Kalpa the next day. Simple.'

'To me a lush carpet of pine needles or spongy grass is more welcome than the most luxurious Persian rug': Meadows near Chitkul

I make some phone calls to hotel owners, book a room at Rakcham for the next night.

The road glides past the hydro-electric project at Karchham, and the lush green valleys and apple orchards at Sangla slowly being choked by hotels, shops and roadside eateries. 14 kilometres from Sangla, an arched signage over the road indicates that we have reached Rakcham.

Wedged between barren mountains on one side, and the Baspa River cradled by snow-covered mountains on the other, Rakcham at 9,514 feet has some 800-odd inhabitants who live in deodar wood houses that would cost a fortune in any Indian city.

For stray visitors or trekkers choosing to spend a night, there is just the one hotel, Rupin Riverview—where we have our booking—and some tents along the Baspa.

At first glance, Rakcham seems to be caught in a time warp. There are no newspapers, no post offices, and no police stations. We do not even find a local market. But for the gurgling river and the cawing of a yellow-billed chough, we have just walked into a silent movie.

After a quick lunch, we drive down to Chitkul: at 11,320 feet, the last and highest village close to the Indo-Tibet border.

Long stretches of the road are bordered by beige-and-white glacial erratics in all shapes and sizes. Pawan, his mood lifted, points to them with his free left: 'See those? They roll down every winter from the mountains, along with the snow.'

Erratics take their name from the Latin word *errare*, and may often be carried by glacial ice over hundreds of kilometres.

It is an impressive pile-up of erratics, interspersed with shining green pine trees, tall yellow grass, shrubs with red leaves, and sudden small rivulets gurgling over yellow moss-wrapped pebbles.

Where the road falls steeply off the cliff, fat, gummy, light brown pine cones sit on wide, velvet-green leafy canopies of trees that seem to rise from the crevasses below.

I get off the car and peer over the edge. The valley with its winding sea-green and white river lies at the base of the mountains. The first row of ranges on the far side has sparse vegetation. Thin, sparkling-silver mountain springs trickle down to meet the river. Roads zigzagging through the vegetation are like the random strokes of an artist's pencil. The second mountain range, towering beyond the first, is snow covered.

The motor road ends at Chitkul, a cluster of one and two-storeyed wooden village houses and granaries. Quaint wooden ladders lead up to square padlocked doors. In their backyard, ladies are winnowing grain, or drying their long hair in the sun.

But the poetry seems to end right there. Satellite TV antennas are sharing space with carved wood cornices. There are more hotel rooms than village homes. Hotels have popped up on the wide open meadow rolling towards the mountains, built one ahead of the other to compete in their offer of great views. The garishly painted structures have taken away the solitude, the quaintness and the beauty of the village altogether.

Even as we watch, mini buses arrive and offload tourists by the dozen. They bring with them the decibel levels of their crowded cities.

Some tourists bulldoze their way through an odd combination of chowmein, parathas, and omelettes at a local restaurant. Ironically, they discuss how the hotel boom in Chitkul has overshot ground reality, leading to rooms lying vacant even through the seasonal rush.

Elsewhere, the altar of the local temple dedicated to goddess Mathi—said to have been built 500 years ago—stays padlocked. On the courtyard, locals gather for an election rally. 'Come, come, listen to our *neta,*' one of the party members urges us aggressively.

'Listen to me,' says the jade-green Baspa River too, gurgling as it bounds past rocks. 'Listen to us,' say the snow-covered ranges, 'and you will still be able to hear the shifting snow.'

Sumita and I walk towards the Baspa, and slowly, its steady murmur fills our souls.

We return to Rakcham by tea time. The small balcony of our upper-floor room in Rupin Riverview opens out to the Baspa River Valley.

Wild red berries add their colour to tree-loads of ochre leaves. Pine trees are heavy with cones. White pebbles line the green-blue river waters, and beyond them stretch the buckwheat fields. A short bridge over the calm river mostly sees four-legged traffic: herds of cattle led by a solitary villager. A glacier on a nameless peak, framed by the fretwork of our window, gleams gold with the last rays of the sun.

When night falls, dragging the temperature uncomfortably down with it, we troop to the dining hall for warm soups. It is a pleasure to discover that the owner's corner in the hall also doubles as a miniature library. Well-thumbed books have been left thoughtfully behind by past travellers. I pick up some on Himalayan birds and both Sumita and I happily tuck us in bed, looking forward to an enlightening read.

Outside, an almost full moon shines its light over the snow-tipped mountains, and Baspa glistens like a streak of lightning.

This is a trekkers' heaven, but we are not here to trek. This is a heaven for anglers, too, for the Baspa River yields brown trouts. We are not planning to fish either. For us, Rakcham means falling off the map for 24 hours. And in these 24 hours, we have managed to pack in aeons of peace.

NAKO

'NH 22 is the worst maintained National Highway,' Pawan grumbles, more to himself.

He means NH 5. A couple of years ago, National Highway Authorities of India decided that the National Highways travelling in a north-south direction would be even-numbered, and the ones going east to west would be odd-numbered. All the numbers of existing highways changed to fit the plan. Pawan, like many of his driver clan, has not updated his database.

NH 22 now runs somewhere in Bihar.

Since we have not travelled over all the national highways yet, we take his statement about NH 5's dubious distinction with a game expression. But we do see why any driver would gripe about the sections we are driving on.

The former National Highway 22—the road we are now on—has featured in History TV's *IRT Deadliest Roads* series. This is what *www.dangerousroads.org* has to say about it:

> *'National Highway 22 is one of the world's deadliest roads. Located in India, the road has dangerous cliffs, poor bridges and tunnels, heavy traffic and very bad conditions....*
>
> *'The road starts asphalted in Ambala... in the state of Haryana. Suddenly, arriving to Kalka..., in the foothills of the Himalayas, the road becomes a mountain road with extensive hairpin turns. The conditions at this point are extreme. Heavy traffic,*

> *dangerous cliffs, poor bridges and tunnels on a very narrow road poorly surfaced.*
>
> *'After Kalka, the road winds up to the Himachal Pradesh and ends in Khab, a small village near the India-Tibet border.... The road is still a lifeline for the local people....*
>
> *'.... In many places the road is bordered by a drop of hundreds of meters (many hundreds of feet) unprotected by guardrails.'*

From the backseat of the Tavera, I offer an apple to Pawan to cheer him up.

He does not extend his hand. Instead, in a solemn tone, he says: 'One minute, Ma'am.'

Almost instantly, I know why he needs that minute or 10: very slowly, but surely, the car is skidding backward, downward.

Pawan manages to kill the engine, half open his door, and wriggle out of the rolling car.

Does he plan to ditch us and save his life?

We freeze in our seats like a bunny out of its burrow with a falcon drawing circles in the sky over its head.

He goes behind the car, picks up a medium-sized boulder, and wedges this against the rear right wheel. Gets back into his seat, and starts the car again. This time, we scramble over and across the skid zone.

Suitably chastened, we continue the journey in silence. Bright yellow signboards pop up now and then on the Sutlej side of the road with warnings:

> *'Shooting Stone Zone. Narrow Road Ahead'.*

Sand-coloured craggy mountains now rising steeply on our left have been gouged out to make the road. As sweet revenge, they do seem quite capable of launching large and small boulders at will on suspecting traffic.

If it is any consolation, the Sutlej River Valley is not too far below the road at this point. So our tumble downward would not be a prolonged, slow motion, heart-stopping-before-you-hit-the-water affair, but telegraphic:

Boulder hits car. Car splashes into Sutlej. Three killed on the spot.

'Look up, don't look down,' I tell Sumita. I do the same.

The sky is cornflower blue, with or without the colour polariser filter on my lens, and like the feathers of an enormous swan—'the feathered glory' of Zeus, may be—pristine white cirrus clouds form patterns on it, patterns that change with every mile we cover. The gods are good, and choose not to rain boulders on three insignificant travellers.

A gushing waterfall makes a dramatic appearance. A mountain lizard approaches a chunk of coconut thrown carelessly by the roadside. It is an ugly black, with warts all over its body, cream dots on its back, and a vicious red mouth that stays open and poised over the coconut till our car has passed.

To state the obvious: I am not in love with anything remotely reptilian.

A little past noon, we halt at a small roadside shop for a tea break. The village lady who owns the shop is busy cutting up tomatoes. She could give a Mukimono guy a run for his money: each cut tomato looks like a bright red flower in full bloom.

'What will you use them in?' I ask the lady.

'I will dry these in the sun, and put them in dal later,' she answers shyly. She is preparing for the onset of winter that would bring with it an acute shortage of fresh vegetables.

In a small pram near her, a little child smiles in its sleep. At the rickety table outside the shop, a robust youth wolfs down a lunch of kidney beans curry and rice, and generously helps himself to what looks like a heap of roasted grasshoppers.

Grasshoppers?

I forget courtesy for a minute and lean over to take a close look at his food. It is a plateful of deep-fried red chillies, with their curled up stems still attached.

At Khab village, where Spiti River gurgling down from Spiti valley meets the Sutlej rising from Manasarovar, we leave NH 5. Nako is not far away.

'Nako village, at 12,018 feet, has more open spaces, and then there is the lake too,' the receptionist at Hotel Kinnaur Kailash has warned us, 'You will find Nako much colder than Kalpa.'

Truer words have never been spoken.

'Water has frozen in the taps,' says the lone guy manning Lake View Guest House. 'You won't be able to stay here. We will put you up at Reo Purgil instead. It is under the same management.'

Hotel Reo Purgil offers us a sunny ground-floor room, with tall glass windows and a balcony overlooking the village. Unlike Lake View, which would have allowed us to gaze upon the blue waters from the warm confines of our room, Reo Purgil is a short walk away from the lake.

A walk versus running water in the taps. Running water wins.

Our hotel is named after Reo Purgyal (22,362 ft), one of the highest peaks of the Zanskar Range. Its name means 'a demon'. It is a peak that would reveal itself to us easily and often during our stay at Nako, at its splendorous best with dusk.

In the room next to us, amid a humongous pile of clothes, bags, mattresses and electronic accessories, a couple of young foreigners try a hand at Indian drums. They are the only other guests during our stay, barring the occasional tourists who drop in for a bio-break or a cup of tea on their way to colder zones.

It is past 2:30 pm. Manish—caretaker, guide, probably chef, too (unverified data: the kitchen is in the basement and accessible through a narrow and dingy passage of stone steps)—can only offer us the ubiquitous noodles for lunch. Bland, but piping hot. Dinner, he promises, would have rice, dal and egg curry: a princely fare in such parts.

A little before sunset, we walk the narrow strip of road to the lake, and scramble down a steep embankment to reach the still waters.

The first thing that strikes us is the silence, so deep that we almost hear the lone sheep munching on sun-dried grass by the shore. The lake glistens in the late autumn sunlight: a fragile sheet of translucent glass that mirrors the flare of yellow leaves on the willows and poplars encircling the pebbled shore, and the blue mountain ranges beyond.

Someone has built a little chorten by the lake. I spend some time adding a couple more uneven pebbles to it, an exercise in balancing. At the top of the embankment, a herd of cream and brown sheep scuttle over loose stones, their coats superbly blending with the rugged brown soil. The shepherd remains unseen.

With the setting of the sun, the chill factor increases, and we return to Reo Purgil. Manish brings tall glasses of tea, the strings of the tea bags wound conveniently around spoons for re-dipping. There is the customary power cut, and the candlelit hour—spent cosily under the thick blankets—is filled with the pleasant anticipation of dinner.

Rice, dal and egg curry arrive with the return of electricity, and live up to expectations.

Returning to the lake and its surroundings the next morning, we have an unexpected escort, a dog with a lovely cream coat and gentle eyes like pools of honey. She leads us up the slopes next to the lake. We huff and we puff, but do not lose sight of our four-legged guide.

She takes us to a ridge with an aerial view of the deep green-blue Nako Lake and the quiet village that stretches from its shore to the foothills of the distant, snow-brushed ranges. About six satellite TV antennas shine like tiny suns from one or two-storeyed homes.

Atop the hillock we have climbed are three white chortens within square, covered spaces and one a little away, standing out against the azure sky. At our feet, little red berries grow in abandon on thorny bushes that jut out from the edge of the cliff.

Sumita finds a wide boulder to sit on. Very close to her, the dog crouches on another boulder: its tapering top barely holds her huddled paws. They sit in silence, their faces away from the sun, and look at the lake and the village while the dog quietly enjoys an occasional ruffling of its furry neck.

After a long while, we come down the mountain, the dog trotting alongside. But while we try to find biscuits for her at the two small grocery shops, the dog quietly walks away. She came to us without expectations, and after a golden hour of canine-human bonding, chose to end the relationship as easily as she had begun it.

Guru Padmasambhava is believed to have walked through this region, and Nako village still bears his footprint. We do not know where this is.

'Let us ask Manish,' Sumita says.

Manish hails from Jharkhand, and has worked in Delhi for a while before settling down at Nako. He is eager to take us through the narrow lanes and bylanes of the village. Petite prayer wheels are everywhere: right in the middle of a lane, hiding in a nook in the wall. Old ladies offer prayers at these recesses. Younger women wash grain at their doorsteps, or lug twigs in conical cane baskets slung across their backs. They all wear *thepangs* to shield their heads from the sun.

We reach the tiny, dark, one-roomed monastery that houses the sacred footprint. The stone with the extra-large footprint stands vertically at the base of an idol of Guru Padmasambhava.

As offerings, there are:

Yellow, plastic flowers in a vase.

A couple of coins stuck on the imprint.

A half-eaten apple placed near the heel.

I wonder about the half-eaten apple.

Walking back to the hotel, we step into Nako's only souvenir shop next to the tiny branch of a bank. An old man is sunning himself outside the shop. He scurries in at our approach.

'Where are you from?' he asks.

'Kolkata.'

'I have been to Kolkata, seen the Howrah bridge!' He stretches his arms sideways and flaps his palms to show us the impressive size of the bridge.

The shop is stashed with semi-precious jewellery, small masks, statuettes, *thangkas*. Sumita spots some singing prayer bowls: metal bowls that come with a small cylindrical piece of polished wood. Rubbing the wood along the outer rim of the bowl in a circular motion produces a sound that could pass as the 'Om'. The prayer bowls at this shop are made of brass, and have engravings both inside the bowl and on its bottom.

'What are you charging for a prayer bowl?' I ask the old man.

'₹ 800,' he says, without batting an eyelid.

It is way overpriced. We try to bargain. Manish stands by the shop door wearing a scowl.

'₹ 600 for you,' says the old man. 'And I will give you the stick for free.'

The bowl should not cost a rupee more than ₹ 300, Manish silently and furiously gestures from behind.

The shopkeeper does not budge from his rate. Sumita really likes the bowl, so I buy it at ₹ 600.

We have been ripped off, and we know it.

To Manish, this is unforgivable stupidity. He does not say as much to his guests, but during our journey back to the hotel, we get a very clear view of his stiff back.

TABO

All in the space of two hours from Nako, we glide into an entirely different landscape. Green mountain slopes turn barren and various shades of deep brown that crease vertically into themselves until the very horizon where the blue peaks have been blessed with snow. For most of the stretch, nothing grows except wild cacti, and even these are not green, but many shades of yellow and russet, wrapped into tight bushy balls by a fickle yet strongly blowing wind.

It does not seem to have changed much, this area visited by Rudyard Kipling's Kim:

> *'At last they entered a world—a valley of leagues where the high hills were fashioned of the mere rubble and refuse from off the knees of the mountains....*
>
> *'"Surely the Gods live here!" said Kim, beaten down by the silence and the appalling sweep and dispersal of the cloud-shadows after rain. "This is no place for men." '*

The road winds along the higher ridges like a blue racer snake. Far below us, at the base of the black-brown ranges, some attempts have been made to plant trees. The result is an abrupt patch of green and orange amid a desert-like land, a magic carpet waiting to fly. The Sutlej meanders along its valley, looking like a wispy, pale green brook from where we stand.

Landslide prone zones are a uniform dull grey, with glacial moraine travelling down to the sides of the road and blocked partially by boulders bound with steel wire. Here, work at road repair seems to go on throughout the year, barring the deadly white winters. Many of the workers are women, some with babies at their breast. A toddler, his red monkey cap a striking contrast to the grey dusty road, plays with an old cricket bat and a ball.

At places, textured, sand-coloured hillocks rise up from the precipice side of the road like colossal termite dens. I almost expect giant termites to stroll out of them and flex their muscles in the manner of Hopper, the grasshopper from the Walt Disney movie, *A Bug's Life.*

Our driver Pawan talks of a family he had brought to this area some years ago. 'They were going from Kalpa to Tabo,' he says. 'When I drove them to these parts, they were so frightened by the bleak landscape that they insisted on turning back. For hours, we had not seen a single soul, let alone chai shops. I had to reverse the car and take them to Nako, where I managed to put them up for the night. The next morning, another team arrived at Nako from Shimla. Since that team was also going to Tabo, my passengers decided to accompany them. So our cars travelled together.'

Cars on this road are few and far between. When a loaded truck does appear behind us, it seems like a toy vehicle against the huge mountain ranges that tower at its back.

As we reach Tabo on an afternoon of lukewarm sunlight and roll down the car windows, we are hit by a surge of cold wind and dry mud.

A film of dry mud settles everywhere in Tabo, at an altitude of 10,000 feet: on parked cars, on the furry coats of stray dogs, on birch trees with bright golden leaves, on the scarves that local women tie around their nose and mouth to keep these from clogging.

The woman who lets us into Trojan Guest House has an air of irritability that is thinly veiled. She is the caretaker's wife, the mother of his two children. 'I cannot prepare lunch,' is the first thing she says. 'Go to the restaurants near the monastery, they will give you food.'

We are the only guests this late in October.

Our luggage is taken to a ground floor room, a basic affair with a double bed, a table, and two wooden, upholstered chairs. We follow. A steel jug stands on the table. 'That is your drinking water,' the woman tells us, 'just changed the water this morning.'

We are thirsty. I take off the lid of the jug to infuse a few drops of Zeolin, our water purifier. Find a dozen dead flies afloat in their watery grave.

'I just changed the water,' the woman insists. Then, with a sigh, 'Okay, I will change again.'

In a restaurant near the monastery, it is tea-time. Convivial men sit around holding white enamel mugs with blue rims. The mugs in their calloused hands are warm but empty: the tea is over, their tales are not. They shift a bit on the bench to make enough space for us, smile and continue the conversation. The lady owner rustles up a meal of rice and kidney beans for Sumita, Pawan and me. It is hot, simple, and very welcome.

'Have you just arrived in Tabo?' the lady asks after we have paid and thanked her for the fare.

'Yes.'

'Take these apples. Fresh from my garden, but I have only these two left.'

'Thank you, and don't worry,' I say, accepting the gift, 'we will share.' Pawan gets one. Sumita and I will have the other.

As we walk out of the restaurant and into the remains of the day, twilight glows: on the few village houses; the mud chortens of the Tabo Monastery; tall, gold-leafed birches with their intertwined pale cream boughs; lone standing poplars with their green, matte gold and burnt orange leaves; on the million pink, succulent leaves of a tree I have not met before. Beyond them rise the hills, and far, far away in the still blue horizon, a few snow-swept peaks raise their heads.

Tabo Chos-hkhor or the Tabo Millennium Monastery (established: 996 AD), a UNESCO World Heritage Site, is a complex of mud buildings and stupas. The accommodation for the monks and the

Millennium Guest House for tourists are, however, painted brick buildings with the whitewashed walls and traditional black-and-maroon bordered carved-wood window frames that we have seen across north-east Himachal.

Tabo Monastery has been called the Ajanta of the Himalayas. The paintings in the main temple—there are nine temples and four decorated stupas—go back to the 10th-11th centuries.

A half-open wooden door leads us to the large porch of Tabo Chos-hkhor the next morning. A wood and iron bench with a backrest occupies the centre of the porch. Local villagers, many of them women, sit on it and around it on the dusty ground, a knee raised to rest the right wrist while they air their cracked feet and their opinion.

Their talk revolves only around the approaching elections. 'Consider the benefits promised by the different parties,' say the veterans, 'and only then cast your vote.' The others nod.

They have not come to visit the monastery; they do not glance at the thin trickle of visitors.

The door to Tsug la Khang, the main temple, is locked. I manage to find an old, bespectacled lama in the traditional maroon robe and smart black boots near the Millennium Guest House.

'Please could you open the monastery for us?' I ask.

'Could you come back on Monday?' he says.

'I am afraid we won't be here till Monday.'

He calls up a student of the monastery from his mobile phone. After a while, a chubby, genial young lama in yellow and maroon clothes arrives to show us around.

The entry to Tsug la Khang is through the door on the south wall. Once in, we turn left to go into the old entry hall. The guardian figure of Vajrapasa (Cho-Kyong) is seated here, right knee forward and the left leg extended. There is a sculpture of Ganesh, a favourite God from the Hindu pantheon. I wonder how he found a place in a Buddhist monastery, then remember that artists and sculptors from Kashmir were commissioned to work here by Yeshe Od, the reigning Tibetan king.

The Assembly Hall has the Vajradhatu Mandala, or the Diamond Realm. In Vajrayana Buddhism, the Diamond Realm is a metaphysical space inhabited by the Five Wisdom Buddhas: Vairochana, Amitabha, Amoghasiddhi, Akshobya, and Ratnasambhava, and other deities associated with them. All the statues have haloes around their heads, in bas-relief, the style of the halo similar to the Pala Age bronzes. At the far end of the hall is a huge image of Maha Vairochana, rather, a combination of four statues seated back to back. His eyes are half-closed, his expression ecstatic.

The entire monastery is said to have been built on the basis of the mandala concept from the *Sarva Tathagata Tattva Samgraha Tantra*, a text translated into Tibetan by Rinchen Zangpo (958-1055 AD).

In my search to understand the Vajradhatu Mandala, this is what I find from Eva Lee, an artist on a Fulbright research project called *Indo-Tibetan Mandalas: Blueprints for Discovering the Nature of Mind and Reality*:

> *'.... there are literally hundreds of tantric deities, each with unique mandalas representing different sets of details and qualities specific to his or her teachings and practice. All varieties transmit fundamentally the same Buddhist wisdom and compassion, but each deity provides a different identity with which practitioners, according to their particular personality, can relate to or find affinity with....*
>
> *'Although intricate, aesthetically compelling, and often mysterious to the non-practitioner, mandalas are meant for religious use and are not intended as works of art for museum or private collection....'*

The deities before us are three-dimensional, stucco sculptures that jut out from the walls, seated apparently on air with their feet at a level above our heads. Each has a name beginning with Vajra: Vajra Dharma, Vajra Tiksna, Vajra Ketu, Vajra Hasa and 29 more, their complexions ranging from sunset red to midnight blue, their eyes piercing or serene as they look down at us from dimly lit walls covered with paintings of Buddhas, bodhisattvas, tantric deities and Bon goddesses. The paintings, like those at Ajanta, have been done in a continuous and sequential manner.

One by one, we explore the Dromton Temple (Brom-ston Lha-khang), founded by the main disciple of the great teacher Atish Dipankar Srigyan, the Initiation Temple (dKyil-kHor-khang), where monks are initiated, the Bodhisattva Maitreya Temple (Byams-Pa Chen-po Lha-khang), with its carved wooden door frame and 20-feet high painted mural of the future Buddha Maitreya, and the Golden Temple (gSer-khang). The Golden Temple gets its name from the belief that a layer of gold-dust as thick as a yak's skin was once spread over its inner walls.

Invasions, an earthquake and the natural passage of time have left their mark. The painted mud walls are cracked or swollen in places. Inch by inch, this treasure house of Indo-Tibetan art is crumbling into dust.

On a cliff-top close to the monastery, there are caves once inhabited by the monks. A narrow, paved road goes halfway up the slope. I climb up the rest of the sheer rock face literally on all fours, amazed at the fitness of the lamas who would have walked and hiked this route three to four times a day. Sumita stays on the road with my camera, marvelling at this opportunity of photographing me in the primate mode. Fills up a lot of frames with my considerable rear end.

The inside of the caves are sooty, with tiny niches that must have once held butter lamps. Some caves are now littered with empty beer bottles.

With nothing to hold on to, and shingles shifting and sliding underfoot, climbing down is far more difficult. I am forced to slide down on the much-photographed part of my body, using my heels as brakes.

On the firm surface of the road, Sumita is laughing her head off. 'You look such a sight,' she says.

'Move away from my path,' I tell her solemnly, 'if I lose my grip, I will come rolling down on you, and both of us will hurtle down right through the row of trees to the village below.'

She turns to look at the drop behind her. Stops laughing and scuttles to her right.

We take a circuitous route back to the guest house, past an apple tree stooping with fruit, and the local post office. The cream pillar holding its low iron gate has a crudely drawn bird in flight and the India Post logo.

When we return to the guest house, there is no electricity to turn on the geyser. It doesn't actually matter—the washroom taps are dry.

Sumita goes in search of the caretaker's wife, finds her busy negotiating a deal with some travellers. They have just arrived, and would like a room. In the absence of an advance reservation, the cash they pay will be pocketed by the caretaker. They have sensed this and are trying to bargain.

'There is no electricity. No water, either,' Sumita tells the woman. 'Could you do something?'

The travellers seeking a room change their minds fast, and disappear. The woman is furious. 'You made me lose clients,' she screams at Sumita. 'Just let my husband return and we will see what he has to say.'

Even when the power is restored, there is no water. Apparently, only Lama, the caretaker, knows how to switch on the pump, and he is not back from his business on the side. Whether, true to his name, he also serves as a lama with the Tabo Monastery is a question we do not get to ask.

When Lama does return late evening, the loss of clients is reported. Deserving an apology for our inconvenience all day, we have instead a confrontational man to handle.

'You have angered my wife. I don't think she will wish to make you any dinner,' Lama says.

'What do you expect us to eat then?' Sumita asks, 'We cannot walk to the restaurants this late, they will be closed.'

'What do I care? I am not going to request my wife. Left to me, I would not give you any dinner,' the caretaker declares. 'If you want any food, go plead with my wife.'

Sumita does have to go ask the wife, and extremely grudgingly dinner is served: a bowl of watery dal, four rotis, and some sad grey,

'Throughout the centuries there were men who took first steps down new roads armed with nothing but their own vision': Tabo Millennium Monastery

boiled potatoes broken into small lumps by hand and then fried—for microseconds, and in half teaspoon oil—with cumin seeds.

I should have known. Anything called Trojan—whether a horse or a virus, or even a guest house—can and will spring some unpleasant surprises.

The single latch on the inside of our room door is wobbly at best. By common consent, Sumita and I drag and pile our entire luggage behind the door before retiring for the night. My sturdy tripod is folded and promoted to the bed, to serve as a weapon if need be.

Eva Lee, the Fulbright scholar on mandalas, also says:

> *'In real life situations, I think of mandala principle as Buddhism-in-action in the sense that your immediate surroundings is your mandala, and all the people you encounter are part of it, too. You have Buddha-nature within you, and so do they. With awareness and practice that comes from meditation, you have at every moment the potential to actualize compassion and wisdom in what you think, what you say, and what you do.'*

We do not feel the 'Buddha-nature' within us tonight.

DHANGKAR

A laggard sun has made sure that the craggy snow peaks in the far horizon stay swathed in a veil of mist, though never out of sight.

When specks of white dulled by the listless light show up on the tallest spur among the barren ranges to our right, Pawan veers off the Samdu-Kaza Road and on to an 8-km-long dirt track winding uphill to Dhangkar Gompa (12,774 ft), one of the five major monasteries of the Spiti Valley.

The *gompa,* or monastery, comes in two parts:

A couple of shining new red-cream concrete buildings at the tiny village of Shichilling. Utterly unremarkable.

The 1,000-year-old original mud-and-stone structure in an equally minuscule village of Dhangkar, perched precariously on a rocky projection a 1,000 feet higher. Completely dramatic.

Of course we feel the punishing need to hike up the shifting, crumbling dry mud track to the endangered monastery. Arrive breathless at a little red door. It wears the oversized metal knob of a knocker with a long rope—multi-coloured silk ribbons pleated together and ending with a tassel.

We do not have to yank at the rope, the door is open. The narrow stone staircase beyond it has a 'Save Dhangkar' signboard on its wall, and opens out to a small shaded porch, where a single lama sits at a small table outside the sanctum door.

The youth, mid-20s at best, has a booklet of flimsy yellow paper: entry tickets that cost ₹ 25 each. He is Tonba, a man of very few words.

The ridges on his shaved oval head mirror the ridges of the mountain he lives in. Sunken in their grooves in an ascetic face, his eyes are lonely and dark as the interiors of the sanctum with its Vairochana statue and its crumbling sacred texts.

Depending on how one looks at it, solitude can be a sanctuary or a prison.

Dhangkar village also harboured a prison once. Nonos, the former rulers of Spiti Valley, were harsh dispensers of justice.

Balancing delicately on the highest cliff behind the monastery are the remains of Dhangkar Fort, the home of the Nonos across several generations.

The 50-year-old World Monuments Fund, a 'non-profit organisation founded in 1965 by individuals concerned about the accelerating destruction of important artistic treasures throughout the world', lists Dhangkar as one of the world's 100 most endangered sites. This is what their website has to say:

> *'The Dhangkar Gompa is one of five major Buddhist monastic centers in the remote region of Spiti near the Tibetan border. Portions of the gompa, or temple, are still being used for worship, while other sections have been closed.... Built using traditional materials of mud, stone, and timber, the monastery contains a series of fifteenth-century wall paintings. The gompa is in an advanced state of deterioration caused by geotechnical instability as well as neglect and inadequate maintenance.'*

The 'geotechnical instability' is understandable. I claw my way up a ridge behind the monastery walls to a spectacular sight: the confluence of rivers Spiti and Pin. The valley lies far, far below, where the two teal-blue rivers—difficult to tell apart—have drawn erratic DNA patterns. Menhir-shaped brown palisades sculpted crudely, ravaged and then sculpted again by the wind and the snows rise randomly from the slopes that keep the valley locked in.

'It's not the mountain we conquer, but ourselves': Spiti River Valley, Dhangkar

I see:

Next to the half-dry river bed, a stretch of farmers' fields separated by dun-coloured aisles, their black-grey earth shorn of all crop.

Pencil-thin dirt tracks leading down to the fields, and up again, zigzagging across the slopes that grow nothing but yellowed balls of wild cacti.

A slow-moving caravan of loaded, depressed black donkeys trudging up a track.

The stubborn, even insane, urge of man to take over and inhabit every corner of the world, however inhospitable the terrain.

KAZA

A ramshackle market, one and two-storeyed houses on the slopes dominated by the colourful pagoda-style structure of a monastery and some russet cows welcome us to Kaza (11,980 ft), the headquarters of the Spiti Valley.

The Spiti belongs to the Himachal Pradesh Tourism Development Corporation (HPTDC), and is the biggest hotel in Kaza.

'Biggest' is not synonymous with the best, though. While we have a large room and a large TV set, power cuts are frequent and long lasting (read, days). Rooms do not have heaters, and the plush double bed has just one blanket per person and a large, common *rezai* for two.

The sky is overcast with slate-grey, menacing clouds that are right now descending vertically over the barren Kunzum Pass, named after Goddess Kunjum (Durga). She is believed to reside in a temple on the Kunzum top and guard the pass.

'Is it going to rain?' we anxiously ask Devraj, the hotel's Man Friday.

'It doesn't rain here, the climate is too cold for that,' Devraj says, 'the water drops freeze. We will have snowfall.'

The power returns for a while. We switch on the television. News channels are full of film clippings. It takes a while to connect the films with a common thread: director Yash Chopra.

Yash Chopra was shooting his last film *Jab Tak Hai Jaan* in Ladakh just a couple of months ago. He was in love with mountains. First, with the ranges in Kashmir that often formed the backdrop of his films.

'All the world is made of faith, and trust, and pixie dust': Ki Monastery, near Kaza

Then, when the strife-torn land allowed no safety for him and his crew, he had shifted his gaze to the Swiss Alps.

In Ladakh, to guard against the killing altitudes, Chopra's shooting team had a doctor on call. Apparently, at 80, he stayed the fittest in the team. To die, then, of dengue in Mumbai, his own city.

Tabo had no television. The news of his death is a day old.

With a little pop, the TV screen fades out. The electricity does not return again throughout our three-day stay.

There are no other tourists when we arrive at The Spiti. But when we go down to dinner, the dining hall is full of talkative guests. A large group of tourists is here by accident. Literally. On the Manali-Gramphu-Kumzum Pass road, one of their cars almost fell into a gorge.

They are relieved to have found a place to stay, some hot food on their plates.

They are so relieved to be alive tonight.

It is an inordinately long, freezing night, lit by a candle and the passing headlights of infrequent cars creating myriad abstract images on the walls.

The morning dawns sunny. All of Kunzum top is covered in snow. The night temperature—we are told—was somewhere in the range of minus six to seven degrees. This morning, it is still below zero.

On the ground outside our first floor window, puddles of water have turned into dirty sheets of sleet. A sheet of sleet covers the top of our car. After what must have been an unimaginably tough night in the open, furry brown and black dogs are looking for the sunniest spots to curl up and snooze.

Seven kilometres from Kaza, Ki Monastery (13,500 ft) is the oldest and largest monastery in Spiti Valley. A layered fort with at least a dozen levels stacked with maroon and white buildings atop a high slope leading up from the village, it has three domes of a fold mountain as its backdrop. Fully visible, and impressive from a turn in the road much below.

It is a steep, altitude-burdened hike from the car parking zone: first, along a winding and windy tar road, then a flight of wide stairs. Finally, we are into a level passage with the customary row of large prayer wheels leading to the monastery courtyard.

Ki has been attacked by the Mongols in the 17th century, caught in the war between Ladakh and Kullu, damaged by Dogra and Sikh armies, a fire and a violent earthquake. All of which probably explains the current labyrinth of corridors, steps and rooms that seem to have come up over the years. Architecturally speaking, it is built in the Pasada, or the fort-monastery style.

Portions of the altar inside the room labelled Kutung have a generous embedding of semi-precious stones. The *thangka*s on the walls on all three sides look ancient. Photos of the Dalai Lama and the Potala Palace hang from a low rafter.

The Zimshung, said to be the highest point in the monastery, shares a common terrace with Kutung. Corners of the different terraces are embellished with small, skull-topped posts with black flounces, or beautifully engraved brass pillars. An awe-inspiring view of Spiti River and the mountain ranges unfolds below us. Layers of an unfamiliar red grass are the only vegetation by the river bed.

It is cold on the terrace. Lips-turning-blue, nose-losing-sensation cold. Throw in windy.

A few lamas walk around the terrace in circles to keep themselves warm. The sound of chanting reverberates from behind the closed doors of the Mani Lhakhang.

I remember a conversation between Mr Chang, the High Lama, and Miss Roberta Brinklow, an Evangelical missionary, in James Hilton's *Lost Horizon*:

> *'What do the lamas do?' she continued.*
>
> *'They devote themselves, madam, to contemplation and to the pursuit of wisdom.'*
>
> *'But that isn't doing anything.'*
>
> *'Then, madam, they do nothing.'*

> *'I thought as much.' She found the occasion to sum up. 'Well, Mr. Chang, it's a pleasure being shown all these things, I'm sure, but you won't convince me that a place like this does any real good. I prefer something more practical.'*
>
> *'Perhaps you would like to take tea?'*

We would like to take tea. We would like that very much.

Just then, one of the lamas requests us to follow him. Bending low to keep our heads from 'denting' the low roof of a narrow, tortuous, stone staircase, we are guided into the dark monastery kitchen.

Strangely-shaped pots and pans sit on the shelves lining two adjacent walls. The centre of the kitchen has a fire going. Lamas huddle around it on wooden benches. They gesture to us to sit down.

The lama who has brought us in offers two glasses of hot, black tea.

Coincidence? Mind-reading? Right then, it is of no consequence. Watched over by many curious yet gentle eyes, we gratefully drink the tea, then record our 'views' in a much-thumbed guest-book.

Needless to say that the feedback is positive.

Higher up, at an altitude of 13,795 feet, Kibber village sits in a bowl-shaped valley ringed in by snow-laden mountains. Eighteen kilometres from Kaza, it is the highest village in the world to have its own polling station during the elections.

We stop by two signposts saying, among many other things, that this is the 65-km Chicham-Kibber Road, and that its construction, between 2004 and 2006, was estimated at ₹ 35.47 lakh, but the final expense went up to ₹ 59.42 lakh. On the two signboards and their zebra-striped iron posts, I count 11 tricoloured palms: the logo of the Congress Party.

A cluster of maroon-and-white homes dot the barren mountain face ahead of us like a flock of cranes.

This is Kibber.

To our distant left, at the base of another barren range, is a smaller cluster of white flecks.

That is Chicham.

An old woman walks up the road we just traversed with her grandson, a sunny toddler in an orange pullover, faded blue jeans and a round red cap.

Kibber's village folk are used to strangers. Both of them smile at us. The lady stops to have a chat. Our completely meaningful conversation has a smattering of Hindi and Paharia and a whole lot of smiles to fill the vocabulary void.

'We have a good hospital at Kibber,' the old lady says, 'and a senior secondary school.' There are 18 teachers at the school. 'I am the school peon.' This, with a small thump on her chest and a proud, gap-toothed smile.

At so high an altitude, Kibber residents manage to grow only potatoes and herd sheep. Through the punishing winters, when the snow ensures that no crops can grow, they are forced to survive mostly on meat. The school stays open, and the teachers, though they are all from a more temperate Mandi—at 3,425 ft—do not ask to go home because of the excruciating cold.

I take the old lady and her grandson's photos against the large chortens at the centre of the Chicham-Kibber Road. Then the toddler readily extends one of his little grubby fists to me, and the other to his grandmother, and somehow I, too, am in the frame.

The old lady throws us a final, sunny smile and bends low. Like a joey, her grandson climbs into a shawl pouch tied to her back. Two heads bob in unison as the school peon ambles down the gravelly path to the village.

LANGZA

In one of the numerous Net surfing sessions before this journey into the Himachal Himalayas, I had come upon a photograph of a huge Buddha statue on a mountain top. I felt drawn to it instantly, inexplicably. The caption said the photo had been taken at Langza, a village beyond Kaza.

With an altitude of 14,435 ft, less than 200 inhabitants, and the fairly dangerous winding road that leads to this village, Langza stays hidden from the regular tourist route, its Buddha seen as a distant, fleeting vision by alert travellers driving to Manali from Kaza.

From base-station Kaza, we set out the next morning in quest of Langza. 'Did you find out the directions to Langza?' I ask Pawan before he starts the engine.

'Yes, yes, I checked with the hotel staff,' he replies, and drives off. Takes a left turn soon, crosses a one-vehicle bridge over the Spiti River, and pulls up confidently by the cream-coloured walls of a single-storeyed monastery. On a slope a little above it, is a large golden statue of the Buddha. The hill continues its rise behind the statue, ending halfway below a single, massive, serrated mountain partially covered in snow.

This is not the figure I saw on the Net.

'This *is* the statue you wanted to see, Ma'am,' Pawan insists. 'There isn't any other.'

I am not convinced.

Many ladies sit on the porch of the monastery, chanting. It has a comforting cadence. They have been chanting at a stretch for three long years—we would learn later—except during the really harsh winter months. Men stand around, listening to the chant. I approach a gentleman who might speak English. He does.

'Please could you tell me the name of this village?'

'This is Rangrik,' he replies.

'Is there any other Buddha statue as large as this one, maybe larger, around these parts?'

'Oh yes, there is one at Langza.' He points to the other shore of the Spiti River, to a distant monastery atop a slope: 'Do you see that monastery?'

I notice the speck of white, the tiny village houses at its feet. They are familiar.

'We have been there. That's the Ki Monastery.'

'Well, Langza is beyond that, and higher. Take that same route, and keep going.'

We thank him. A crestfallen Pawan retraces his route.

It is a seemingly endless and lonely road to Langza. There are no other cars in sight. Something moves on the menacingly rugged, cider-brown mountains, sending down a shower of small stones. It is a well-camouflaged team of barasingha, the antlered deer. The only other sign of life is a bush covered with wild red berries.

The car comes to a halt near the top of a barren hill. Two thin trails made by the regular footfall of Buddhist villagers lead to the statue on its edge. Panting a little from the altitude gain, we walk the trail.

The Buddha towers over us, easily six times the height of an average human being. He faces a panoramic range of snow-draped mountains against an azure horizon. His attire orange-yellow, his expression serene.

A yellow-billed ebony-black chough glides gently over the black curls on the Buddha's head. In the homes below the hill, villagers go about their usual chores, but no sound travels up to us. We sit down a little distance behind the statue, gazing at the snowy peaks in companionable silence even as our breathing returns to its normal pace.

'I never get tired of the blue sky': Langza village

Village women walk up to us with an offer of butter tea. These are our early days in the Himalayas: we are not adventurous enough to try local food. 'Later, perhaps,' we tell the ladies, not wishing to disappoint them.

A little girl with unkempt hair approaches us with a fossil. 'Would you like to buy *chaudua*? *Phossil*? ₹ 150 only,' she says.

It is an ammonite, probably the most widely known fossil, with a ribbed spiral shell. These marine creatures lived between 240-65 million years ago, and had one thing in common with the dinosaurs: they went extinct around the same time. 'Ammonite' originates from Ammon, the Greek ram-horned god. Ammonites were cephalopods, a group of predators that includes the octopus, squid, cuttlefish and nautilus.

Strange as this may sound, fossils like the ammonite lie scattered amid the rocky grounds of Langza. These are from the Tethys Sea.

The Britannica website has this to say:

> *'Tethys Sea, former tropical body of salt water that separated the supercontinent of Laurasia in the north from Gondwana in the south during much of the Mesozoic Era (251 to 65.5 million years ago). Laurasia consisted of what are now North America and the portion of Eurasia north of the Alpine-Himalayan mountain ranges, while Gondwana consisted of present-day South America, Africa, peninsular India, Australia, Antarctica, and those Eurasian regions south of the Alpine-Himalayan chain. These mountains were created by continental collisions that eventually eliminated the sea. Tethys was named in 1893, by the Austrian geologist Eduard Suess, after the sister and consort of Oceanus, the ancient Greek god of the ocean....*
>
> *'Tethyan deposits can be found in North America and Eurasia (especially in the Alpine and Himalayan regions) and in southern Asia (Myanmar and Indonesia). Limestones are a dominant sedimentary facies of Tethys. These sediments are often very rich in fossils, indicating an abundant and diverse tropical marine fauna....*
>
> *'East of the Alpine region, the Indian Plate was moving northward approaching the Asian Plate. Tethys closed during the*

> *Cenozoic Era about 50 million years ago when continental fragments of Gondwana—India, Arabia, and Apulia (consisting of parts of Italy, the Balkan states, Greece, and Turkey)—finally collided with the rest of Eurasia. The result was the creation of the modern Alpine-Himalayan ranges, which extend from Spain (the Pyrenees) and northwest Africa (the Atlas) along the northern margin of the Mediterranean Sea (the Alps and Carpathians) into southern Asia (the Himalayas) and then to Indonesia. Remnants of the Tethys Sea remain today as the Mediterranean, Black, Caspian, and Aral seas.'*

In India, it is illegal to even collect, let alone buy or sell fossils. The little seller goes away, disappointed. Sumita and I spend a while more with the Buddha, building a little chorten of pebbles at his feet. Like mighty waves frozen in time, the snow-covered, sun-dappled mountains have our backs.

UTTARAKHAND

CHAKRATA

It is 5:00 am and dark inside our air-conditioned compartment of the New Delhi-Dehradun Nanda Devi Express. A darkness heavy with the rhythmic jangle of the wheels muffled by the glass windowpanes and the clear, discordant snores that rise from varying mounds of flesh on unvarying berths. It is difficult to distinguish the bass from the soprano: all mounds are uniformly covered in white, crumpled bed sheets.

There is a third sound. Distinct, familiar. It is my mobile phone.

'Calling from Chakrata,' begins the male voice on the phone. It is Chauhan Chetan Singh, one of the owners of the accommodation we have booked. 'There has been a minor landslide between here and Dehradun,' Chetan says. 'The car we sent to pick you up is stuck at the spot. It may take a while for the road to clear. I am trying to get another car to receive you at the station. It has already crossed the landslide zone, and will get you till Vikasnagar. Please get off there and wait for your car.'

'Who is the driver?' I ask, 'How do we find him at Dehradun?'

'Name's Niki. I have messaged his number to you. Dehradun has a very small platform, you will find him easily. Please don't worry,' says Chetan.

Pp 136-137: 'Climb the mountains and get their good tidings': Trishul Peak from Kausani

Facing page: 'If I had to choose a religion, the sun as the universal giver of life would be my God.' At Chilmiri Neck, Chakrata

'If you don't climb the mountain, you can't see the view':
Yamuna flows around a hillock, near Chakrata

The day has not begun well. The train wheezes into Dehradun station at 7: 15 am, two hours behind schedule. It is a relief to find Niki.

Even after we have loaded our luggage and are ready to go, Niki does not start the engine.

'Is there a problem?' I ask him.

There is one, and it is at the moment trudging out of the station: a crotchety old lady lugging a massive suitcase. She has booked Niki's car. We are the hitch-hikers.

Her displeasure at this invasion of her privacy and her car is as subtle as the Great Wall of China. I shift to the front seat, next to Niki. Sumita retreats to the far corner of the backseat even as the lady dumps the suitcase near her knees. To establish her rightful claim to the car, she keeps us waiting and stomps off to have her morning cuppa.

After a couple of hours, Niki drops us at Vikasnagar. Post Sumita's tentative attempts at armistice in that while, the old lady has recovered her mood enough to smile and wave us goodbye. Good riddance, more like.

Our car has not arrived yet. I call up Chetan. 'Your driver Dinesh will be with you in 10 minutes,' he says. 'Relax, have a cup of tea.'

We act on the suggestion, and before the last sip, Dinesh arrives with three things: a white Scorpio, a wave, and a sunny smile. We are off to Chakrata.

Nestled between the Yamuna and the Tons (Tamas) rivers, Chakrata, at 6,949 feet, is a quaint cantonment area established in 1866 by Colonel Hume, 55th Regiment, British Indian Army. Roughly a 100 kilometres away from Dehradun, it is still an Indian Army base and a restricted area for foreigners.

The snow-laden Gangotri-Yamunotri ranges make a grand appearance as we drive past Chakrata's lone cinema hall. It is run by the Army and civilians are allowed in only for Sunday shows, says Dinesh. Photographing the hall and its surroundings is prohibited.

We seem to have arrived early in the tourist season, like the *gurash,* blood-red rhododendrons swaying on the branches in profuse clumps. It is the state flower of Uttarakhand.

At the head of the rough, bouldered ramp leading up to the porch of Hotel Himalayan Paradise, a tall, lean gentleman signals with his arms like an aircraft marshal on a runway, and our car zooms up to the hotel grounds.

Dinesh introduces us to Chetan, for it is none other. He is an ex-colonel of the Indian Army, Dinesh would tell us later, unsure about the 'ex' bit: apparently Chetan still gets calls from the Army and may go away for a stretch.

Chetan introduces us to Bruno, a large four-pawed veteran settled in the centre of the hotel porch. The early afternoon sunlight ripples through his golden flanks. Age sits heavy on his shoulders and has dimmed his liquid brown eyes. He responds with one bass 'Woof', and a mild thump of his tail.

Kalu or Kallan introduces himself with a sudden sharp lunge at my knees and rounds of staccato barks. At three months, he is a black-and-brown powerhouse of German shepherd energy and—we soon discover—most always covered in *transferable* dust. That is natural. Kalu is an explorer with a special focus on ornithology. He and I connect that instant. Sumita believes in friendships that grow slowly. A belief strengthened by the discovery that our new friend has not yet learned to keep his milk teeth out of our trouser edges.

From the front balcony of our first-floor room, we have a clear view of the distant southern slopes. While the hills that rise immediately behind the resort are lush green and peppered with birds, the southern face of the mountain range, we note, is barren.

Our room has:

Walls of deodar wood.

A polished-wood fireplace.

A wooden loft that can sleep two more guests.

A wooden ladder to access the loft.

I do not like the implication.

'Trees do not grow on the south side,' says Chetan, reading my look. He sounds like he knows. This is what I would read in a scientific article later:

'In general, for the northern hemisphere, south-facing slopes receive more sunlight and become more xeric and warmer, supporting drought-resistant vegetation and less conducive for tree growth, while north-facing slopes retain moisture and are cold and humid, supporting moisture-loving plants.'

In the evening, we speak to Chetan about an incident troubling our minds: the rape and murder of a young woman at Chakrata a few months ago. The report on outlookindia.com said:

'11 November 2014 | Society

'Dehradun: Taxi Driver Rapes Tourist, Murders Her and Her Friend

'A Delhi-based woman tourist was allegedly raped and murdered and her male friend killed by a taxi driver and his three accomplices here, police said today.

'The 27-year-old woman and her 24-year-old male companion had arrived in Dehradun on October 21 to celebrate Diwali, but were reportedly missing after two days, Vikasnagar Circle Officer Swapan Kishore Singh said.

'The four accused, including the cab driver, Raju, Bablu, Guddu and Kundan, have been arrested, and were being interrogated, he said.

'One of the accused has confessed during interrogation that he raped the woman before killing her, police sources claimed, adding that this can be confirmed only after her body was found.

'The incident happened on October 23 when the victims were returning in the taxi from the Tiger Falls about 30 km from Chakrata near here....

'The sources said that the accused confessed that the woman's body was dumped in the Yamuna river near Lakhamandal while her friend's body was thrown from a cliff about two km from there....'

'The two of us have been travelling among Himalayan townships for years now,' I tell Chetan. 'We've always found the hills very safe, safer than our cities. Then we read about this incident... it has shaken our faith.'

Chetan looks thoughtful. 'Of late, I have been dreading that something like this would happen. Only, I had thought it would be the other way around, one of our local girls being molested by visitors.... There have been tourists who play loud music in their cars, drink, party....'

The driver was not from Chakrata, he says, but Vikasnagar, closer to the urban influences of Dehradun. 'And then, if you ask your driver for drugs, wear shorts and bathe in the waterfall...' his voice trails away.

So rape only happens to women who are not dressed right, who happen to travel with a boyfriend, who take drugs? We do not match those criteria. Does that make us absolutely safe? We know he does not have an answer to that. We do not ask the question.

I produce a scrunched sheaf of printouts about the places we plan to visit. Chetan ignores most of the sites on my list.

'The sunrise view from Chilmiri Neck is good. You could then visit Chaani-Churani, and the temple coming up at Bisoi,' he suggests. 'You won't have these mentioned in your printout.'

We are back in the Scorpio at 5:45 am the next morning. Destination: Chilmiri Neck tabletop.

The eastern sky is turning red. Dinesh drives faster on the winding roads.

We reach in time. Unlike at most other sunrise viewpoints on the hills, here we are the only witnesses to the play of colours behind the rolling blue ranges. The hills closest to us are the deepest blue, the shade getting lighter as they recede further and further into the now orange horizon.

With the arrival of the great golden orb, birds fly out of the thick green foliage surrounding the flat mountain top. Magpies. Tits. Others that we hear, but cannot see.

Churani hilltop is an hour away. An hour brimful with rhododendron bursts by the roadside, verdant green fields, red-roofed village homes and on a barren branch pointing to the sky, the silhouette of a bird with tousled head feathers.

Chaani-Churani is a huddle of rugged stone huts that seem to have been loosely thrown together by a Howard Roark in answer to a trekker's core belief—'your mountain is waiting'.

Trekking season has not begun yet. The spartan one-room huts are unoccupied. Before them, a stone path meanders through free-growing grass barely contained by a crude fence. Beyond that fence tumbles the valley, and far beyond the green terraced valley, like the frothy crest of a Tsunami wave frozen in time, stand the Gangotri-Yamunotri ranges.

The cook, informed of our arrival, is waiting around. He rustles up a breakfast of scrambled eggs, diced potatoes fried with cumin seeds, and roti. We have a choice of beverages: black tea, or *matha*, the cool buttermilk sent up from the cook's home. I do realise the buttermilk was meant for his consumption and has been offered to us on an impulse, but quaff most of it. Sumita prefers the familiarity of tea.

A full stomach encourages indolence. We sit on logs outside the huts, content to gaze at the snow-covered ranges.

This is the Jaunsar-Bawar region. 'Locals here are sheep and cattle grazers,' says Dinesh. 'They also grow wheat, peas, ginger and potato. The sheep are shorn in summer, and their wool is shampooed and made into shoes and coats. These are worn by our *dadas* and *pardadas*. The wool is special. It doesn't get wet unless you dump it in a lake.'

He points out the Yamunotri, Gangotri and Kedarnath peaks, counting them on the fingers of his left hand, starting with the little finger. 'Badri Peak is lower; from here you cannot make out which one it is.'

I mention the huge deluge of June 2013, caused by unusually heavy rainfall and the bursting of the Chorabari Lake. River Mandakini rising from the Chorabari Glacier (12,779 ft) near the lake had swelled, and torrents had come gushing down from the mountains behind the Kedarnath temple. Within 15 minutes, a 15-feet-high wall of water, silt and boulders had pounded the Kedarnath region, completely washing away thousands of pilgrims.

'I was at Kedarnath the day before that flood,' Dinesh says softly. 'I had taken a Bengali family on a pilgrimage. The Chakravarti family.'

'How did you get away?'

'It had been raining. Heavy, very heavy showers. I did not like the look of the sky. I am a local, we go by our instincts. I told Mr Chakravarti that we should leave. They had not visited the temple yet. The wife wasn't very willing. But they listened to me, and we left.'

'Around 5,000 people died in the flood, right?'

'That is what the government says,' Dinesh is sceptical. 'We think it must be about 15,000-20,000. So many villagers went missing. If they are not dead, how is it that they have not been found?'

He looks up at the sunny blue sky: 'Shiv*ji* saved our lives that day.'

The white dome of a temple on an adjacent hill glows in the sunlight. 'That is the Shilgur temple,' says Dinesh. 'The view from there is very good. *Aap jaana chahoge*?'

Yes, of course we would like to go.

It is not as easy as we think, though. Trekking on what seems a never-ending upward trail past a meandering stone wall, we are about to give up. Just then Dinesh calls out from a narrow goat track below. He urges us on.

Voices of villagers grazing cattle on the other side of the wall float over to us. I manage to photograph a bulbul, a soaring eagle. We climb up an entire hill side and down its opposite slope, only to climb up the next hill with its burst of red rhododendrons.

Taking a break on a flat, rectangular outcrop, we are hedged by ankle-high bushes crowned with purple, yellow and light blue flowers. The valley stretches for miles below, its houses tiny from this height.

Puja is held at the small Shiva temple every Sankranti day. The idol looks peaceful. The temple looks neglected.

On the way back, we halt at the Chakrata Market for lunch. A long and indecisive walk to practically the other end of the market, and then we find Sher-e-Punjab. Walls blackened with the soot from a wood-fire. Rickety wooden tables topped with a layer of tin. Business is brisk. A meal of dal-chawal-chana sets our tongues on fire. Local children eating the same fare at the next table seem to have no issues.

Cherry trees are covered with blossoms. Pines hang heavy with cones. Fallen rhododendron flowers carpet the base of their large, gnarled tree trunks as we set out again for a sunset view from Chilmiri. The journey ends sooner than expected. Clouds have hidden the snow-capped ranges. They are heavy with rain. Near the lone cinema hall, monkeys swing from pine to pine.

Weather holds the next morning. That is good news. Today, we go into the beautiful forest of Deoban. The name is a derivative of *Dev-van*: where the gods live. There is a forest rest house inside, and a walk uphill leads to Vyas Shikhar, the peak where Vyas is said to have written *The Mahabharata*.

The old man at the check post before the forest says we do not require a permit. That is bad news. 'Your car won't go far enough for a permit,' the man explains. 'Many trees have fallen along the route. About 60 of them.'

Driving on nevertheless, we pass an Army training centre. Boulders with 'Guerrilla Country' and 'Spiders' Colony' painted on them proclaim that this is a restricted zone. Soon, the car comes to a halt near the fallen trunk of a huge deodar tree. We get off and start walking past it. Dinesh stays back in the car. He has a cold.

This is a different world. All there is is the swishing of wind amid the chir pines, deodars and firs. And bird call. They come in all colours and sizes, scarlet, medium; orange, extra small; yellow and green, large.

In and around Chakrata, we would see at least 25 bird species.

Deep into the forest, where the sunlight does not penetrate, waterfalls are still frozen. Patches of snow on the ground are strewn with fragrant cones and acorn. In the horizon seen fleetingly through the treeline on the edge of the road, the ranges are a light blue, mist-covered mass, their glaciers but a memory.

I capture a long-tailed scarlet minivet in flight, and a parrot gyrating on a branch in an obvious attempt to draw attention. More and more trees block our path. We need to sit astride the wide trunks of some to cross over and continue walking.

We have a sudden, unusual and desperate urge to mark our territory. All that buttermilk and tea.

Sumita and I take turns at the base of the slopes to our left, one of us looking out for that stray woodcutter. There is no one walking the forest path.

A very short while after, in the just-dried slush on the track, we find four paw prints clustered in an almost linear row.

Each paw print seems to have three toes.

Sixth sense says we might be watched. I take quick photos.

'Get close and stay very close to me,' I tell Sumita.

'Why?'

Sumita needs a rock-solid reason for any sudden change. I remember a time I had bruised her arm trying to drag her away from the path of a fast-moving snake: she had not seen the snake.

Sixth sense precludes reasoning. I bring in a dramatic whisper.

'Don't ask questions now. And keep your voice low.'

We hasten our pace a little. We have not found the forest rest house yet. Even if we had reached the end of the road, there would still be a five km trek uphill to Vyas Shikhar. But it was too early in the season to try that, the slope would be snow covered.

Best to turn back.

When we return to the car, Dinesh shows us a foot-high Shiva temple on the edge of the cliff, built in the memory of one Raunak Singh who had accidentally fallen to his death at this spot in 2013.

Dinesh is now intent on getting me some bird shots. With his help, I spot a couple of Oriental white-eyes. A chough circles overhead.

At Jadi village, children in bright pink and orange pullovers and long, sun-browned hair falling over their very dusty faces play on the slopes by the road. Village women sun themselves on a ledge above. They smile readily for a photograph. When I show them their photo on my camera screen, I make friends for life.

Every year, a couple of researchers from Pune arrive in Chakrata, and driving them during their trip has been enlightening for Dinesh.

'The researchers have told me that a long, long time ago, this entire region was under the sea,' says Dinesh. 'Stones from here were sent abroad, and they proved this belief.'

He means the Tethys Sea.

On the huge boulders towering by the roadside, there are small shrubs with succulent leaves. Dinesh plucks off some leaves, and rubs them on his palm. They turn into clumps that look like little balls of dried papier mâché. 'You can use these to light a fire, even on snow,' he tells us. 'They showed this on Discovery channel. Our elders would carry some in their pockets, to light their pipes.'

There are coal deposits on these mountains, but due to strong iron content, these have never been mined. The researchers have told Dinesh that there could be diamonds amid these deposits.

'When I heard that, I wanted to give up driving and immediately start digging,' Dinesh adds. 'But I found out that the cost of mining would be much more than the cost of the diamonds. If I found any, that is.'

The misty mountain views at Deoban have left us disappointed. Eager to cheer us up, Dinesh drives to Lokhandi, where not just the Yamunotri Range, but peaks from the Tibet ranges fence the horizon.

'This is why we call the Himalayas *rakshak*,' Dinesh says reverently. 'They protect us from invasion.' He loves to see the mountains every morning. They make him happy, and at peace.

The road is snow covered in patches. Boots sink in with a scrunching sound, and the cold seeps through them to my socks. To our left, three little cherry trees defy the snow at their feet by sending up clusters of frail pink blossoms. But they are no match for the trees we would see next, at Kanasar.

On the way to Kanasar, we meet Dinesh's brother, driving in the opposite direction. He is carting dried leaves for his sheep and goats. The leaves are tied with string into large round bundles, and look like mammoth balls of natural loofah.

Surrounding a wide meadow with lush green grass, the deodar trees at Kanasar have been standing for centuries.

'No one is allowed to cut down trees around here,' says Dinesh. 'Villagers can collect the ones that have fallen, without being penalised. The logs from fallen trees are called *maafi ki lakdi*.'

There are 200 village houses. Every alternate year, 100 houses take turns to collect such wood and store it for future use.

Some of the tree trunks at Kanasar measure 3.75 metres, 5 metres, even 6.35 metres. There is a signboard fixed on one of the majestic trunks. It bears a uniquely worded message from the tree:

> *'Main ek buzurg vriksh praani hoon, bol nahin sakta, phir bhi main Kanasar devta se aapki yatra/parivaar/bachchon/vansh ke sukh samriddhi ki kaamna karta hoon, aapse prarthana karta hoon ke aap bhi mere vansh-praniyon (ped-paudho-van praniyon) ki suraksha ki khayal aapne bachchon/parivaar ki tarah rakhenge. Dhanyavad.'*

Loosely translated, it means: 'I am a very old tree. I cannot speak, yet I pray to the God of Kanasar for your happy journey and the prosperity of your family, children and lineage. I request that you too take care of my family (trees, creepers and animals in the wild) just as you would take care of your own children and family. Thank you!'

It is an ideal place to do nothing. We squat on a fallen tree and watch the world go by. A local lady visits the small Shiva temple near the meadow with her husband. She has her hair wrapped in a deep pink scarf. With hardly any cajoling, I get her to pose with Sumita on the sunny greens.

And then it is lunch time. At Koti, an ancient village a stick's throw away, a roadside restaurant offers a homely, delicious meal of freshly cooked sarson saag, roti, dal, rice and pickle.

Deodar logs burn in the oven.

'If you live in a house built of deodars, you'll never fall ill,' says Dinesh, as he tears a piece off a soft roti. 'The fragrance stays on. The word deodar comes from *Dev-daru*: gods are said to live in these trees.'

I know the fragrance. Earlier in the day, I picked up a deodar wood chip from the roadside. The heady fragrance lingered on my fingers and inside the car for a long, long while.

Koti's azure horizon is defined by the Mundali Range. The wide tar road winding through the village is edged by flower-laden trees:

white blossoms on a cherry tree; tiny pink ones on an aloo bukhara; more pink blossoms on another cherry tree.

Local boys Manoj and Harish pose for me against the white blossoms, their soft baby cheeks and pixie ears a contrast to the very formal expression they assume.

When we return to the hotel at the end of this fulfilling day, Kallan gives us a boisterous reception. He then proceeds to diligently eat the red mud layering our boots.

Later that evening, I show the photograph of the three-toed footprints to Dinesh and Chetan. They exchange knowing glances.

'*Baghira*?' Chetan asks Dinesh, speaking in Jaunsari. Dinesh nods.

'*Kothi?*'

'Deoban.'

Chetan nods an affirmation.

He confirms that they were the pugmarks of a leopard poised for a leap. And yes, the leopard might have still been around.

'*Shayed woh kahin upar baithey aapko dekh raha tha,*' Chetan says.

LAKHAMANDAL-BISOI

The road to Lakhamandal is arduous, practically a dirt track that entwines itself around the mountain range, past the villages of Kwasi, Gouraghati and Kandoi. It is tough to be a passenger on this road, and tougher to be a driver.

Dinesh is undaunted. He has a smile and a courteous word for every driver coming from the other direction. It seems a custom in these parts of Uttarakhand, this meeting and greeting like ants and the sharing of information: the latest on the fellow driver-villager's well-being, the condition of the roads he has just travelled on. Most of all, it is the sense of companionship on long and lonely journeys.

Here, in the Jaunsar-Bawar region, the inhabitants, Jaunsaris, believe they descended from the Pandavas. Across the rest of Uttarakhand, too, legends from *The Mahabharata* envelop most ancient sites. Lakhamandal is no different.

The *Adi Parva* of *The Mahabharata* has a section on *jatugriha,* a palace built of lacquer, a highly inflammable material. The citizens of Hastinapura were eager to see Yudhishthir, the eldest Pandava, ascend the throne. This was intolerable for Duryodhana. He sent the Pandavas with their mother Kunti on an excursion to Varanavati, where the palace of lacquer was constructed for them. The plan was to set the palace on fire at night, while the Pandavas slept.

Thanks to wise Vidura's tips, the Pandavas were aware of the plan. One night, they themselves set fire to the palace and escaped through a tunnel dug for them. A tribal woman and her five sons sleeping in the palace were burnt to death, and the assumption was that the Pandavas had perished.

Lakhamandal is said to be the spot where this *jatugriha* had been built. Nothing remains of the palace, and that is how it should be, given that it had completely burned down. But a temple that the Pandavas had built still marks the spot.

The Archaeological Survey of India, Dehradun Circle, does not mention the Pandavas in the context of Lakhamandal, though. Its note on this temple says (*excerpt unedited*):

> *'Dedicated to Lord Siva, this temple, popularly known as Lakeswara, was built between 12th -13th cent. A.D in Nagara style. However, fragmentary inscription of Chhaglesa and Prashasti of Princes Isvasra (circa 5th-6th centuries AD), revealed that the antiquity of the site goes much earlier then the existing temple. The Prashasti of Princes Isvasra, belonging to the Royal race of Singhpura, described the construction of a temple in honour of Siva, for the spiritual welfare of her deceased husband Chandragupta, the son of king Jalandhara. Remains of brick temple datable to 5th structures AD, below the ruined* (sic) *of stone temple in the complex is* (sic) *the earliest structural activity at the site.*
>
> *'Recent scientific clearance carried out by ASI revealed large number of structural remains in the temple premises including remains of flat roofed temples assignable to 5th -6th Cent. AD which through* (sic) *new dimension in the history of the temple architecture of the Central Himalayan region.'*

The temple holds pride of place among old village houses with their intricate wood carvings. As we climb the steps to the temple compound, two teenage boys take complete charge of us. They insist that we first visit a couple of ancient stone statues some distance away from the temple.

'These are Bhadra and Veerbhadra, *dwarpalas* (gatekeepers)—also called Jay and Vijay in a different age,' they say.

'Earlier, it was believed that if we placed the body of a dead villager between these two statues and chanted hymns, the villager would be brought back from the dead.'

I learn later that Bhadra and Veerabhadra are *dwarapalaka*s of Shiva's abode, while and Jay and Vijay guard Vishnu's abode.

Our self-appointed guides point to a wide stone platform with a Shivalinga rising from its centre: 'That is the Drum Yudhishthir Linga. Village elders say that there's food stored under the Linga, enough to last the whole world for two-and-a-half days in times of famine.'

'The British had tried to break open the Linga once,' one of the boys says, 'when two huge snakes had emerged from it. Half of the diggers died of snake bites, the other half ran away.' The boy speaks fast, his excited narration lending colour to his cheeks and to his story.

Finally, an old priest takes us inside the temple. His speech is slurred, probably the effect of an untreated stroke, and his front teeth are missing. I had hoped to verify the young boys' accounts with him, but that does not seem possible.

In the innermost sanctum, there are about 20 or more stone statuettes. Even in the dim light, we are able to recognise Parvati, Vishnu, Ganesh and Shiva. All exquisite sculptures carved out of black stone.

The outer sanctum has a statue of Parvati seated on Shiva's thigh, with their sons Ganesh and Kartik at their feet. 'The sons were born here,' drawls the priest.

There are wooden idols, too. Replicas of *dashavatars,* the 10 incarnations of Vishnu, have been carved on a long wood panel.

'When the archaeologists came here and started excavating, they found all these statues,' the priest adds. He takes a long time to complete his sentences, articulating each word painfully. 'There were just so many statues; so many that they decided to let most of them remain underground.'

Reserving the best of his stories for the last, the priest shows us a small footprint on a slab of stone. 'And *that* is the imprint of Parvati's foot.'

For us, that is a little hard to believe.

The teens point out a hill nearby and say that King Virat had ruled from there.

I find this passage in *Urbanization in Garhwal Himalaya: A Geographical Interpretation,* by Surendra Singh:

> *'Second was the kingdom of Raja Virat who ruled the Doon, Jaunsar Bawar, western Garhwal and parts of Sirmaur Hills. Varnawat was perhaps the name of this kingdom covering the parts of upper Yamuna Basin and western parts of Ganga Basin.... Perhaps the present Jaunsar Bawar region may be the ancient Varnawat because the extensive ruins of Lakshagriha the palace... are scattered at Lakhamandal.... Pandavas escaped unhurt and reached another town known as Ekchakra which was also known as Chakrawati. It later came to be known as Chakravata, Chakrauta.'*

If Lakhamandal was where *jatugriha* had been, then the tunnel through which the Pandavas are believed to have escaped must also be close, I tell Dinesh. And it is, indeed, a short drive away.

'*Prachin Pandava Gufa* (ancient cave of the Pandavas)' says the signboard. Local children play *pittu,* the traditional Seven Stones game, just inside the mouth of a cave that leads to an extremely dark, narrow, claustrophobic space. A male voice speaks to us from within. He claims to be a priest.

'Do come in,' the priest says.

Warning bells toll in my head. Dinesh has not accompanied us inside. Besides, I cannot see a thing in the complete darkness; I can only hear the man.

'How far inside do we need to go?' I ask the priest.

'Just crawl towards where I am sitting, you cannot go any further,' he assures us in the dark.

There are just three steps into a low tunnel which ends abruptly. The priest squats on the top step. Sumita and I cram on the bottom one. 'This is the spot where the Pandavas came out of the tunnel,' says the priest. 'They kept piling up mud behind them so they could not be followed.'

Somewhat used to the darkness now, we prod the tunnel wall with our fingers. There is a small shower of grit.

'The stone walls of the tunnel had a sandy component. So, over the years, the tunnel roof has caved in, sealing off the passage completely,' the priest adds.

The sunlight outside is blinding. Back in the car, Dinesh tells us how the Badrinath temple was taken away from Shiva by a conniving Vishnu.

'One day, Shiva and Parvati were sitting inside the temple, when they heard a baby crying to be let in. Parvati wanted to let the baby in, but Shiva knew who it actually was. He told Parvati that if she let the child in, they would have to leave the temple, and would never be able to enter it again. But Parvati did not listen; she let the child enter the temple. Once inside the temple, Vishnu, for that is who it was, assumed his own form, and took over the temple.'

This is what sets Dinesh apart from the drivers who we have travelled with earlier, this eagerness to share what he knows of his land.

Driving back to the hotel, he shows us a tree. 'That is the bhimal tree,' he says. 'The bark is used to make rope. It is first soaked in water, for months, and then twisted into shape. All the local women use this rope.'

A common kestrel hovers in the late afternoon sky. We manage to spot a verditer flycatcher, a pied bush chat and a variable wheatear.

Our Chakrata stay is coming to an end. 'On your way to Mussoorie, ask Dinesh to take you to Bisoi, my village,' Chetan says. 'There's a temple coming up there, it will be the largest in Uttarakhand.'

Three years have gone by in the making of the temple, and work is still on, says Dinesh as we start off for Mussoorie the next day. A Mahasu Devta temple exists at the venue already, but a much larger one is being built.

Mahasu is a derivation of Mahashiv, Dinesh tells us. According to ancient lore, a demon lived in these parts of Uttarakhand. He would eat at least one man from the nearby villages every day. In one of the villages named Mandrath, a Brahmin decided to pray to Shiva to end the demon's tyranny. In answer to his prayers, Shiva instructed

Devladli Devi, one of his women devotees, to send her four sons to fight the demon. Her sons surrounded the demon from all sides, and killed him in battle.

Later, when the Brahmin was ploughing his fields, he discovered four Shivlingas. These four were named after the four sons of Devladli Devi: Mahasu, Pavasi, Vasik and Chalda. Together, they came to be called Char Mahasu.

The villagers rejoiced, and Shiva was worshipped as Mahasu ever after. There is a 9th century Mahasu Devta temple on the banks of River Tons (Tamas) at Hanol, 95 kilometres from Chakrata.

As with folklore, there are several versions of this story, each a tad different from the other. The temple at Bisoi has its own story, too, says Dinesh.

'A villager falsely accused of a crime was being taken away in chains. He began to pray to Mahasu Devta. Even as the villager prayed, his chains fell off. The rusted chains are still inside this temple.'

The half-finished wood-and-stone temple with ornate carvings is an impressive structure already. But we are denied entry into the compound that holds both the old and the new temples. Dinesh has a word with the priest in Jaunsari, their mother tongue. All we get of the conversation is a vehement shake of the priest's head. We know he will not be convinced, though we do not quite know why.

I walk up and down the road next to the temple. Photograph quaint village houses. We cannot bring ourselves to leave yet.

Then Dinesh drops a bomb.

'If only you were not married, you could have gone in,' he says with sadness.

'But we *are* single,' I exclaim, 'both of us.'

He is overjoyed. 'Then nobody can stop you from entering. You are *kanya*s, embodiments of the goddess.'

Fortunately, the priest agrees. Before he changes his mind again, the *kanyas* quickly walk down the steps leading to the temple compound.

The old temple is actually a small house. A narrow corridor with a low, sloping wooden ceiling leads to small rooms. One holds tiny brass thrones with equally tiny idols on them. The next has the *doli* or the palanquin in which the idols are usually carried.

As the priest puts the tika on our forehead, a small boy begins to play the nagara, the temple drum. Puja is about to begin.

Across the compound, craftsmen from Gorakhpur are carving out images of many a god on the wooden panels. The temple inauguration will see a surge of media personnel, Dinesh foretells. A hundred drums and bugles will be played. The inaugural worship is usually so impressive that people go into a trance.

It is not difficult to imagine that day. But today's worship is a quiet one. The priest has some time alone with the gods. Standing in a pile of fragrant deodar wood shavings, we gaze at the snowy mountain ranges in the distant horizon. And listen to the drum beats.

MUSSOORIE

Lazily strolling along Camel's Back Road, we have our first view of Bandarpoonch Peak. 'And thereby hangs a tale.'

Says *The Ramayana,* Ram sent Hanuman the Monkey God to find Sita. Hanuman discovered her in the demon Ravan's kingdom, Lanka. He had a word with Sita, and then allowed himself to be captured by the demons. The demons wrapped Hanuman's tail in an oil-soaked rag and set fire to it. Hanuman raced through Ravan's palace, setting the whole building on fire. He then flew to one of the snowy Himalayan peaks to cool his burning appendage. And that was how Bandarpoonch—'The Monkey's Tail'—got its name.

In a quiet corner a couple of steps off the left of the road is a tea stall with a viewpoint and some iron benches.

'This is a very old viewpoint built by the British in 1928,' says the old man running the stall. 'Dogs and Indians were not allowed here then.' His tea is good, the view even better.

Nearby, a couple fiddles with a telescope. The snow-clad peaks are not in focus. The man points the telescope towards his wife. She giggles. The telescope owner looks on, indifferent.

Ours is an enlightening walk, with quotes of Nirankari Baba on regularly placed signboards along the road. 'Peace, not pieces,' we learn.

Complete with giant pieces—bishops, pawns, kings, queens—a huge chessboard made with black and white tiles adorns the terrace of a hotel on a ledge far below the road. Despite the road signs apparently pointing in its direction, the Durga temple remains hidden. A youth on a sputtering scooter rides up and down Camel's Back Road. There is a nauseating smell of diesel.

We pass private estates, and the Camel's Back Cemetery. John Lang, the Australian writer and barrister who had represented Rani Laxmibai in a lawsuit against the British sleeps here. So does John Hindmarsh. Hindmarsh had been among the few survivors of the British Light Cavalry of 600 soldiers who, after a misinterpreted command, had charged towards the Russian guns during the Crimean War (1854). I remember being fascinated by their story many many years ago, in Lord Tennyson's poem '*The Charge of the Light Brigade.*'

Birds flit from tree to tree over our heads. A man with Garhwali costumes on hire has a quiet smoke while another with a telescope wants us to take a look at the mountain peak shaped like a camel's back that has given the road its name.

At the tourist office, an official is fending off questions from foreigners. A young lady asks where she could see some wildlife.

'At Rajaji National Park, Ma'am. But that is far from here,' the official says.

'You could have visited the park from Rishikesh,' I add. A sad, faraway look comes into her eyes. 'I did go to Rishikesh, to immerse my father's ashes in the Ganga. I was not there as a tourist....'

'So what should a tourist do in Mussoorie?' she asks me. I suggest she visit Landour, Sisters' Bazar, Chaar Dukan. The tourism official is relieved at this transfer of roles, and is listening with interest.

I point to Landour on the tourist map. Her eyes light up. 'My father studied here, many years ago,' she says, tapping on Woodstock School. I tell her about the many authors and actors who have bungalows in Landour. 'Oh so it's a sort of an artistes' colony?' One could call Landour that, I say.

At Kulri Bazar, the two old gentlemen who own Cambrige Book Depot tell us that author Bill Aitken has just left (pointing to the empty revolving chair placed at the entry to the shop), and that Ruskin Bond drops in only on Saturdays.

'The richness I achieve comes from Nature, the source of my inspiration':
Tulips, Mussoorie

'Bond does not entertain guests at his home any more,' they add. 'He is busy writing again. Prem, his adopted son, has just had a stroke, so Rakesh and Bina, Prem's son and daughter-in-law are regularly visiting Prem at a Dehradun hospital.'

By next Saturday, we would be at Landour, and have no plans to walk downhill all the way to Mussoorie, we say.

'You can still get your books autographed by Bond,' one of the old gentlemen tells me.

It is a simple process. A reader buys a book, fixes a sticky note with his or her name on it, and leaves the book at the store. A lady who lives close to Bond's house carries the books to the author every morning to get them signed. She brings the books back to the store by 10:30 am.

We buy books. Inside mine, I write my name on a post-it and add a note to Bond, reminding him that I had met him in Kolkata, and had gifted him my book of children's short stories. In Sumita's book, I say that she loves the hills, and wishes to stay on them forever.

'Pick up the books tomorrow evening,' the gentleman says. 'They will be signed and ready by then.'

A bright red cable car riding on a 400-metre ropeway takes us up to Gun Hill (7,200 ft). Until 1919, every day at noon, a shot would be fired from a cannon placed here so the locals could set their watches.

However, a signboard at the site says that this practice was a constant source of worry, since 'the boom was produced by charging it with moist grass, cotton waste and gun powder… on one occasion, the barrel was overcharged and a lady in a dandy down below found a ball of grass fall into her lap! Soon after, an absent-minded gunner forgot the ram-rod in the barrel and it shot straight out, crashing through the tin-roof of a nearby house!'

The firing had to be discontinued, and during the Second World War, the gun was melted down as part of the war effort.

A flat hilltop now encircled by stalls that do brisk business, Gun Hill allows other modes of shooting. I aim for some beautiful valley views at dusk, children turned out prettily in hired ethnic wear. Hand my camera to Sumita and take potshots from an airgun to burst a few balloons.

Our day ends with bowls of soup at Kalsang Thai Corner, high up on Trip Advisor's list of recommended restaurants in Mussoorie. My soup does not stay down. By 5:00 am the next morning, I have thrown up ladles of it five times. An Avomine sees me back in bed, fighting waves of induced drowsiness.

A day wasted.

Left to entertain herself and feeling lonely, Sumita walks down to Cambridge Book Depot in the evening to collect the autographed books. To cheer me up, she buys a little box made entirely of colourful toothpick sized sticks bound together by threads, a small wooden ship named Cyprus, and a finger-length copper bugle.

Bond has signed the books and added one-line notes.

Mine: 'To a successful future!'

Sumita's: 'With love from the hills!'

I feel well enough to blow into the toy bugle. It gives out an ear-piercing shrill note. Utterly unbecoming of a guest at a heritage hotel.

The next morning, it is destination Everest. Not the peak, but Park Estate, the house of Sir George Everest in Hathipaon.

We drive past the Company Garden, a monastery, a Tibetan school. Our driver is engrossed in the cricket commentary over the crackling car radio. India is in the semi-finals of the World Cup.

Surveyor General and Superintendent of East India Company's Great Trigonometrical Survey, Colonel Sir George Everest bought Park Estate in Hathipaon (7,080 ft) near Mussoorie in 1832. He spent the next decade in India.

Sir George had brought in the most accurate surveying instruments of the times. In the course of the project, he and his predecessors had measured the meridional arc of 11.5 degrees from the Himalayas to Cape Comorin, the southernmost point of India.

The instruments and the observation posts were at times a cause for concern among the locals. Zalim Singh, a landowner from the south of Delhi believed that an observation post overlooked his zenana, the women's quarters. He even offered to pay for its relocation.

Sir George replied mockingly:

> *'The zamindar must have money in superfluity to be willing to incur so vast a charge for an object so insignificant as that of removing 10 or 20 paces... an edifice which, since it must surpass all circumjacent dwellings in height, would equally command a view of his zenana...*
>
> *'Persuaded ...that our telescopes which invert have magic powers, and are able to turn women upside down (an indecent posture no doubt and very shocking to contemplate), it is natural enough that they should assign to us the propensity of sitting all day long, spying through the stone walls at those whom they deem so enchanting.*
>
> *'But the Great Trigonometrical Survey is a department of hard work, and not of idleness, ...and men who sit up all night and all day, with barely time for sleep or meals, have rarely leisure for such trifling as Zalim Singh anticipates, even if their taste were so ill*

> *regulated, and their lot so forlorn, as to become a prey to such... speculative amusement.'*
>
> *(Courtesy: Historical Records of Survey of India Vol 4 By Phillimore; Published 1958)*

Sir George's house on a flat-topped hill is now in ruins. At some point, the walls received a coat of white paint. They are now a canvas for a hundred lovers to write their names with charcoal. The F-word crops up, too. For the local cattle, the cool interiors or what remains of it make for a pit stop.

But visitors do arrive, their numbers enough to make Ritesh, a student of class VI, run a tea stall with his parents.

'Why is this area called Hathipaon?' I ask Ritesh.

'Why is Kolkata called Kolkata?' he counter questions. I give him the story.

'There is a marble mine nearby,' Ritesh says. 'The dug-up area resembles an elephant's footprint (*hathi*: elephant, *paon*: foot). Foreigners visit the mine,' he adds. Quite a few of them tend to pick up a piece of marble as a souvenir.

Wishing Well, a short turn away, is the only natural well in the Himalayas. The signage proclaiming this is broken, the writing barely legible.

It is now the Washing Well. Local women wash their clothes on the raised platform encircling the well. Their children gape at us, wondering why we are there. A statue of Shiva sits in a small, dark temple nearby.

Cricket commentaries do not help in navigation. The car takes a wrong turn, and we arrive at Landour hours later than expected.

LANDOUR

Tabor Cottage built in the 1850s has five rooms on offer, with names like Lilac, Yellow or Blue. The bed covers and the walls match the name of a room, and the keychain bears it, too.

The meals are ordered from Rokeby Manor, the most expensive cottage in this chain. Our lunch arrives in plastic bowls. We are served in style, though, at the narrow, sunny dining room which was once probably just a corridor leading to the kitchen.

Inspiration is everywhere; from the smart sayings on the dining room wall to the poster in our Blue room which says 'It is only when it is the darkest that you can see the stars'.

From Tabor, the road climbs downhill past St Paul's Church where Jim Corbett's parents were wed. We pass the crossroads named Chaar Dukan—the first four establishments to come up here were Bipin's Tiptop Teashop, Anil's Coffee Joint, Surbir's Cyber Café, and a bank—on our way to Doma's Inn.

Doma's Inn nestles in one portion of Ivy Cottage. In the other, a longish flight of red steps leads up to author Ruskin Bond's apartment.

We have no plans of barging in on him. But while we are looking up the steps, a man climbs them and the green door at the head of the stairs opens in answer to his knock.

A familiar round face wearing a pair of golden, round-frame spectacles pops out for a brief moment. The author peers out at the man, and in the process notes our presence at the foot of the steps. The door closes. When the visitor comes down, we cheekily ask him whether this is the famous author's house.

'Yes, but he is *not* home.'

'So who were you speaking to?'

'Just someone who lives in the house.'

He is obviously not a good liar, but his loyalty is unquestionable. We take pity on him, and embed an answer in our question:

'Was it the caretaker?'

'Oh yes, yes, *that*'s who it was!' he says, and scurries away.

Doma's Inn has a cosy nook for a coffee break, and we settle for a honey-lemon tea and a cold coffee before the long trudge uphill and back to Tabor, past the Landour Language School and the Kellogg Memorial Church. Huge rhododendron trees are in bloom along the roadside. A foreign tourist rides a rented scooter downhill. She looks tense, does not return a smile.

Mist comes up over the Mussoorie-Landour valleys even as we return to the cottage. One by one, lights begin to twinkle in the twilight. Insects tap dance on our glass panes.

Two men come out from Yellow and switch on the lounge TV. India has lost the match.

The next morning, an over-ambitious urge to walk all the way downhill from Tabor Cottage to Landour Bazar sees us at a U-turn offering a view of the red roofs of Landour. The Bazar is still a long, long way down the hill. Two old men are coming up the curve.

'Could you please point out the Clock Tower to us?' I ask them.

'Oh, that has been broken down,' says one of the men.

'It was in front of Narang's hotel,' adds the other. 'The hotel could not be seen from afar. So Narang broke it down, promising to build another one.'

'Public did not object,' says the first gentleman. 'They believed him. He hasn't built another clock tower yet.'

They lumber uphill, old heads nodding from age and frustration.

A military cantonment since 1827, Landour (7,500 ft) was a Convalescent Depot for wounded British soldiers. Traders followed them uphill and set up shop. Then the military invited civilians to build homes at Landour, and 78 bungalows with exotic names came into being.

The nurses who looked after the convalescing soldiers gave Sisters' Bazaar its name. Just a few shops now make up the bazaar. Pre-briefed by our travel guidebooks, we walk into Prakash Brothers for bottles of pomegranate preserve. Prakash Handicrafts next door has a lady at the counter, lot of handicraft on sale which are not sourced locally, and books written by local authors.

I leaf through a book by Bill Aitken.

'It will cost you 50 rupees more than the cover price,' says the lady. 'It has been autographed.'

'If I had a flower for every time I thought of you... I could walk through my garden forever': Magnolias in bloom at Mussoorie

Bill Aitken's book waits for a buyer as we take the tree-lined route to Lal Tibba.

Over our heads deodar, cedar, Himalayan oak, chir pine, blue pine, West Himalayan fir, Himalayan maple and rhododendron reach out and touch one another to form a canopy of fine green lace that sways in the wind. In the Landour Cemetery, a bunch of blue magpies cackle on a red tin box. Their chatter merely enhances the ambient hush. Two dogs stroll among the headstones, sniffing at nothing in particular.

A brightly painted fence and some steps go up to actor Victor Banerjee's house slightly above the road. His magnolia tree is in full bloom, and a dog rests under it, just his snout visible from where we stand.

Right there, we disobey the last of the Ten Commandments: 'You shall not covet your neighbour's house; you shall not covet your neighbour's wife, or his male servant, or his female servant, or his ox, or his donkey, or anything that is your neighbour's.'

We covet. His house. His dog, even though we can only see its snout. His magnolia tree.

Definitely his magnolia tree.

But here's the thing: We are not Victor Banerjee's neighbours. If we were, we would have our own cottage, *and* our dog, *and* our magnolia tree.

Definitely *our* magnolia tree.

For the weekend tourists zooming past us in their Innovas and SUVs, Lal Tibba has two concrete structures with three floors each. There are balconies and terraces with red railings from where the mountain range can be viewed at leisure, and for a price. To add to the experience, there is a pair of binoculars, a telescope, and beverages from the restaurant below.

But the evening is upon us, and light is fading over the mountains that now wear a reddish hue.

Lights have set Landour hills aglow by the time we return to Tabor. For dinner, the chef is willing to rustle up dal, gobi, salad and hot rotis.

He adds a bowl of great-tasting yoghurt too. 'I have the simplest tastes. I am always satisfied with the best,' Oscar Wilde speaks from a small poster on the dining room wall. We tend to agree, sinking tired bodies into soft white beds.

Sumita is still in bed when I sneak out on a bird-watching trail the next morning. It is unproductive. A bunch of rhesus macaques have taken over the cottage porch and the surrounding trees. Quite a few of them have babies clinging onto their backs. The birds have been silenced by these bullies. A lone blue streak flies from tree to tree, staying out of camera range. I know it is a verditer flycatcher.

One of the macaques makes an ugly face at me. I retire offended to the cottage and occupy the wide window seat to gaze idly at the Mussoorie-Landour valleys through the clear glass panes. All of a sudden, the verditer flycatcher flutters to the window. It soft perches on the narrow window sill, and looks at me with round, curious eyes. I stay perfectly still. It lingers awhile, swishing its tail. Takes wing.

Post breakfast, our return trip to Lal Tibba past Alyndale and Seaforth Lodge is a pleasant walk punctuated by great quotes painted for some odd reason at the base of roadside bins. The one on a tin board nailed to an oak lingers in my head: 'Every Great Oak was once a little nut that stood its ground.'

The mountain slopes are dotted with quaint little bungalows of the rich and famous. Galvanised tin roofs of cottages below the road are dazzling octagons in the morning sunlight.

A white-haired gentleman in dark glasses stops before us.

'So you are into photography?' he asks with a smile and a faint nod at the DSLR hanging from my neck.

'We are into everything,' I say.

He laughs, introduces himself. Tony Malik has lived in Landour with his Tibetan wife for the last 30 years. His daughter, now in Chicago, is interested in photography.

'She had taken this photo of Grand Canyon,' says Malik. 'It was published on the *National Geographic* website—that's the Holy Grail for photographers, isn't it—with a nice comment about the lighting.'

His adopted daughter from Nagaland is into publishing. 'Her book of poems, *Echoes of Spring*, has a foreword from Ruskin Bond. Bond loved one of her poems about the whispering pines.'

Tony Malik tells us about the forthcoming Mussoorie Writers Mountain Festival, in October. That it is organised by Stephen Alter, actor Tom Alter's cousin, at Woodstock School. That it is older than the Jaipur Literary Meet.

'You will find Tom Alter's house on the road past Sisters' Bazar. Then there are the houses of Prannoy and Radhika Roy, and their daughter, Devina. William Bissell of Fab India fame and his wife have a home, too. 'So, yes, this is your walk,' Malik ends with a flourishing sweep of his hand.

Children from Wynberg-Allen School are on an excursion to Lal Tibba. Their chatter fills the terrace of Dabbu's Café as they take turns to look through the telescope. Snow-mantled Swargarohini I (20,512 ft), II (20,495 ft) and III (20,371 ft) and Bandarpoonch I (20,722 ft) and II (20,020 ft) grab the most attention.

Café owner Rajinder Singh Rawat comes up for a chat. We learn: that the honey in our tea comes from the Valley of Flowers; that Rawat comes from Kanda village; that he walks two hours each way, every day.

'At home, we make a paste of ginger, garlic and honey. I have a spoonful before I set out,' he says. 'The ginger is for the heart, it regulates breath. The honey gives energy, the garlic keeps us warm.'

Lal Tibba is named thus, Rawat tells us, for at sunrise the mountain range turns red, and the same hue tinges anyone standing at this point.

He makes us look through the telescope in the direction of the Surkhunda Devi Temple on the distant mountains. The temple is not visible to our unfamiliar eyes. 'You can trek up, or take a horse ride. If you can do neither, break a coconut at the bottom of the hill,' suggests Rawat, 'Devi accepts.'

On an adjacent hillock stands a maroon-roofed cottage half encircled by tall pines. The path leading up to it from the road has an iron gate and a marble slab next to it that reads:

Nahata Estate
1990
(Formerly known as
Childer's Estate 1829)

'Childer's Estate was first sold for one lakh, a second time for 25 lakh and then sold again for 150 crore rupees,' says Rawat. 'It has 310 acres of land.'

The school children have left. With some reluctance, we leave Rawat's blissfully quiet terrace with its mountain views and start walking back to Tabor.

Strains of a song rise from Kellogg Memorial Church. The gate is open. Inside, a lone youth stands at a podium, singing Hindi songs in praise of Jesus. The sanctum and the hillside are alive with his melodious voice. We are the only listeners in the pew.

Tabor Cottage has an interesting collection of books. I am reading *Silk*, by Alessandro Baricco. It is set in France 1861, when an epidemic threatens to wipe out the silk trade. I am close to the end, where the protagonist Hervé Joncour has begun 'to allow himself a pleasure that hitherto he had always denied himself: he would talk of his travels to those who came to call on him. He would tell his tales slowly, seeing in the air things that the others did not see.'

RISHIKESH

In this magical hour of an October dawn, the distant hills are a soft blue silhouette. Mist embraces the hills, the trees and the calm river, veiling colours and fudging contours. As I stand on the hotel terrace, mist touches my face too: lightly, with the tentative fingers of a long-lost friend.

But the leaves covering the branches of the tree next to the terrace are a bright, parrot green. Even as I watch, several hundred leaves rise into the air with one accord, their elegant long tails sweeping the mist away, their bright red beaks open in the excited chatter only a flock of parrots can make. Another day has begun at Rishikesh, Uttarakhand.

Of the thousands driving into Rishikesh every day, the pilgrims move on to Badrinath, Kedarnath, Gangotri or Yamunotri, the trekkers journey to the Valley of Flowers in Hemkund. The rafting enthusiasts learn to paddle and Eskimo roll on the bubbling green river.

Rishikesh is a day's halt for us as well. We will drive down to Duggalbitta, and trek or ride onward to Tunganath temple at 12,000 ft. We plan to spend the night on Tunganath premises, trek all the way up to Chandrashila Peak before dawn the next day, and watch the sun rise over an uninterrupted vista of the Kumaon and Garhwal Himalayas.

Jeet, our driver, picked us up the previous day from the Delhi airport. He had been briefed about two ladies from Kolkata and had serious apprehensions about driving a demure, sari-clad duo on a pilgrimage. We—and the prospect of adventure we bring with us—are definitely not what he expected.

Long-legged foreign tourists stride purposefully in the narrow lanes and by lanes of Rishikesh, lugging their world in colourful backpacks. They are here for that yoga expert, who would help them bend their bodies and mend their minds. For the musically inclined, sitar, tabla, flute and harmonium lessons come at ₹ 200 per hour.

If communication with the local guru is an issue, language classes in Hindi begin at ₹ 80, also an hourly rate. The language lessons offer a double bonanza: they help the foreigner communicate his needs, and regale his indigenous listener. Someone who has listened to chaste Hindi spoken with a pure Parisian accent will know what I mean.

There are many enlightening things to do in Rishikesh. But we choose near-total indolence. Sail across the Ganga in a red-and-yellow ferry boat. Feed the fish readymade balls of wheat flour bought from a shop. Once across, I try photographing a saffron-clad sadhu sitting cross-legged near the Ram Jhula. He tries to take a swipe at my camera with his long bamboo staff, establishing in an instant that I should desist from any activity detrimental to my well-being.

Walking past the Rameshwar Temple, we soon abandon the congested lane advertising everything from reiki to cooking to Kathak and take a flight of stone steps down to the Muni-ki-Reti.

The long stretch of sparkling silver sands dotted with boulders is empty but for a yawning mongrel and a turbaned sadhu. From the latter's barely-disguised fluster, we seem to have disturbed an important download. After that, we take care to look before we step among the boulders.

The river shore is a good place to laze about and watch the continuous stream of tiny, foam-tipped waves. Rafts sail by. Occasionally, a helmet-wearing rafter tumbles into the water, and clings on to the edges of the raft like an overgrown tadpole.

Having had our fill of the sun and the sands, we walk across the Lakshman Jhula to the 13-tiered Tryambakeshwar Mahadev Temple. Daunted by the number of stairs, we do not pay the gods a visit. Instead, we watch a monkey couple on the bridge. One of them carries out a free bug-removal service, while the other lies perfectly still.

My online research on the official Garhwal Mandal Vikas Nigam (GMVN) website had revealed a list of all possible trekking gear one could hire from the tourism centres along with their rental fees. We pay the GMVN Trekking and Equipment Centre a visit.

Officials at the Centre take a sceptical look at the 'two very urban ladies in jeans' team.

'You will not be able to stay the night at Tunganath,' one of them says. 'The facilities are too basic.' He shakes his head. 'It will be too cold.' He shakes his head again. 'No, not possible at all.'

'So what do you suggest?' I ask politely.

'Trek up to Tunganath and Chandrashila and return the same day,' he suggests. 'People at Chopta could arrange it for you.'

'We've heard it will be very cold on Chandrashila, and that GMVN rents Hollofil jackets. Could you lend us a couple? We return to Rishikesh in two days.'

'We can't give you jackets right now. The ones we had were worn out. They were auctioned.'

'Haven't you bought new gear, then?'

'We will buy some, certainly. A committee has been formed; they will be meeting soon to decide what to procure,' he says.

Stillness defines the dusk at Triveni Ghat. Triveni: where the Ganga, Yamuna and the Saraswati rivers meet. Yamuna and Saraswati stay hidden. Ganga flows on.

A handful of priests and devotees gather for the evening worship of the Ganga. Large brass lamps, their wicks dipped in oil, stand on small iron stools balanced precariously on the pebbled shore. Devotees light tiny boat-shaped earthen lamps and coax these into the river. The current catches hold of them; makes them dance.

The *arati* begins. The sound of bells and chanting fill the air. With each sweeping arc of the priests' lean arms, the wicks in the brass lamps burn brighter, until the little teardrop-shaped lights blur into one big flame. The faces of the devotees fade into the darkness.

When the cold night wind comes inland from the river, only the smell of burnt wicks lingers.

CHANDRASHILA

The well traversed and talked of route to Kedarnath and Badrinath is something that every Indian wishes to follow at least once in a lifetime, and it could have been an obvious choice for us too. But somewhere in the labyrinthine maze of all that one had read long ago and half forgotten, a different peak stood waiting, enveloped in legends and surrounded by almost the entire range of Garhwal and Kumaon Himalayas.

So it was that Chandrashila, or the mountain of the moon, came to be the high point of our itinerary.

Legend said Chandrashila was a peak where the moon had done penance. So had Ram, for killing Ravan. It was a peak that watched over Tunganath—at 12,000 feet, the highest temple in Asia. Tunganath belongs to the Panch Kedar group, the third of the five Indian temples said to have been built by the Pandavas to worship Shiva.

Post the Kurukshetra war, Rishi Vyas had suggested the Pandavas worship Shiva to atone for their sins of killing their cousins, the Kauravas. No one asked Shiva what he wanted. Clearly, forgiving the Pandavas was not part of his plan, for Shiva chose to evade the Pandavas in the guise of a bull. He was discovered and caught by Bheem, and in the tussle disintegrated into six parts. Five of these body parts fell at Kedarnath, Kalpeshwar, Rudranath, Tunganath and Madhyamaheshwar in India, and the sixth, at Pashupatinath in Nepal.

The Pandavas built the temples around these body parts to worship Shiva. Bit by bit. They were probably forgiven.

Available statistics said we would need to strike base at Chopta, over 200 kilometres from Rishikesh. The four-km uphill trek to Tunganath temple would be on a six-foot wide rock-paved road. One could hire horses too.

For the almost two-km trek from Tunganath to Chandrashila Peak, towering at more than 13,000 ft, we would need to rely on our feet and our stamina, tested sore at high altitudes thanks to the low supply of oxygen. For a breathtaking—literally or otherwise—view of the sunrise over the Garhwal and Kumaon ranges, it would be best to spend the night at Tunganath, and gasp and claw our way up to Chandrashila before dawn the next day.

Armed with nothing but advice from the tourist officials at Rishikesh, we begin the journey from Rishikesh to Chopta, halting only for short lunch and tea breaks. And one long break: to witness the blending of the very different hued waters of Alakananda and the Mandakini rivers at Rudraprayag. The small red and yellow temple at the confluence does not have a priest. It has a priestess; the only one of her kind we would meet on this trip.

From Rudraprayag the road forks out for Kedarnath and Badrinath. We take the Kedarnath road, which would lead us to Ukhimath, where the Omkareshwar temple is the winter home of the Kedar and Badri idols, and onward to Chopta.

We know Chopta has very very basic hotels. We are to stay at the Mayadeep Herbal Resort in Duggalbitta, six kilometres before Chopta.

It is love at first sight. Duggalbitta, with its almost complete lack of mobile connectivity and complete lack of electricity welcomes us with half-hidden waterfalls and green and gold hillocks teeming with Himalayan blue magpies. Their clean silvery hair glinting in the sun, grey langurs cause frequent showers of red-gold leaves as they lope over the black branches of tall deciduous trees.

The road just above the resort has a tea shack. It comes with:

Teasing views of the Kedar and Kedar Dome peaks.

Omelettes sprinkled generously with coriander leaves that grow on a small ledge just below the shack.

A clown called Jeet running up and down the almost empty road, his mobile phone raised high above his shoulders. He is trying to connect with his girlfriend.

In the evening, the moonlight turns the hillocks into large, looming silhouettes too close for comfort. Workers at the resort light a bonfire in the open. The few guests huddle around the fire in their assortment of woollens and exchange travel tales over the merry splutter of fragrant logs.

The next morning, Jeet drives us to Chopta. We stand under the welcome arch at the start of the Tunganath trail. Sumita rings the brass bell hanging from it with gusto.

Today, we plan to trek up the path to the Tunganath temple, but only do a third of the total trail and halt at a large green meadow, almost in the shadow of Chaukhamba and Kedar peaks. This is the Tunganath *bugiyal*. In the name of acclimatisation, we will just loll about all morning and soak up the sun.

At 10:00 am, the cobbled trail is already warm from the sun and gives off the odour of dried horse dung, scattered liberally. Horses and mules heave and snort past us on repeat journeys to the temple. They carry oddly hunched human bundles, first time riders of all sizes and fitness: children round-eyed with apprehension, ladies suppressing a shriek every minute and still letting out quite a few, and men—most of them old—wearing fixed, nervous smiles.

'Please be careful,' an old man says to me, tilting precariously on the saddle as his mule heads towards us at an erratic pace, 'This has no brake or gear that I can control.'

'It is not down in any map; true places never are', Herman Melville would have said. The verdant *bugiyal* is a discovery to be made by every single traveller, enjoyed, and tucked away like a glossy green leaf into the book of happy memories. Around us, tall trees covered with lichen sway their branches in the nippy, refreshing wind.

Dumping our windcheaters and trekking poles, we bound down the grassy slope, watch lazy cirrus clouds drift over the snowy mountains etched in a deep azure sky and have syrupy sweet tea at the lone tea stall by the path.

Jeet is overjoyed. 'Ma'am, I have often brought tourists to Rishikesh, but never driven this far before,' he says. 'This is so beautiful.'

Beyond the tea stall with its assortment of noodles, chips packets, cold drinks (stored in ice cold water from the local mountain springs) and logs of wood stacked among the rafters is the dark interior of a stone walled room. Its lone window offers the most majestic view of the Chaukhamba. This could be where the owner lives. Going by the number of sheets spread on the floor, it is probably let out to trekkers as well.

We return to Duggalbitta for the night. The next afternoon finds us on the trail again, this time on horses. Jeet has gone ahead. He, too, wishes to trek up to Chandrashila.

Five minutes into the ride, Sumita's horse decides to go off the trail. He hurtles into a gradient dotted with tree trunks, almost throwing her off.

This is not a good start. We have one guide for both our horses. He clutches at the tail of the errant horse, just managing to stop him. I holler at him.

'I cannot take charge of both horses,' he says, 'that horse won't go without his owner.' Indifferent to the hold on his tail, and the protesting rider on its back, the horse is meanwhile making a meal out of fallen leaves and dry grass.

'So where is his owner? Why isn't he here? Call him up right away, or we aren't going,' I tell him.

His owner Dinesh Chauhan sent for and secured, the horse undergoes a transformation. He trots up the rest of the trail like a docile fawn, nudging his owner's elbow with his nose ever so often.

The paved path gets steeper as we ride, and the horses stumble now and then. The sun has gone under a clutch of billowy clouds, radiating white bars of light over the blue mountains.

'The ranges could not be viewed from Chandrashila this morning,' Dinesh says, 'but the clouds might clear tonight. If, by 3:00 am, you are able to see the moon, begin the trek to the Chandrashila Peak. Otherwise, go back to bed.'

We reach the Tunganath temple precincts at dusk. As we dismount and try to get our legs to work, complete strangers sitting around makeshift tea stalls give us a rousing welcome. At close to 12,000 ft, norms of urban societies with their well-lit cubic homes and clinically precise offices fall away. No one waits for a formal introduction: we are already connected by our common passion for the same glorious mountain.

The cold is seeping into our bones, so we are glad to get inside the dimly-lit outer sanctum of the impressive stone temple. A handful of travellers have gathered there already. In the semi-darkness, we sense the presence of stone statues along the walls. Golden statuettes shine in the inner sanctum, lit by brass lamps. Behind them is the ancient stone linga. The evening *arati* and the chanting of Sanskrit hymns take us centuries back in time.

Outside, it is totally dark. We grope our way into a tea stall. While we have tea, two weather beaten men toss rotis over a log fire. The flames light up the crags on their happy faces. In a few days, they will carry the golden statuettes down to their village. The temple will remain closed for winter, covered in snow, and watched over by the lone linga.

Tunganath premises have no electricity, and no running water. Our tiny room in the temple guest house smells of urine and burnt candle wax. For fear of carbon monoxide poisoning, we have put out the lone candle.

By 8:00 pm, we are in our sleeping bags still swaddled in all our woollens. Two thick blankets cover the sleeping bags, but both feel soaking wet. We remain ramrod stiff with the cold.

Our breathing is shallow. Sleep, out of the question.

When we open the door at 4:00 am, a blast of cold wind hits our faces. Turning to avoid it, we see the most mesmerising sight ever:

the entire snow-covered Garhwal Range bathed by the light of a huge full moon.

We stand there a whole minute in complete surrender, while the overpowering beauty fills our hearts.

The two-km trek to the Chandrashila peak is over broken shales of rock, slippery from hidden streams, some shifting position underfoot. The route is narrow, curving and steep, and the moonlight reveals deep precipices.

Torches begin to appear way below us. More travellers have joined the trek. Younger. Fitter. *Faster.*

To Jeet's great disappointment, we are not able to hold onto our lead. Even though he carries my tripod for me, and towards the end, my 5-kg camera bag as well, Sumita and I are the tailenders.

The bright red flag of the Ganga temple on the peak finally becomes visible. We scramble up the last of the scraggy boulders to stand on Chandrashila Peak: a narrow, uneven ledge surrounded by deep chasms. To our right are the distant Trishul, Nanda Devi, Panchachuli and other peaks of the Kumaon Himalayas against an orange sky, and before us, much closer, stand the Garhwal peaks. Around 20 men and 3 women wait on the windswept top, freezing blue fingers on camera buttons.

And then, like the lone red stage light marking out the most poignant moment in a play, the sun rises.

One by one, the snow on Chaukhamba I (23,419 ft), Chaukhamba II (23,156 ft) Mandani (20,318 ft), Kedarnath Main (22,769 ft) and Kedar Dome (22,411 ft) turns pink, then a brilliant gold. Golden light bounces off our happy faces, and off the tall, bronze grass growing at our feet.

All the shutters go off together. The men cheer. Total strangers bond.

Climbing down is easier in daylight. When we reach Tunganath, the priests are washing the temple compound. Another beautiful day on the mountains has just begun.

After a particularly steep downward slope, we come to a tea stall by the winding route. An old man sits by the shop. His thin face is

'In the midst of winter, I found there was, within me, an invincible summer': Chaukhamba or Badri Peak at sunrise, from Chandrashila

full of wrinkles, vertical grooves caked with dirt. He makes us some black tea.

While we sip the hot brew gratefully, a mouse hare arrives. It chooses to sit close to us, looking at us with bright, beady eyes. The old man chats about Mokkumath, his village below the mountain. He would return to it soon, post Deepavali. This whole mountain would then be covered in snow for six months.

The man gets up suddenly, goes behind his shop and rings a large bell with all his might. The sound echoes all over the range. Then he returns to sit with us again.

'Why did you do that?' we ask him, surprised.

In a gentle, soft voice, he explains, 'You see, a lot of people climb up the mountain to have darshan at the Tunganath temple. But this is a difficult, steep climb, and many feel very tired. They want to give up and go back. But if they hear the bell, they think they have almost reached the temple. Then they keep climbing. And once they reach me, I tell them that they just have a little more to go before they see the Shivalinga. That's why I ring this bell every half hour or so.'

He is an illiterate villager of indeterminate age. But thanks to him, hundreds of devotees succeed in climbing up to a temple at 12,000 ft, every day.

If I close my eyes, I still hear the sound of his bell. And because it holds people like him, it is still a beautiful world.

DEORIA TAAL

Caught in the hypnotic orbs of our car's headlights, the lone barasingha pauses a while, turning its elegant head and long antlers towards us. Watchful, yet unafraid. Its healthy, dust brown coat shines in the light. A second or two before it moves on, gracefully stepping off the winding motor road and into the dark forest.

A half hour later, we reach Sari, a village on the Ukimath-Chopta road. Jeet switches off the ignition. It is exactly 5:00 am, but as with all hilly regions, the cold, silent night still has its mantle over us. The path ahead is moon lit, and the Saptarshi or Ursa Major constellation shines overhead. Then, from afar, the fresh breeze brings with it a sweet tinkling of bells. Suraj Singh Negi's mules are on their way.

The pre-dawn three-km ride is along a steep, cobbled and narrow path sharply, at times almost vertically, winding up the mountain. The three mules—Jeet has sought permission to accompany us again—and their owners keep a steady pace, the sounds of their hoof beats and bells punctuated by monosyllabic instructions from the owners to turn a curve or keep close to the rock face.

The riders are lost in thought.

Sumita rides first. Each time her mule stumbles on loose shale, she has this vision of a free fall backward, her mule falling on Jeet's, Jeet and his mule landing on me and my animal, and throwing all of us off the cliff.

Jeet rides second. He relives his wedding day horse ride (no, he is not married to his girlfriend). A firecracker had burst near the horse's hooves, too close for the quadruped's comfort. Jeet was almost thrown off. That 'almost' is suspect: I have only the groom's version.

Jeet's mule, used to leading a convoy, is now trying its best to overtake Sumita's at an extremely narrow turn of the uphill track. He suddenly makes a thrust from the left, where, an inch from his hooves, the track has tumbled down into a dark chasm. *'Arrey yaar, tera* left indicator *toh jala de,'* Jeet exclaims at this unexpected jolt, even as the mule handler snatches and tightens the rein.

Things are in control.

The lights of Sari and other neighbouring villages twinkle far below and to our left. Behind us, far away in the horizon the Chandrashila summit is starkly visible, a peak we conquered two days ago. The moonlight makes silhouettes of us all, hooded figures riding into an enchanting fairy tale.

Around 8,000 ft, just when the moonlight is fading and the sky turning lighter, the mountain top suddenly opens out to a tree-lined valley, and a huge freshwater lake comes into view. This is the Deoria or Devariya Taal where, according to local belief, devas or gods would come down to bathe.

We wait for dawn. At a shack some distance away from the lake, Jeet celebrates his survival with a double-egg omelette.

Deoria Taal, locals say, is the lake mentioned in the *Aranya Parva* (*aranya*: forest, *parva*: chapter) of *The Mahabharata.*

After their 12-year exile in the forest, the Pandavas were still undecided where to spend a year incognito. Around this time, a Brahmin came to them with a request: the sticks he used for igniting his sacrificial fire had got entangled in the antlers of a deer, and the deer had run away. Could the Pandavas help him retrieve the sticks?

The Pandavas went in search of that deer. In the forest, they felt very thirsty. Sahadev, the youngest Pandava, was sent to look for a lake, and he discovered one. But when he bent to drink from it, a crane standing by the lake told Sahadev that he would have to answer some questions before he could drink the water. Sahadev ignored the crane, began to drink from the lake, and died instantly.

One by one, Nakul, Arjun and Bheem followed the same path to the lake. They too ignored the crane's warnings and died. When Yudhishthir, the eldest Pandava, came to look for his brothers, he was stunned to see their bodies lining the lake.

The crane warned Yudhishthir not to drink from the lake without answering his questions. Unlike his brothers, Yudhishthir agreed to answer. The crane then took the form of a Yaksh, the spirit guarding the lake, and asked him profound questions. Yudhishthir answered them all without hesitation. Satisfied, the Yaksh, who was in reality Yamadharma, the God of Death, and Yudhishthir's spiritual father, brought the four Pandavas back to life.

At dawn today, there are no cranes by the lake. Nor people. The tranquil waters hold the reflections of Chaukhamba, Kedarnath and other snow laden peaks of the Garhwal Himalayan Range. The long finger of a still invisible sun touches their tips hesitantly, making them blush, and the lake does an instant playback.

In slow motion, scant clouds over the peaks turn orange. The lake mirrors that too. And then, the still waters ripple with the sudden flip of a cormorant's wings, the surrounding meadows turn a golden yellow, and the lake, an emerald green.

Campers arrive with colourful tents and begin to set them up by the lake. The spell is broken, the allure remains. We return to Duggalbitta.

Some time before dawn the next day, Sumita and I hear the shuffle of stealthy feet outside our door. We are on instant alert, though reluctant to leave the warm blankets and investigate. There are some soft, scraping noises on the door for a while, but no one tries to open the lock. After a while the sounds stop. We fall asleep again.

Morning reveals a sheet of tissue paper slid under the door. Scrawled on it are a smiling face and the words 'Happy Birthday'.

I yank the door open. On its outer flank, chrysanthemums and marigolds stuck with cellotape surround another note, on another sheet of tissue paper. This has a sketch of three balloons, and the words 'Happy Birthday 2 U FROM JEET.'

I have two questions. The first, for Sumita. I know the answer, though.

'How did he know it was my birthday?'

'I told him.'

The second question is for Jeet.

'Where did you get the flowers from?' I am afraid I know what is coming.

'From the resort garden, Ma'am,' Jeet says with a cheeky grin.

An early checkout is in order.

BINSAR

A couple of langurs swing in wide arcs from tree to tree, their direct glances sizing us up. Over our heads, rufous-naped and yellow-breasted tits take deep breaths of the cold mountain air till they turn into tight feather balls and then release it all in a high-pitched burst of song.

The leopards remain elusive, letting us know of their silent presence only through a fresh pugmark. Left a couple of hours ago, on the half-dried mud track through the pine, oak and rhododendron trees in Binsar Wildlife Sanctuary (6,600 ft), Kumaon.

The track goes past the government rest house, and up to Zero Point with its magnificent, if distant, 300-km array of Kumaon Himalayan peaks: Kedarnath Main (22,769 ft), Chaukhamba (23,419 ft), Trishul I (23,360 ft), II (21,949 ft), III (19,711 ft), Nanda Devi (25,645 ft), Nanda Kot (22,510 ft), Nagalaphu (21,030 ft) Panchachuli I (20,846 ft), II (22,648 ft), III (20,709 ft), IV (20,781 ft), and V (21,119 ft).

Zero Point is also called the Jhandi Dhar (*jhanda*: flag, *dhar*: the pole that holds it) Peak. This is where the British Union Jack—or a white flag according to some accounts—would be hoisted to announce that 'King Ramji Sahib' was 'at home'.

The king in question: Sir Henry Ramsay, commissioner of Kumaon from 1856 to 1884.

Ramsay, the local lore goes, was once riding his horse through Binsar when a spot of land caught his attention. He asked some villagers what the area was called. They told him it was *khali*, or empty, as nothing ever grew there. Ramsay bought 25 acres of this land and built a bungalow amid orchards, naming it the Khali Estate.

In the 1900s, Pandit Jawaharlal Nehru's sister Vijay Lakshmi Pandit and her husband Ranjit Sitaram Pandit bought the estate. In her evocative memoir, *Prison and Chocolate Cake*, their daughter Nayantara Sahgal reminisces:

> *'Khali weather was pleasantly warm and drowsy in contrast with the plains, and that summer Papu's honeybees seemed to fly even more busily from flower to honeycomb and back to flower. Daisies and wild orchids carpeted the hillsides. We climbed trees in search of luscious purple berries, and ate plump, juicy yellow ones on our porridge every morning. We discovered a way of making table mats by plaiting pine needles and stitching them together.'*

When we walk into the residence-turned-resort of Khali Estate for a three-day stay, we are not aware that it had hosted Gandhi*ji* and three of India's Prime Ministers: Nehru, Indira Gandhi and Rajiv Gandhi, the latter as a child.

Nehru loved Khali. In the letter he wrote to Indira Gandhi from Ahmadnagar Fort Prison, Nehru suggested she spend time at Khali with Rajiv, so the child could learn to love the hills.

> *'I should like him to become acquainted as early as possible with the Himalayas, have sight of the snow covered peaks, looking down into the deep valleys and breathe the fragrant and health giving air of the pine clad hillsides.'*

So they could experience the hills better, Nehru is believed to have suggested they take the bridle path to Binsar from Almora and not travel by car.

Evening has landed softly among the trees, with the patter of dew. In the sprawling drawing room of Khali Estate, the fireplace is aglow with crackling logs. Madan, a scruffy man on the staff payroll, shares Khali's history with the guests.

Going by his narration, impeccable English is history, too.

There is a foreign couple among us. The old lady and her husband have just returned from a trek into the forests.

'The forests have black beers,' Madan tells them. 'Did you find any?'

'Beer?' asks the lady, confused.

'He means bear,' says another guest.

'Yes, yes, bear. You see, we Indians pronounce it beer,' Madan continues with a smirk.

'We Indians'—who do not pronounce 'bear' as 'beer'—fume and bear it.

'Oh, *bear*! No, we didn't meet any.' The lady laughs nervously.

Khali had enamoured its illustrious residents. Its charms remain, and we are youngsters again as we ride the swings in the sprawling lawns, loll in the hammock, gather pine cones until we have no hands left, and discover shining green cucumbers and bursting pomegranates on the creepers and trees behind the bungalow. While the absence of mobile towers and television sets helps recreate our childhood, the only teenage tourist at the estate wakes up before dawn and goes birdwatching with the guides.

Binsar is much more than the estates. Charmed with the beautiful landscapes, Ms. Marianne North, a 19th century British traveller, artist and naturalist, had painted them during her stay with the Ramsays. *From Lady Ramsay's Garden, Temple in a Dell* and the glorious *Panch Choola from Binsur with Oak Trees and Grey Apes in the foreground* are exhibited in the Marianne North Gallery at Royal Botanic Gardens, Kew.

Amid a green meadow shaded by tall trees sits North's *Temple in a Dell*: the Bineshwar Mahadev Temple which gave Binsar its name. It dates back to the 16th century, believed to be built by King Kalyan Chand of the Chand Dynasty that ruled Binsar from the 11th to the 18th centuries. The quaint little altar nestles a Shivalinga, constantly bathed by water that drips from a pot hung over it.

'Binsar' is a British distortion of 'Bineshwar' that might in turn be a distortion of 'Vishveshwara' or the Lord of the Universe: Shiva.

The quiet, cool glade urges us to hit the pause button for good. But there are long walks to be taken amid the woods with the apples from the breakfast buffet bulging in our pockets, all the while breathing in the air heavy with the scent of pines. There are a hundred trees to sit under when our legs tire, with the butterflies and bees hovering overhead and the occasional village buffalo mooing to announce its presence. And there are just these few precious sunrises and sunsets to warm the cockles of our tired hearts.

KAUSANI

'You can never get a cup of tea large enough or a book long enough to suit me,' C.S. Lewis had said. For tea-drinking travellers, there is nothing like a hot cup of tea from a roadside stall at the end of a long drive. Our cups on this nippy afternoon are special, made from fragrant tea leaves fresh from the Girias Tea Factory across the road. We have just reached Kausani, and going by this warm welcome, we have a good feeling about our stay.

Our resort has a balcony with a 350-km view of the Kumaon Himalayas. The full impact of that hits us at sunset, with the three golden prongs of Trishul (I, II and III) holding most of our attention. When T.G. Longstaff climbed Trishul I in 1907, it marked the world's first ascent of an over 7,000 m peak, and a conquest of a summit held sacred.

Trishul Peak is named after the trident of Lord Shiva. Folklore: Shiva was once returning to Mount Kailash with his consort Sati, from her father King Daksha's palace. When they came to the Kumaon Himalayan Range, Sati felt thirsty. The Alakananda River flowed nearby. But since it had originated from the feet of Lord Vishnu, Shiva's attendant Nandi did not like the thought of Sati drinking from it. So Shiva plunged his trident down. The waters of Nandakini River surged from the earth, and the Trishul Peak came into being.

Kausani, at 6,201 feet, was named the Switzerland of India by Mahatma Gandhi, who had penned his treatise on Anashakti Yoga here. The Anashakti Ashram is dedicated to him. In one of its dimly lit rooms is a bunch of photographs from Gandhi's life.

A river runs through it: Gomti flows by the Baijnath Temple, near Kausani

Some tourists have put up at the ashram. They sun themselves on plastic chairs on the manicured lawn.

'Do you need to be a Gandhian to stay here?' I ask a gentleman.

'No, no, anyone can book a room,' he replies. 'But we have to attend the morning and evening prayers.'

The Himalayan views from the porch are awesome, and a Bengali artist has very helpfully painted and named all the peaks on a rostrum. We scramble up on it to identify the peaks.

From natural peaks to manmade curvilinear spires: The Baijnath (Vaidyanath) temple complex sits by River Gomti in Garuda Valley, 19 kilometres away from Kausani. These 9th-12th century temples were built in the Nagara style probably by the Katyuri rulers of Kartikeypura. The stones in the structure are said to have been joined together by an *urad* dal mix. The most impressive statue is that of Goddess Parvati, made of grey schist.

Just outside the temple compound lies a big, round stone. I have read somewhere that nine men are usually able to lift the stone, each of them using just one finger. We cannot verify this—apart from the two of us and our driver, not a single soul is around. I try giving it a shove with both hands. The stone does not budge a millimetre.

Looking for a guide and a tour plan for the second day, we walk into A.K. Pant's Aradhana Restaurant at Kausani's small market. The genial owner is an ex-Army man, and readily offers the services of his teenage son, Neeraj.

A day with the quiet and serious Neeraj reveals the insider's view of Kausani. While our car waits, we climb up a hillock with a small Hanuman temple for a grandstand view of his village and River Kosi running through it.

On a high range far away, a white dot shines in the sunlight.

'That is the temple of Budha Pinaknath,' says Neeraj. 'It is an eight-hour trek from the mountain base. The strongest of our boys find it difficult.' For us, Neeraj has selected a less strenuous trek: 'I am taking you to the Rudradhari caves and waterfall.'

We get off the Kantali village road for a two kilometre trudge into the forest. Stumble over boulders, and hike up and down narrow, steep mountain trails through oak and chir pine forests. The day gets hotter. Like errant children, we pause at every little stream next to our path, and dip our fingers in the cool waters gurgling over moss-green boulders.

Village women trot downhill with huge bundles of grass on their heads, their pace decided by gravitation. Blue magpies ride the cattle grazing in the forests, and peck out bugs from their twitching skin.

The last lap under a canopy of tall trees is arduous. Gasping up a series of steps roughly cut into the mountain slope, we suddenly see a sunlit opening below us. It leads to the small, dark and mysterious Rudradhari cave temple. The waterfall crashes down from an adjacent hillock, and forms a small pool next to the cave.

Neeraj takes a bucket from the temple. He fills it at the pool and urges us to wash our grimy hands and feet before he takes us inside the sanctum with its small marble statues. He lights the lamp. Sumita and I happily ring the cluster of brass bells hung from the low and rugged stone roof. There are no priests to chant a hymn or ask for a donation, and this moment of peace is all ours to prolong.

Our young guide has other plans. 'I want you to visit the Someshwar Temple,' he says.

Someshwar town is 11 kilometres from Kausani. A walk through the congested Talli Bazaar and a narrow passage between village homes, and we are at the 12th century temple built by Raja Som Chand of the Chand dynasty.

Most of the statues date between the 11th and the 15th century, and some have lost their features to time. Somehow, this vulnerability narrows the chasm between the divine and the human. That the idols are still worshipped with fondness is evident from the abundance of sandalwood paste on their time-ravaged faces.

The evening light falls on a trident stuck on the temple porch, and scatters into a million golden rays. It marks the end to a good, satisfying day.

'You know your homeland very well, Neeraj,' I tell the soft-spoken boy. 'Would you like to be a guide when you grow up?'

'I want to join the Indian Army,' he replies.

'And why is that?'

'They give you food, uniforms.'

MUNSIYARI

Thal onward, the Ramganga River dances along our route, its blue-green water straight out of the first 3D birthday card I had received long ago. The little waves dashing against sun-whitened rocks are for real, though, and the laughing, gurgling waterfalls playing 'peek-a-boo' from bushes by the wayside make you want to get off the car and laugh with them.

The lashing rains have left white gashes on the mountainside, a grim reminder of floods, landslides and losses. The road winding along the mountain range is often dangerous. Our car rocks sideways every now and then, sending little pebbles flying down to the deep crevasses.

But the rains have also fed the rivers and the waterfalls, and Birthi, the largest waterfall on our way to Munsiyari in Pithoragarh district is bounding down the rock face in a surge of white, billowy foam. The shrubs around it are green, and little white spiders with a human face painted on their backs are busy building their matching white webs.

The road lopes past the windy Kalamuni Pass, with its quaint orange Kala Muni temple and a striking black goddess Kali carved on the wall, and is smooth again, climbing gently up to Zara Resort, our home for the next three days.

Munsiyari is a stash of picture postcards mailed to the deep, unsullied recesses of the traveller's heart, and not one of these fail to deliver. In that late winter afternoon of our arrival, our welcome gift is a splendid view of Mt Nagalaphu and the Panchachuli Range, through the large glass panes of our Panchachuli suite.

As with all relatively remote destinations, mythology has its pride of place here. The five peaks of the Panchachuli Range are believed to be the five *chulhas* (clay ovens) used by the Pandavas to cook their food on their final heavenward journey. As if to dispel our disbelief, the setting sun lights the five peaks with the fiery glow of embers, and smoke-like clouds provide the finishing touch to the ovens.

Days begin incredibly early in the mountains, much before sunrise, and once we wipe away the dense mist from the glass panes the next morning, the ranges appear again, this time in their pristine white splendour. Before the village home next to the hotel, smiling women in bright coloured clothes are busy stuffing cut grass into sacks.

The women are always at work, carrying loads of chopped wood or hay on their heads up and down winding mountain paths that we—empty-handed city breds—would be huffing and puffing on, tending to their vegetable gardens, feeding the cow, cooking for their family.

It is only around 3:00 pm, when the afternoon sunlight falls just so on the steps leading to their room, that the older women take a break, sharing the warmth and the hookah among themselves in silent harmony. The younger sit with their faces in the shadow, holding chubby-cheeked kids in their lap.

The next morning, we have an intense urge to laze about with mugs of warm coffee and simply gaze at the ranges. But Ramesh, our guide, is ready, and the day, full of promise. We drive down to the Goriganga River, its light green waters wetting the sun bleached pebbles on the shore. The pebbles just below the surface of the clear water are multi-coloured and collectibles for the child in everyone. I sit cross-legged on a large white rock right next to the rippling water, pretending to meditate. The waves sneak up and wet my shoes with a splash.

Eight kilometres from Munsiyari, a long flight of stairs leads off the motorable road and down to Dar Kot village. Half way down, the stairs open out to a green level ground with three small temples for

'The sun does not forget a village just because it is small': Damayanti Pangtey looks out of her home in the ancient village of Dar Kot

Durga, Kali and Shiva. Adorned with bells, and brightly painted, they make the backdrop of the sky seem a deeper azure, and the world a peaceful place.

We keep climbing down, past the small stage for the annual Ram Leela festival and a tree full of pink pepper (*timur*), until a 100-year-old house looms into view. The carved wooden doors that remain speak of a people proud of their art, but the inhabitants have long moved out to indifferent cities in search of work. Their tomato tree still bears fruit, and Ramesh picks us a handful for our salad.

Dar Kot village lives on its production of Angora and Pashmina shawls. In a five-feet high room, where the only piece of furniture is a two feet-by-three feet bed, Damayanti Pangtey weaves magic on her

'For I would ride with you upon the wind.... And dance upon the mountains like a flame': A portion of the Panchachuli Range, Munsiyari

loom with the fur from Angora rabbits. We sit on the bed, and watch her work the loom.

The rabbits live with their families in cages behind the house. Damayanti brings one out of its cage. Loaded with its burden of grey-white hair, the rabbit is hardly able to move, and snuggles close to our feet for a pat.

'We cut off their hair in the summer months,' Damayanti says, 'then they jump about happily.'

Generous sunlight on the courtyard bathes the diced yak meat set out to dry and the bright red flowers in pots, and its warmth has long seeped into the hearts of the Kumaonis. Damayanti and her sister-in-law Swati readily offer us lunch.

Tempted as we are to taste their home food, we choose not to inconvenience them, and get up to leave. I clutch on to the Angora cap which Sumita has just bought for me. It feels just as warm as its brown-eyed, long-eared owner.

As a gift, Damayanti quickly wraps a fistful of chopped and dried parsley leaves in an old newspaper.

'Take this home,' she says. 'When you cook dal, or a potato curry, heat up the oil and sprinkle these leaves. You will love the fragrance.'

At Nanasen village, labourers are paving a small uphill path off the main road with square boulders. We do not notice the old man sitting on a boulder at the head of the path, until the guide introduces us: 'Master*ji*, they have come to visit your museum.'

The gentleman gives us a big smile, stands up quickly like an energetic teenager, and leads us further uphill till we reach the Tribal Heritage Museum: two storeys of a dedicated man's lifelong efforts.

Dr Sher Singh Pangtey, or Master*ji*, as he is fondly referred to by the locals, has woven bits of history in his old home—itself a relic with exquisitely carved wooden doors and windows.

An avid traveller and trekker in his youth, Dr Pangtey has gone on several treks, and done the Kailash Manasarovar Yatra more than once. He did his doctoral thesis on the Bhotia tribe (originally the

Shaukya tribe), and is a retired professor of the Government Inter College at Munsiyari. He has also written many books on local history and culture.

In his bid to preserve the lost lore of the Johar valley (Munsiyari is considered the entry point to this valley) and its tribes, he has visited all Bhotia homes in Munsiyari to collect numerous relics from the past. He is the bridge that connects the youth of Munsiyari to their history, and they love him for it.

On the wall adjoining the entrance, a small strip of paper gives us the GPS position of the museum, as well as the altitude (5,980 ft). Not just a meticulous man with a penchant for detail, but an eager storyteller with twinkling eyes, Dr Pangtey shares with us details of how the ancient Shaukya tribes lived their life.

Since agriculture could not flourish at this altitude, the men of the region were involved in the salt trade between India and Tibet. Milam, north-west of Munsiyari, used to be the frontier trading post on the ancient Indo-Tibet trade route. After the Indo-China War in 1962, trading ended and the Bhotia traders migrated to towns and cities.

A typewritten application for such a trade permit, the paper yellow with age, catches our eye. It is from Bala Singh, a trader, to the Political Officer in Gangtok, Sikkim. It says:

> *'I beg to state, that we, the following traders dealing with Western Tibet want to export 25 loads of China ball tea from licence holder M/S Panna Lal Kishan Lal, Calcutta, to Western Tibet. It is therefore requested that we may kindly be granted export permit. We were also granted such permit last year.*

Shri Kushal Singh	*– 5 loads*
Shri Bala Singh	*– 5 loads*
Shri Mahendra Singh	*– 5 loads*
Shri Bala Singh Pangtey	*– 5 loads*
Shri Prahlad Singh	*– 5 loads*
	25 loads'

'I trust that the current knows where it is going. I shall let go, and let it take me where it will': Ramganga River on the way to Munsiyari

For his museum, Dr Pangtey has collected the saddles that once belonged to the traders—complete with colourful rugs thrown over them for the riders' comfort—as well as handmade leather bags that they would sling across their chests.

Some of the embroidery on the bags still remains. With a bit of polishing, these would be coveted by any urban male. The bags, the sturdy, fawn coloured leather shoes and the coat brushes in Dr Pangtey's collection show that the men, despite their hard and dangerous lives unfolding across difficult mountain passes, were proud of their appearances.

*Hookah*s of different styles line a shelf, and rusted swords hang from the rafters. On the floor sits an ancient version of a distiller used to make wine.

There are life-sized models of women, dressed in traditional clothes and jewellery, and quite a few of the shelves are filled with ornate copper, clay and wooden pots and pans.

Dr Pangtey takes down a bellow hanging from a hook on the shelf.

'Women used this to blow on the burning logs in their oven.' He blows air into it with gusto to show us how the leather and wood contraption was used.

On the next shelf are crow-sized birds sculpted out of wood. Master*ji* takes one and slides the wings outward to reveal two compartments.

'These were meant to keep sindoor (vermillion). But these days the ladies prefer plastic containers,' he says, a tinge of regret in his voice.

The library section holds books written by Dr Pangtey, old documents, photographs. There is a photo of Jabbu, a cross between a cow and a yak. (In Ladakh, it would be called Dzo.)

The feedback book in the museum speaks of visits by foreigners. Richard and Diana Parker of Hertford College, Oxford University, UK, write: 'This reminds us of the esteemed Pitt Rivers museum (The Pitt Rivers Museum cares for the University of Oxford's collection of anthropology and world archaeology) in Oxford and is even more characterful.'

Dr Paul Wagner from Germany says that this is a 'Very important private initiative to honour cultural heritage. Good luck.'

On our way out, we take another look around the museum. Rusted swords, crude coat brushes, faded trade permits bring to us the sound of hooves on hard mountain trails. The odour of horses and tired riders on the salt trading route from Tibet blend with the smoke from the elegant hookahs glowing in the late afternoon light. Back in their cottages, the women bring out leather bellows to light the fire, and apply vermilion on their foreheads from ornate, bird-shaped wooden cases.

The trade route may have become a trek route, but Munsiyari's present is still no less beautiful than its past. A mild climb to a flat mountain top the next morning takes us to the Nanda Devi temple. Bright flags flutter from the freshly painted structure, its white dome matching the incredibly white ranges facing it. The idol of the goddess is small and fair, with calm, beautiful eyes.

Guide Ramesh talks of an annual festival and fair when the mountain top is quite transformed, with numerous stalls and throngs of locals offering puja.

But for now, we are happy with the wide, empty space cradled by the cold mountains. I make friends with the shy black and brown ponies grazing on the green. They breathe on my palm and gently swish their long silky tails.

For now, our lives are perfect.

NEPAL

KATHMANDU

I have a strong dislike for forms that I need to fill in long hand, printed forms that come with numerous infinitesimal boxes and expect me to wring out my life's details onto them, one uppercase letter at a time.

Immigration forms are the worst, for they also induce a fear of rejection.

I remember my trip to the US for a 15-day professional assignment. The official at the immigration counter in Atlanta took time to sift through all my papers and then asked me, 'So how long do you propose to stay?'

It was all there before him, a neat sheaf of papers with my ancestral, health and project details printed in fairly large fonts. I assumed he could read. After the longest 36 hours of my life spent inside cheap flights and crowded terminals, I could not resist saying, 'Well, the business visa is for three months...' All the strands of golden fur on his thick, pink neck rose of one accord, and he made a move as if to rise, too. I hastily ended my sentence with '...but I have no plans of staying beyond a fortnight.'

It was quite an encounter with American paranoia, a memory reinforced by a body search on my way *out* of that country the said fortnight later. Since then, I always wait for the official at any

---

Pp 210-211: 'My religion is very simple. My religion is kindness': Boudhanath Stupa, Kathmandu

Facing page: 'If we think we are bound, we are bound': Puppets at Kathmandu Durbar Square

immigration counter—usually male, hefty and poker-faced—to look up from the form I have handed him and announce, 'Ma'am, I cannot let you in. Step aside and let the others pass.'

What happens when you step aside? Do you do a Tom Hanks at the terminal? Do they let you live indefinitely on the edges of the runway, with the stray pigeons?

Sumita does not share my dislike of forms. She just does not *do* forms. Her quota of longhand writing—she firmly believes—begins and ends with her signature. That I will be the one filling up all possible forms, hotel guest registers and feedback logs through the trip is her pre-condition to any of our journeys. If I disagree, well, she would rather stay home.

If you have got to do something, you have got to. The Arrivals hall at Tribhuvan International Airport, Kathmandu is cold at 4,386 feet, crowded. I can never remember my passport number, and with some trouble ferret out the blue book from a bag choking with essentials. Sumita waits patiently behind me, her passport and blank immigration form in her hand.

Supporting the flimsy six-inch form against a three-inch wide window ledge, I scribble in my details, the point of the pen making little holes in some of the boxes. All the while, some Malaysian ladies peer over my right shoulder in the hope of making some sense of the form in languages absolutely foreign to them: English and Hindi.

Afraid that they would end up copying my details onto their forms, I use gestures—polite, if a little hysterical—to guide them to the nearest security officer.

We live through immigration, the deafening thuds of travel cases thrown brutally onto conveyor belts and reeking washrooms to finally find ourselves outside the airport.

Nothing could have given us a better welcome than the burst of violet flowers on what I think is a jacaranda tree. The smiling moon-face of Bikram, our local travel agent, is a poor second. Just to be certain, I ask him the name of the tree. He turns around, discovering it for the first time.

Bikram: '(*Clears his throat*) I don't know, Ma'am.'

We would come across jacarandas in riotous bloom all over Nepal.

On the way, Bikram does point out the Pashupatinath Temple and the statue of Tenzing Norgay. Then he delivers the bad news: he would not be around to guide us through the trip.

'I am trekking to Everest Base Camp,' Bikram says, 'for the Everest Marathon. It is held every year on May 29. But don't worry; my partner will take care of you.'

The road ambles past Baidehi Fancy Bazar, Kaiser Gallery, Narayanhiti Palace Museum and the Garden of Dreams. Then, with a sudden turn, we are honking our way into the heart of Thamel—*jhamel*, or chaotic, as the locals call it—its narrow lanes honeycombed with a zillion outlets: handicraft emporia with their brass prayer bowls, woollen shawls, wooden masks, and magnificent paintings, mountaineering gear shops, foreign currency exchange booths, restaurants, cafés, pubs, and nightclubs.

This is hardly a road, but there are numerous bikes. There is hardly a pavement, but loads of pedestrians. It all seems familiar.

It all seems Indian.

At the end of a muddy by lane off the market madness is our oasis of a hotel. Clean room, caring staff, unpretentious decor.

Quiet, it is not.

A laptop-wielding belligerent young woman working with some non-governmental organisation has taken over the cosy, common dining space and turned it into her office. Over our entire stay and through every single meal—hers and ours—she would be holding loud meetings with her team.

She is an Indian, also a guest at the hotel.

It is quieter in Narayanthan, a roadside village at the base of the Shivpuri hill. In a sprawling complex, Budha Nilkantha (literally, 'Old Blue Throat') lies on the coils of Sesha Nag the 11-headed snake, at the centre of a lake that represents the cosmic ocean. This is a five-metre long statue of Narayan or Sleeping Vishnu sculpted out of a single black slab of basalt in the Licchavi-style. It dates back to the 7th or the 8th century.

'God is a circle whose center is everywhere and circumference nowhere':
Budha Nilkantha, Kathmandu

'Nilkantha' is an epithet used for Shiva, not Vishnu. *The Rough Guide to Nepal* has this to say:

> *'The myth of Shiva's blue throat, a favorite in Nepal, relates how the gods churned the ocean of existence and inadvertently unleashed a poison that threatened to destroy the world. They begged Shiva to save them from their blunder and he obliged by drinking the poison. His throat burning, the great god flew up to the range north of Kathmandu, struck the mountainside with his trident to create a lake, Gosainkund, and quenched his thirst—suffering no lasting ill effect except for a blue patch on his throat. The water in the Sleeping Vishnu's tank is popularly believed to originate in Gosainkund, and Shaivas claim a reclining image of Shiva can be seen under the waters of the lake during the annual Shiva festival there in August, which perhaps explains the association. Local legend maintains that a mirror-like statue of Shiva lies on the statue's underside.'*

Pigeons and mynahs perch on the deity's thighs and arms, carrying on their own dialogue.

The temple theme seems to be golden yellow:

Narayan wears a yellow dhoti.

His garlands are of fresh marigolds.

A bowl of ripe yellow bananas rests on his body.

Santosh, the teenaged priest, wears a yellow kurta and a matching yellow dhoti.

There are devotees from Bhutan, from the south of India, local men and women crowding at Narayan's feet with garlands and coloured powder. While we wait for a moment alone with the statue, I make friends with Santosh. Shy at first, he soon opens up.

'Do you study?' I ask him.

'I study scriptures at the residential school. Thirty-five of us stay here. You from India?'

'Yes.'

'Narendra Modi your new Prime Minister?'

'That's right.'

'Isn't it very hot in India?'

'In summer, it is. Not so throughout the year.'

'India is full of mosquitoes.' He has a cheeky smile. This is not a question, but bait.

'No, that's not true, Santosh. Visit India, so you can see for yourself.'

When I do find the space to take a photograph, I find that Budha Nilkantha's eyes, like those of Santosh, slant upwards at the corners.

Driving down from Budha Nilkantha to Boudhanath, we make a discovery: shop names in Kathmandu are an entire inventory of Nepal's religion, culture, geography and fauna. Budha Nilkantha Money Transfer, Budha Nilkantha Digital Colour Lab, Kumari Hardware, Sagarmatha Cement, Yak Auto Parts, and Yeti Fabric Limited are outlets that line the road.

Buddha's large eyes slanting upward at the corners watch us from the square tower of Boudhanath, Asia's largest stupa. This was a staging post for the Tibetan traders travelling between

Kathmandu and Lhasa, who would pray at the stupa for a safe journey over the Himalayas.

The structure, with a wall-to-wall length that almost equals a football field, abounds in symbolism.

The plinth stands for the earth.

The dome signifies water.

The square tower represents fire.

The spire is the air.

The umbrella on top is ether.

The 13 levels of the spire are the stages that a human being should cross in the journey towards enlightenment.

It is a bustling, happy place, the pristine white stupa encircled by monasteries, restaurants and shops. Little lamas crowd around colourful shopfronts. A bunch of schoolchildren pose for a photograph on the stupa. Planes fly overhead at regular intervals, their silver bodies reflecting the bright sunlight. A hundred over-fed pigeons puff their chests out and strut like dignitaries all over the stupa grounds, occasionally deigning to peck at a carpet of corn. Green, plastic bowls of bird feed are stacked suggestively beside women squatting under umbrellas.

The midday sun shows no mercy as we reach Pashupatinath. This Shiva temple is considered the sixth of the Kedar group of temples known as the Panch Kedar in India. It is a centuries-old practice—oft-contested by the people of Nepal—to appoint Indian priests at this temple.

Non-Hindus are not allowed in. All they get to see at the entrance are the hump, the rump and the privates of a huge golden statue of Nandi, Shiva's bull, who sits facing the temple.

I am not allowed to take my camera. Sumita goes in first, then returns to wait with it while I take the tour.

'You may need to hurry,' she says. 'Apparently, they will close soon, and open only after 5:30 pm.'

Stone slabs of the ruthlessly sunny compound make toast of my bare soles, and I reach the sanctum at an inappropriate trot. A toothless old man smiles affectionately at my endeavour.

For a month now, the temple priests have been on strike. They are demanding a 25 per cent share of the temple earnings from 'special worships'. There have been no special worships all this while.

Long, thick iron chains hang from the sanctum's ceiling. As I join the queue outside a knee-high wall for a glimpse of the idol, some of the priests grab the chains to swing out of the sanctum, Tarzan-style.

Temple doors are silver and gold plated, ornate. There are carvings everywhere: on doors, on the rafters, on bells that swing from the rafters. The four-headed idol of dark stone, made darker with ritual smearing, has gold plated eyes. Stone statues of kings and saints on their haunches face the sanctum.

We have been listening to Hindi and Nepali songs on Radio Bagmati all morning, but River Bagmati is not on song, burdened as it is with the city's debris. And its journey past the Pashupatinath Temple complex is dotted with bodies brought in for cremation. Wails and smoke hang heavy in the air. At a home for destitutes nearby, old men sleep on a porch stacked with logs used in cremation.

It is a sobering dusk.

Night falls by the time we hit the lane to our hotel. 'Sister, sister, come have a look,' a man calls out to us from a curio-choked shop. We turn to see him following us, and quicken our steps a little. 'I am after your money,' he says, laughing at our fear.

Psychedelic lights surfacing from the Dancing Girls' Bar in a basement lend a touch of mystery to the alley. At the foot of the narrow stairs that lead to the basement, two burly men are counting thick wads of notes.

Legend goes that all of Kathmandu was once a lake—this has geological evidence, too—and the hill bearing the UNESCO World Heritage Site of Swayambhunath rose from the waters. So it came to be called *swayambhu*, or 'self-arisen'.

An enormous brass-plated *dorje* (thunderbolt) sits at the head of a long stairway leading to the stupa. Called a vajra in Sanskrit, this represents the power of enlightenment that destroys ignorance, but is itself indestructible.

Emperor Ashoka is said to have paid Swayambhunath a visit. It takes us a good couple of hours to walk by the array of soot-blackened idols, stupas and temples spread over different levels, and watch women queue up for worship with an offering of eggs.

Our ambling leads to the less crowded Saraswati temple. I go in to get a photograph. A jot tired, Sumita decides to wait outside.

A minute later, she calls out my name.

'Sohini... Sohineeeee....'

It is a high-pitched, urgent whisper.

I come out to investigate, and find her rooted where I had left her, clutching my tripod and a Coke bottle which carries our drinking water. She is bug-eyed with fear.

A large male rhesus macaque sits by Sumita's leg. He has his arms firmly around her thigh. He looks at me and flashes a healthy set of teeth.

A tourist couple and I take in the situation. 'Do something,' the lady urges her husband. He and I do not make any sudden moves, just urgent, guttural but purposeful shooing noises. The monkey releases his hold, and circles Sumita, fixing her with his stare. She slowly and stubbornly tries to move her belongings out of his sight. In a swift move, he snatches the Coke bottle. Unscrews the cap with deft, experienced fingers, pours some of the water on the ground and licks it. Apparently satisfied with the result, he gulps down the rest of the water, throws the bottle at our feet, and walks away.

Swayambhunath is—quite unceremoniously—called the Monkey Temple.

Named after the Monkey God, the Hanuman Dhoka Palace at Kathmandu's Durbar Square houses a good museum, with, among other things, the massive tusks of the royal elephants Suvarna Prashad and Kiran Prashad, and photos from King Tribhuvan's 'royal babyhood'.

If Hanuman Dhoka is for the kings and the temples for the gods, the Kashthamandap, the wooden pavilion said to have given the city its name, is for the commoner. Locals say that the structure was built around the 12th century from a single *sal (Shorea robusta)* tree. Inside, the four corners have idols of Ganesh: Karya Vinayak, Surya Vinayak, Jal Vinayak and Ashok Vinayak.

A rest-house next to two ancient trans-Himalayan trade routes, the Kashthamandap was once a storage centre for traders on their way to Tibet or India. From their times to ours, generations of Malakar flower sellers and Sarafi (Afghani) money exchangers have sat on Kashthamandap's steps. People pray, ring bells on their way to work, or just share a quiet smoke.

Flower sellers also sit under multi-coloured garden umbrellas on the brick-paved steps of the Maju Dewal, their stacks of bright orange and yellow marigold garlands draped over the auburn bricks. With a nine-step staircase forming its base, Maju Dewal, or the Temple of the Queen Mother is an impressive part of the Durbar Square skyline. Built in 1692 by Queen Riddhi Laxmi, mother of infant King Bhupatindra Malla, it comes with an interesting legend.

The Newars, the story goes, loved to live in close-knit communities. So, the king's palace was surrounded by the residences of his ministers, courtiers, priests and his astrologer. The astrologer had a beautiful daughter, and the king was quite infatuated by her. He would stare across the courtyard at the astrologer's home, yearning for a glimpse of the girl.

This did not escape the queen. One day, she sought permission from the king to build a Shiva temple. Little knowing what was in store, the king granted her wish. The queen built the temple right across the Durbar Square, totally cutting off the view of the astrologer's house.

Maju Dewal has outlived the king and the queen, and surely the astrologer's daughter too, but this ancient temple and the 537 years older Kashthamandap would both crumble to dust a year later, in the massive earthquake—7.8 on the Richter scale—of 2015.

We do not know it just then, but under our feet, seismic energy is building up and tectonic plates are shifting. Among the Himalayas, an upheaval is long overdue.

PATAN

It is business as usual in Patan Durbar Square, a UNESCO World Heritage Site since 1979. As we buy the entrance tickets and put on our tourist tags, an old man pays homage to a vermilion-smeared stone statue of Vishnu's Narasimha avatar, boys sit next to large stone lions and watch life go by, and women line up yellow plastic containers at the Manga Hiti, a trough where three spouts shaped like crocodile-elephant mouths dispense water. On the red-brick courtyard, pigeons decide their pecking order over a generous sprinkling of corn.

One bird stays absolutely still. Perching dangerously on a cobra's hood, its nimble body is poised for flight. When it does fly, the elephants that guard the Vishvanath temple will amble across to Manga Hiti for a drink, and King Yoganarendra Malla will return to his palace.

The elephants are made of stone, the bird, of brass. King Yoganarendra's statue that sits on a pillar with his queens by his side is of brass, too. Yoganarendra disappeared in 1705.

At Patan, probably built by the Kirat dynasty in the 3rd century BC, expanded by Lichhavis in the 6th century AD, and then by the Malla kings in the medieval age, legends seamlessly blend with reality.

The legend goes that a serpent of Taudaha Lake had gifted a farmer a magic stone. As long as he possessed the stone, and until an impossible wish came true, he would be immortal.

Initially, this made the farmer very happy. As the years passed, everyone in his family died, and the lonely man did not wish to live

'May God break my heart so completely that the whole world falls in': Old man at Patan

any longer. So he approached King Yoganarendra and gifted him the stone.

With time, the king too was weary with his royal responsibilities. So, after a long thought, he made eight impossible wishes. He announced to his subjects that until these wishes came true, they should continue to attend to his needs.

The king disappeared soon after, but since his wishes have not come true, he is still believed to be alive. It is said that his *hookah* has been kept ready for him in the palace over the last three centuries.

Also called Lalitpur or the beautiful city or Yala, after King Yalamber, Patan, at 4,324 feet, has some of the finest temple architecture. Most of these are at its Durbar Square, now filling up with young women rushing to work, old women limping up the stairs to the temples and men setting up stalls to sell stone and metal statuettes. Two women try to sell necklaces of silver and semi-precious stones to a foreign tourist who already wears a large marigold garland. On a temple porch, an old lady lays out her store of costume jewellery. I indicate that I would like to take her photograph.

'Money, money,' she says instantly, '10 *lupeej*.'

I pay her and take three shots, just for the heck of it. The first was good enough.

The linear array of temples with their finely carved woodwork or equally well-sculpted stone begins with a Krishna Mandir, followed by the Taleju bell, which would be rung by subjects wishing to report their grievances to the reigning king. We walk past the bell toward the Shankar Narayan, Narasimha and Char Narayan temples, one more Krishna temple, one for Vishvanath, and the Bheemsen temple.

A temple dedicated to Bheemsen, the superhuman Pandava, makes us sufficiently curious to visit. His idol on the first floor has a striking red complexion and angry, bulging eyes. He towers over an offender with a raised hand.

There is, but of course, a legend: Bungadyah, or Karunamaya, the Buddhist god of compassion was assigning every god and goddess a specific department to oversee human welfare. He did not plan to assign any chore to Bhindyah or Bheemsen because of the Pandava's short temper.

When Bheemsen got to know this, he approached Bungadyah and said that he at least knew how to add two and two to make four. 'Well then, I will make you the god of the merchants,' said Bungadyah. 'Take care of their business, and see that they prosper.' So Bheemsen became the god of trade and business in Nepal.

King Srinivas Malla wished to build a temple for Bheemsen at Patan, and selected a craftsman from the Shakya community to build an idol of the god. Kalyan Simha, the craftsman, began work on the statue. King Srinivas supervised the progress regularly, and was not happy with the form it was taking: the sculpture did not come anywhere close to his vision of Bheemsen. One day, the king lost his temper, and raised his hand to strike the craftsman. The craftsman

'I'm not afraid of death; I just don't want to be there when it happens':
Statue of King Yoganarendra Malla, Patan

could instantly visualise the fierce image of Bheemsen. This time, his work pleased the king.

In a lane next to the Bheemsen temple, Anjana has her little handicraft shop. She, her father and her brother are all into wood carving, while her mother is a teacher.

Sumita loves one of Anjana's Buddha statues, a meticulous palm-sized sculpture in red wood. It is going to be the latest in her collection.

Anjana is happy with our praise. 'No one cares about the value of art nowadays,' she says.

We do, and while we are at it, a six-inch high Green Tara exquisite in turquoise somehow finds her way into our hearts.

'Faith unlocks the door': Entrance of the Taleju shrine, guarded by life-size metal sculptures of Ganga and Yamuna, Mul Chowk, Patan

Goddess Green Tara (Sanskrit: Shyamatara; Tibetan: Sgrol-ljang) is said to be full of youthful vigour. In Buddhism, the colour green signifies activity and accomplishment.

Our petite Tara's left hand is raised in the *sharanagamana* mudra or refuge-granting gesture, and her right hand is in the *varada* or the boon-granting one. She sits in a posture of ease, yet ready for action: her left leg folded, and the right outstretched.

A little tired with the morning's activity, we walk into an old Newari residence, now a home for the old. In a large courtyard edged with potted plants and little creepers growing from cold drink bottles hung at different levels along the walls, a young woman sits washing clothes. We sit down on the porch for a breather when, in one long bound from the other end of the courtyard, a black-and-brown beauty rushes to meet us. It is a one-year-old German shepherd.

'Down, Sweetie,' admonishes the young woman.

'Let her be,' Sumita says, 'we love dogs.'

Her love is tested soon enough. Sweetie leaps to the porch next to Sumita, and focuses on planting a very wet, very pink tongue on her lips. Sumita slowly turns her face away. Sweetie goes around her to the other side, her hot breath now on Sumita's ear and a tense jawline. It is an intimate moment.

Sweetie is not allowed the lick. Quite unlike a one-year-old, she understands.

In the Museum Café nearby, we make another friend. Birendra Shrestha, an officer—and a gentleman—with the Kathmandu hotel that runs the café, introduces himself.

Shrestha has lived a while in India, 'Falakata, then Roorkee, then Delhi'. He remembers his very first visit to a planetarium, 'that was in Kolkata'.

'We will be visiting the museum next,' I tell him.

'May I offer a suggestion?' Shrestha asks politely. 'I feel you should do the Sundari Chowk first. The museum trip is exhausting; you may not want to do anything else afterward. But the Sundari Chowk should not be missed. The Kathmandu Valley Preservation Trust (KVPT) has just recently opened Mul Chowk and Sundari Chowk for public viewing.'

Founded in 1990, KVPT works to safeguard the architecture and heritage of Nepal. Sundari Chowk is a sprawling courtyard with an oval step-well. Commissioned in 1647, the Tusha Hiti step-well has a bronze water spout with an image of Lakshmi and Narayan riding on Garuda. The niches are packed with tiny tantric idols in metal and stone. A miniature replica of the Krishna Mandir sits on the brink of the well.

The Mul Chowk or the main courtyard has an exquisite golden doorway marking entry to the Taleju shrine, guarded by life-size metal sculptures of Ganga and Yamuna.

The best is to follow. Keshav Narayan Chowk, the palace compound, holds one of the finest museums in Asia, initially funded by the Austrian government. Eight galleries display 200 objects labelled in detail, from an ivory-handled bronze mirror to a metallurgist's reference manual. The latter tells us that the cranial bump for a Buddha statue should measure four fingers in Patan, and six in Kathmandu.

The only bump in our trip in Patan is an old Nepali lady we meet in the Krishna Mandir. The minute she lays eyes on my camera, she warns me that photography is not allowed inside the sanctum. I show her that my lens already has its cover on, and assure her that I do not plan to photograph the temple carvings or the shrine.

After paying homage to the deity, I realise that the temple corridors offer a bird's-eye shot of Durbar Square below. Before I can focus, though, I receive a stinging slap on my arm from the same lady, now screaming murder. Since I have not photographed any part of the temple, the attack is quite unprovoked.

Sumita is furious. In a rare display of temper, she accosts the old lady in a cold, low tone: 'Why did you hit her? And where does it say that you cannot take photographs?'

A little subdued, the lady takes us to a remote corner of the temple to show us a sign in Nepali. We do not know what it says.

'If it is meant for foreigners, this notice should be in English, or at least in Hindi,' Sumita is not convinced. 'Why could you not speak to her first, check whether she was actually clicking photos of the temple?'

The commotion draws more women. One of them approaches us. 'Please forget the incident,' she says, trying to calm Sumita down.

'*Why did she hit her?*' Sumita repeats.

'Let it go,' says the second lady. 'This is a temple, God sees everything.' She runs her palm down my back in a silent apology.

I know I could have the offender arrested for assaulting a foreign national, but I would rather exercise restraint and respect the sanctity of a shrine. Over and above the smidge of vermilion on my now bruised arm, the incident definitely lends local colour to our Patan experience.

BHAKTAPUR

He seems to be waiting for us, a stocky body topped by a bespectacled, smiling moon-face, tanned despite the cap shielding it. The eyes behind the glasses are gentle.

'Do you need a guide?' he says, falling in step as we get off the car and approach the half-village, half-town of Bhaktapur, at 4,596 feet. 'I could show you around, I am Shankar Prajapati.'

He comes at a reasonable rate, and it is good to have a local guide taking us around the maze of lanes that connect the Durbar Square, Dattatreya Square, Taumadhi and Potters' Squares.

All Bhaktapur residents are named after the gods, says Shankar. 'Ours is a city of devotees. There was a time when we had more temples than people.'

Bhaktapur is also known as Bhadgaon, or by the Newari name of Khwopa. It is one of the three ancient kingdoms of Kathmandu Valley—Kathmandu, Patan and Bhaktapur—conquered by Prithvi Narayan Shah and merged to create the country of Nepal.

The three kings were often caught up in trivial conflicts. Jealousy would at times be a reason. There is a story of how the Patan Durbar Square once had a beautiful stone pillar, and Bhaktapur had none quite like it. The king of Bhaktapur was unhappy about this, and wished that the pillar at Patan could somehow be destroyed. One of his loyal subjects thought he could fulfil his king's wish.

This man began to walk to Patan Durbar Square every day, and spend hours with his ear glued to the pillar. Soon, the curious locals

'Art is not what you see, but what you make others see': Temple sculpture at Bhaktapur

started asking him what he was up to. 'There is a worm inside this pillar,' he answered them gravely, 'and it is boring away at the stone.'

One of the locals put his ear to the pillar too, and thought he could hear the sound of boring. He was followed by another, and then another. They all thought they could hear something.

Before long, the rumour reached the king of Patan, and he ordered his men to find out the truth. The pillar was broken down to look for the imagined insect. The man who had started it all was no longer on the scene. He had slipped away to Bhaktapur to convey the good news to his king.

Locals believe that Prithvi Narayan Shah's conquest of the three kingdoms had been foretold. The three kings of Kathmandu, Patan and Bhaktapur had once gone on a pilgrimage to Gosaikund, a holy lake created by Shiva. As an offering to Shiva, who—the kings believed—resided in the lake, the king of Patan immersed a copper bull in the water. The king of Kathmandu offered a silver bull, and the king of Bhaktapur, one made of stone. The copper and silver bulls sank immediately, but the stone bull floated on the water.

The kings of Kathmandu and Patan laughed at the king of Bhaktapur. They said that Shiva was not willing to accept his offering. The humiliated king of Bhaktapur jumped into the lake holding the stone bull, and went under. When he did not rise again, the other two gave him up for dead and returned to their kingdoms.

The king of Bhaktapur did not die. He sank to the bottom of the lake, and met Shiva. He was overjoyed. Shiva, however, had a warning for him. He said that the three kings should unite and rule. If they did not, they would lose all their kingdoms.

'A mask tells us more than a face': Papier mâché mask of Ganesha at Bhaktapur Durbar Square museum

Blessed by Shiva, the king returned to Bhaktapur. He paid no heed to Shiva's warning, though, and did not even bother to share it with the kings of Patan and Kathmandu. The kings continued to squabble. In 1768, Prithvi Narayan Shah, the ruler of a small hilltop kingdom called Gorkha, invaded Kathmandu, and by 1769, he defeated all three Malla kings. The Shah dynasty and the Nepali nation came into being.

Shankar's efficient narration seamlessly connects the rich past and the mundane yet artistic present of Bhaktapur. He pauses a while by the gate of Shree Padma Higher Secondary School. It is flanked by stone statues of Bhairav or Shiva, and his consort Ugrachandi, a form of Durga.

'King Bhupatindra Malla, who had commissioned these stone sculptures had the sculptor's right hand cut off afterwards,' says Shankar, 'so that he could not sculpt similar statues again. The sculptor would not give up. He made replicas of these statues in a place 30 kilometres away. This time, he worked with his left hand.'

Shankar takes us to a golden gate that leads into a 55-window palace. On the gilded arch of the gate, Garuda fights with serpents above the 10-armed figure of Taleju Bhawani, the family deity of the Malla kings. It is a splendid example of repoussé metalwork.

'This gate was built in the 18th century by a craftsman from Patan,' says Shankar. 'The king of Patan was jealous that one of his subjects had worked for Bhaktapur, so he banished the craftsman from his kingdom.'

Just inside the gate, two enormous drums sit in an enclosure. They would be used to alert people about an invasion.

Walking in, we find ourselves before the Taleju Bhawani Temple. Only Hindus are allowed to enter. Shankar sits down next to the armed guard at the door with our camera and leather wallets while we step into a courtyard with the Taleju shrine on one side, and the Kumari's residence on the other.

It is a quiet and somewhat mysterious place. The Kumari does not appear at her window. The guard comes in and orders us out.

'A king may be all-powerful, but he would still be afraid to die,' Shankar tells us. 'King Bhupatindra Malla once dreamt that the spirit of death had come to take him.' To drive the spirit away, the king had a bell installed near the Taleju Temple in 1721. Shankar shows us the bell. 'Every time this bell was rung, it would set all the dogs barking. So, at some point, the bell was chained to stop it from ringing.'

There are stories around everything: the towering temples, statues and step wells that surround the large, sunny squares of Bhaktapur. It is quite impossible, moreover, to do justice to their intricate terracotta, stone and wood carvings in a day. Especially since live distractions abound in the lanes and by lanes: clumps of rice stalks, a golden beige and heavy with grain, rise from blue plastic mats on the ground like giant, over-used shaving brushes. Old men and women arrange them in well-ordered rows, their backs bent with years of toil, barely looking up from their labour. Younger men and women winnow the harvest by hand, the chaff falling about them like a shower of gold dust.

The scorching sun is right overhead, but the narrow, cobblestone and mud-paved lanes that separate red-brick houses are cool. Large clumps of garlic hang from the eaves and rickety wooden balconies, drying in the sun. Beautifully painted scenes of everyday life hang in smart black frames outside a shop. A woman comes running out from within its dim interiors. 'No photos, no photos,' she says.

Shankar meets friends: a lady and her small son squatting at the door to their house. He buys candyfloss for the boy, exchanges a few words.

Three old ladies sit in their doorway, withered faces in the shade, and gnarled feet in the sun. Long strands of red coral necklaces dangle over their bright, printed attire. Irresistible subjects, they are averse to being photographed; it takes Shankar Prajapati's persuasive skills to make them agree.

'Those are real coral beads,' Shankar tells us, 'and do notice the tattoos on their hands. Old folks believe that when people go to heaven and happen to run short of cash, they can sell their tattoos for a good price.'

As I compose a shot, a couple of children start thumping on my stomach. They want chocolates.

In a dingy little shop filled with bicycles, gas cylinders and other odd household essentials, a teenager polishes a metal statue of Tara Devi.

In a god-fearing land, priests enjoy power. We walk past a series of ornate timber and brick buildings that once belonged to the priests. The most significant among these is the Pujari Math, built during the reign of King Yaksha Malla, and rebuilt in 1763. One of its first-floor windows has an exquisite peacock carved out of wood. This 15th-century Peacock Window is considered the finest in Kathmandu valley.

In the naming tradition typical to Nepal—remember Kumari Hardware?—there is a New Café De Peacock, a Peacock Guesthouse, and a Peacock Tea and Spice Shop.

The Dattatreya Temple in Dattatreya Square was made in 1427, from the timber of one single tree. Stone statues of Rajput wrestlers Jayamal and Patta guard the entrance. Armed with our knowledge of struts, columns, and tympana from the Patan Museum exhibits, we are better able to admire the exquisite carvings they bear.

Two old men in Nepali caps lean against huge wooden chariot wheels at Taumadhi Square and watch the world go by. Nepali teenagers throng the upper floor balcony of Café Nyatapola.

The five-storeyed Nyatapola Temple, the tallest temple in all of Nepal, towers over the square. It is dedicated to Siddhi Lakshmi. 'The structure is so strong that even the severe earthquake of 1934 could barely cause damage,' says Shankar.

Nyatapola's staircase is guarded at five levels by stone statues. The lowest level has statues of Jayamal and Patta, each famed to have been as strong as 10 men. They brandish huge maces. A pair of elephants with floral saddles stands on the rung above. A couple of lions wearing bells and two griffons, with the unlikely combination of beaks and rams' horns, follow the elephants. The uppermost level has goddesses

Baghini and Singhini. Each pair of guards is said to be 10 times stronger than the one below it.

Sumita and I gape at the statues. A tourist from the Far East clutches Patta's massive armpit with both her arms for that offbeat photo. Shankar takes a five-minute break on the porch of the Bhiravnath Temple next door and plays on a borrowed flute. It is a happy tune.

'Where do you live, Shankar?'

'My home is at the Potters' Square,' he says. 'I am taking you there.'

The sprawling square is a beehive of furious activity. Hundreds of russet earthen pots are laid out in long, regimental columns. Women work the potters' wheels deftly, or add the final layer of clay to a set of tumblers. In an open kiln, a potter arranges row after row of red pots and covers them first with a layer of straw, and then one of smoking hot fly ash.

A Caucasian lady tourist with a photograph in hand walks from shop to shop, asking the sellers to identify the man she had photographed on her last visit. 'This is his son,' a shop-owner says finally, pointing to a youth. 'You can give him the photograph. Or he can take you to his father.'

At the door of a shop that has its walls lined with paintings of parrots, eyes, and ornate pots, stands a thin, fair girl with light brown eyes. Long arms, gangly legs sticking out of an olive green frock, and two long plaits tied with yellow ribbons. She cannot be more than 12 years.

She holds out a tiny clay elephant.

'Would you like to buy this?' she asks Sumita in English.

'Did you make it?'

'Yes, I made all of those,' says the girl, pointing to a rickety table full of miniatures. Pots, peacocks, turtles, frogs, owls. Buddha heads.

'Sweet,' Sumita says. 'Do you also go to school? What's your name?'

'Yes, I do. I am Purnima. Shall I give you the elephant? Would you like something else, this peacock?'

For 20 Nepali rupees, we buy: a russet peacock; a little russet pot with a spout.

If we continue to hang around here, we might buy the lot.

Purnima's mother comes to stand behind her, smiling indulgently. 'Your daughter is very bright,' Sumita tells her. 'Please see that she completes her studies.' Purnima is suddenly shy as a fawn.

Whether wood, stone, or clay, Bhaktapur's art bears the indelible mark of excellence. Talking of indelible marks, I am considering a tattoo for myself. That extra wad of cash might just help me in heaven.

But here is something to consider: gods occasionally need help, too. On the Dolagiri, or Changu ridge that overlooks the valley of Bhaktapur sits Nepal's most ancient temple, Changu Narayan. A UNESCO World Heritage Site, it dates back to the Licchavi period and holds a shrine for Vishnu.

A story drapes thc temple. A cowherd once bought a cow from a Brahmin named Sudarshan. The Brahmin told him that the cow would give him a huge amount of milk. The cowherd happily took the animal out to graze. Left to herself, the cow went behind a tree and returned

Talk to me: Near Changu Narayan Temple

'The door to happiness opens from the inside': Carved door arch of Changu Narayan Temple

a good while later. When she delivered milk that day, the amount was far below the cowherd's expectations.

This went on for some days, until the angry cowherd accused the Brahmin of cheating. Surprised, the Brahmin went with the cowherd to the fields. He, too, noticed the cow disappearing behind a tree.

The Brahmin and the cowherd followed the animal. They discovered a little dark boy drinking the cow's milk. 'This must be a demon that lives in the tree,' they thought, and with one sweep of an axe, they felled the tree.

Lord Vishnu emerged from the tree. He told the astonished men that he had been under a curse that imprisoned him in the tree. In cutting the tree down, the men had freed him. Overjoyed, the cowherd and the Brahmin built a shrine for Vishnu. The Changu Narayan Temple cradles the same shrine.

It is an uphill walk from the car park through a colourful maze of handicraft shops and *thangka* painting schools. The priest is about to lock the shrine, but relents when he sees us. We have a quiet moment before the silver plated sanctum, and then the doors are shut.

With the compound now entirely to ourselves, we step carefully over the unimaginable volume of pigeon droppings to admire the exquisite stone statues of Vishnu as Narasimha, Vishnu as Vamana, a stone statue of Garuda that dates back to the 5th century, and on a pillar, the earliest inscription of the valley which narrates how the king had pleaded with his mother not to immolate herself on the pyre of his father.

The Living Traditions Museum on the temple compound was founded by Judith Chase in 2012. For over 35 years, Chase has trekked all over Nepal. Her collections and photographs are organised under four sections based on the major geophysical regions of Nepal: Terai, Middle Hills, Kathmandu Valley and Himalayan Highlands.

There are charming artefacts from everyday living. We love the colourful wall and the floor painted with symbols of fertility by the Maithili women of Janakpur. It is a reproduction of the bridal chamber.

DHULIKHEL

I once dropped a two-kg dumbbell on my foot, quite by accident. I had no idea how excruciating the pain could be, nor how prolonged. After a short blackout, I discovered that no bone was broken, but the dumbbell had completely squashed a vein at the base of my little toe. That foot has never been the same again.

However, the dumb act may have given me some idea of the immensity of pain involved in cutting off flesh from one's thighs, quite voluntarily, to feed a starving tigress with newborn cubs. Much as I love tigers, I could not do it. Tiger lovers across the world may unite to save the near-extinct population of striped beauties, but I am sure they could not do it either. It takes superhuman willpower to make such an offering.

It takes a Buddha-To-Be.

First, the story. According to the *Jataka*s, 6,000 years ago, three princes named Great Sound or Dra Chenpo, Great Deity or Lha Chenpo, and Great Being or Semchen Chenpo or Mahasatwo rode into a forest to hunt. They came upon a cave where a tigress had just delivered cubs.

Mahasatwo, the youngest prince, noticed that the tigress was too weak to move. He asked his brothers how he could help the tigress, and they said he could feed it some warm animal flesh. Not willing to kill an animal for the sake of saving another, the young prince offered himself to the tigress.

For this sacrifice, Mahasatwo's spirit reached Tushita, a celestial realm, where he waited to be reborn as the future Buddha. A stupa was built over the spot where his bones and hair were found, and it came to be known as Takmo Lüjin. Locals passing through the forest on full moon nights would often find a tigress pacing around the stupa.

Three thousand and five hundred years later, Gautama Buddha visited the forest, now in Dhulikhel, Nepal, with his disciples Syaribu and Maao Gyalki Buku, and affirmed that he was the reincarnation of Prince Mahasatwo. And the stupa was renamed Namo Buddha. It is one of the three most significant stupas in all of Nepal.

Forty kilometres from Kathmandu and at 5,086 feet, Dhulikhel's claim to fame is the Namo Buddha stupa, and snow-covered Himalayan peaks that might stay hidden even in clear sunny weather.

Sumita and I put up at the Dhulikhel Lodge Resort, one of the few tourist accommodations in the area.

It is a sunny May morning. From the resort, a dirt road through tall pine forests winds its way up a mountain to end close to a row of shacks selling biscuits, momos and tea. A painted red gateway leads to a cluster of white chortens, and a tiny, soot-covered sanctum. Butter lamps burn within, adding to the soot. A little distance away, foreign tourists sit on plastic chairs outside a shack, cradling mugs of tea. They guide us towards a flight of stairs beyond the chortens.

We are looking at a steep hike. Soon, the stairs give way to a winding, sun-dappled mud trail lined by tall trees and multi-coloured prayer flags.

We meet two teenagers on the way, a boy and a girl. They appear somewhat startled. We might have interrupted a lovers' sojourn.

The boy recovers fast. 'Where you from?' he says.

'Kolkata,' I reply.

'Kolkata, India. On holiday?'

'Yes.'

'Have you seen the Taj Mahal? In Agra, India?'

I understand the implied question, the sub-text: 'So you have come all the way from India to Dhulikhel to see the Namo Buddha stupa, but you have not seen the marvellous Taj Mahal in your own country?' We have embarrassed them by breaking into their lair, and so he wishes to embarrass us.

The Taj is probably the most beautiful building in the world, a monument to Emperor Shah Jahan's undying love for Mumtaz Mahal. She was the third of Shah Jahan's seven wives, and died giving birth to their 14th child. European chronicler Niccolao Manucci has said that Shah Jahan did not lose his 'weakness for the flesh' even when he had grown very old.

I can tell the youngster all this, but he is too young, just starting out on the path of what he thinks is love.

'No, we haven't seen the Taj,' I say.

A good while later, we reach a paved clearing. It has an incredible view of all of Dhulikhel. A pole loaded with prayer flags stands at the centre, marking one of the probable spots of Prince Mahasatwo's sacrifice. After all these years, no one can take us to the actual cave. Another hill close by holds a small sanctum, with a stone engraving of the prince offering his flesh to the tigress. A nook close by has statues of the Buddha, the tigress and her cubs.

The Thrangu Tashi Yangtse Monastery, a huge, modern complex in striking maroon and gold is a 1976 addition to the locale. Paintings of 17 Karmapas line the walls of the prayer room. Seven golden Buddha statues look down upon us with compassionate eyes. They are the seven Tathagatas:

Vipashyi, the one with supreme insight;

Shikhi, the one with a crown protuberance;

Visvabhu, the all-protecting one;

Shakyamuni, the powerful sage;

Karkucchandhah, the destroyer of samsara;

Kankamuni, the golden sage;

Kashyapah, the one who protects with light.

Colourful molten wax decorations at the altar also narrate the story of Prince Mahasatwo's sacrifice. On the monastery steps, wind chimes tinkle, and orchids bloom in carefully-tended pots.

Back at the resort, there is no electricity. The intercom does not work. I take the steep, long, winding steps up to the reception and order biryani, listed under the 'Indian menu', for lunch. It should take an hour to prepare it, I am told.

An hour later, we trudge up the steep, long, winding steps to the dining hall. The 'Indian biryani' awaits us: 250 gms of rice, with 50 gms worth of spice.

Turmeric is the only spice.

'Let's stick to the Nepali menu next time,' is all Sumita says.

There is still no electricity. It is a hot and stuffy afternoon. Sumita and I sit on our balcony. We should have a sparkling sight of the snow-laden Annapurna, Ganesh Himal, Langtang, Phurbi-Chyachu, Gaurishankar and Lhotse peaks rising beyond the distant blue foothills. But an unseen haze has risen from the far end of the valley, shielding the entire Annapurna Range from view: though cloudless, the horizon is heartbreakingly empty.

Across the bamboo and pine trees next to the balcony, birds are engaged in an energetic conversation: one that is literally and figuratively over our heads. Today, a la John Keats, 'my imagination is a monastery, and I am its monk'. I imagine that, through their animated chatter, the story of Prince Mahasatwo is being passed on.

POKHARA

An ephemeral light-blue shadow that looks like the upended tail of a gigantic fish towers in the sky just for a few tantalising moments every dawn. Soon, waves of grey rain-clouds engulf the tail.

We are not allowed to forget that vision and get on with our lives: every bookshop that lines the roads of Pokhara showcases its photograph. Every Nepali artist has painted it at least once, and the paintings adorn the walls of street-side cafés and bistros. On crispy winter mornings, so we are told, the Phewa Lake proudly bears its image on the crystal clear waters.

The locals call it Machhapuchhare, the Fishtail Mountain. At almost 23,000 feet, it is the second highest peak of the Annapurna Himalayan Range. Lord Shiva is believed to live on the peak. To respect this belief, Wilfrid Noyce and A.D.M. Cox, British mountaineers of the only expedition undertaken in 1957 to climb this summit, had ended their ascent 165 feet below the top.

Down below, 200 kilometres and six hours from Kathmandu, stretches the enchanting Pokhara valley, a creation of tectonic movement and glacial flood. All that remains of the flood is the waters of the Phewa, Begnas and Rupa lakes. Phewa is fed by a stream, but a dam regulates the flow, which makes it a semi-natural freshwater lake. It is the second largest lake in Nepal. Just about 28 kilometres to its north, straight as the crow flies, is the Annapurna Himalayan Range.

Doongas—red, blue, green and yellow local boats—are tethered to the lakeshore. Little waves lap at the *doongas*, making them rock gently

'To reach a port we must set sail/Sail, not tie at anchor/Sail, not drift':
Boats on Phewa lake, Pokhara

G 10 G
55

against one another in the dappled sunlight like a handful of fallen petals. A boatman offers us an hour's ride on the Phewa. Our boat is blue, its narrow plank-seats red. The oars are blue. The life jackets we must put on are a ridiculous shade of pink.

The locals, I note, have a different vessel of passage. Two *doongas* joined by a wide wooden plank from the edges of which rises a metal scaffold draped on top with a plastic sheet for shade, metal seats. Scaffold and seats painted a fluorescent green. Not enough life jackets.

Placid green waters mirror the rolling, verdant hills, the occasional jacaranda or flamboyant tree in bloom. A cormorant sits on a broken log sticking out of the lake. Honey-coloured cranes with creamy white wings fly overhead.

We anchor a while at a little green island. Six or seven large trees and a two-tiered pagoda-style temple from the 18th century are about all the island can hold.

'Please keep here like sandle (*sic*), shoe and leather goods,' says a notice near the sanctum. Nepalese families wait patiently in a long queue: women, with dainty *sal*-leaf or cane baskets of offerings; men, with little pigtailed children laughing on their shoulders. Those coming out of the temple have bright red tikas on their fair foreheads.

This is the Taal Varahi Temple, with an ancient lore. Ajima, or Varahi, the boar-headed incarnation of Goddess Shakti, had once visited a Nepali village full of wicked residents. To test their compassion, she went from door to door begging for alms. She was refused by all but one, a lady who gave her alms and shelter.

To punish the villagers, the goddess sunk the whole village with a deluge. Only the little patch of land holding the home of the generous lady was spared. This is where the temple stands. On clear days, locals believe they can see the remains of houses at the bottom of the lake.

Legend swathes the Vindhya Vasini temple too, a pristine white structure atop a ridge near Pokhara's old market. Tibetan tantrics were carrying the idol of the goddess from the Vindhya mountain ranges of India to Mustang in Tibet. On their way, the exhausted men put the idol down in Pokhara so they could rest a while. They could not lift it again.

The temple precincts offer a wonderful bird's-eye view of Pokhara. Under a bougainvillea tree bursting with shocking pink flowers, devotees have gathered to offer coconuts.

There is a machine to break the coconuts. It comes with:

A short iron pole planted on a square block of stone.

A broad iron blade attached at right angles to the pole.

A lever to bring down the blade on the unsuspecting coconut.

A thin old man with gnarled, muscled arms to work the machine.

The golden statue of Vindhya Vasini is smeared with vermilion, and the fair, genial old priest in a Nepali cap urges us to touch her feet. '*Khush raho,*' he says, wishing us happiness.

The true story of Patale Chhango or Davis Fall is not a happy one. It is a 100-feet waterfall two kilometres southwest of downtown Pokhara, the spot where the Pardi Khola stream goes underground. In 1961, a sudden gush of water had swept away Mrs Davis, a Swiss citizen bathing in the falls with her husband.

Right across the street from Davis Fall is the Gupteshwar Mahadev Cave, where a huge stalagmite is worshipped as a Shivalinga. With a few adventurous souls, we clamber down a set of very wet stone steps to a pitch-dark tunnel and a damp cavern. A long, vertical breach in the cavern frames the sunlit, thundering waters of Davis Fall gushing over what looks like a rough-cut natural sculpture of Nandi, Shiva's bull.

Travelling down from the Annapurna Range, the roaring Seti Gandaki River dances right through Pokhara in a deep, narrow, hidden chasm. We meet the frothy white river at a gorge under a bridge, and listen to its story from a local guard.

'They were two sisters, the rivers Seti and Kali Gandaki,' says the old man. 'One day, Kali Gandaki, the elder sister, chose to slide down the mountainside quietly. Seti woke up to find her sister gone, and so she rushed down to look for her. Around where we are standing, Seti came across women working on the fields. She was unhappy that the women had to work instead of the men, and plunged down a gorge so she would not have to watch this disgraceful sight.'

Seti continued her journey underground, says the guard, but she never found her sister.

The mountain peaks remain elusive even on a pre-dawn visit to Sarangkot, the village on a hilltop that normally offers fabulous close-ups of the Annapurna and the Dhaulagiri ranges. The luxuriant hills and the terraced rice fields at our feet are a poor compensation.

We spend our days then lounging by Phewa's shores: on stone benches shaded by trees, in wide, cushioned wicker chairs placed

'Mountains are not stadiums where I satisfy my ambition to achieve, they are the cathedrals where I practice my religion': Machhapuchhare Peak from Pokhara

invitingly on the porches of roadside cafés. Like a hundred flowers dropping lightly from the sky, paragliders float down to the Phewa from Sarangkot top. Ultralight aircraft fly over the World Peace Pagoda, a white-gold structure built by Buddhist monks from the Japanese Nipponzan Myohoji organisation.

A Tibetan woman approaches us one morning with her little bundle of goods: bracelets and necklaces in semi-precious stone, friendship wristbands woven in multi-coloured wool. She is a refugee, one of thousands who fled a Tibet oppressed and taken over by China.

'Many of us came to Nepal, many went to India. Nepal, India, very kind to Tibetan refugees, very kind,' she says.

'Would you like to buy a bracelet? I have some very pretty ones.' She lays them out on the stone bench in a neat row. They are indeed beautiful, if somewhat expensive.

I happen to be wearing a bracelet of semi-precious stone, a gift from a cousin. Sumita does not wear jewellery of any kind.

We have no need of bracelets, really.

We buy four bracelets.

The old lady likes the bracelet I wear. 'Very pretty,' she exclaims, touching it softly, 'very pretty.'

'Would you like to have it?' I say on an impulse. 'Here, wear it. Let this be a gift from India.'

Her face lights up. 'Thank you so much.' She takes out two friendship bands, ties them on both our wrists. 'No, no, no money. These are gifts.'

Refuge: a word that arrived from the Latin *re-fugere,* to 'flee backward'. I have my roots in a pre-Partition Bengal, I think I understand homelessness.

Sumita is often the practical soul. 'Did you notice her smile? She had a gold-capped tooth.'

As we cross the street, a man playing a four-stringed instrument walks up. 'Buy Nepali sarangi, Ma'am? Only 1,200 Nepali rupees.'

He plays it well, the bow caressing the strings to produce a lilting melody.

'I don't know how to play it,' I tell him. I do notice the exquisite carvings on the sarangi, though. The wide end has a Ganesh face, the narrow end is shaped like a peacock neck. He notices my admiring glance, plays on with enthusiasm.

'₹ 300,' says Sumita. She has suddenly remembered a travel advisory for Nepal: before you buy, bargain.

The man appears shocked. 'Look at the carving, Ma'am. So good. A 1,000 Nepali rupees?'

'₹ 500. Won't pay a rupee more.' Sumita is firm.

'Okay. Fifty rupees more for a Coke?'

'No. Buy your Coke from the ₹ 500.'

The sarangi changes hands. I cradle it lovingly. The man looks like he has been dealt a big blow, and walks away with a long face.

The next afternoon we lounge at a roadside café with tall mugs of coffee. 'I probably bargained too hard,' Sumita says with a tinge of regret. 'The man sold the sarangi for a loss. I should have paid him a little more.'

Just then, we hear the sound of a drum. It is the same man again, this time with a 12-inch long wooden drum.

'Want a drum, Ma'am?' he says with a grin.

'Want a drum?' Sumita repeats the question for me with a twinkle in her eye. She knows I can play a drum. Better than a sarangi at least, this is not saying much, but still.

'Please, no,' I say, 'not another instrument. We just don't have any space to pack them all in.'

The man continues to play the drum. He plays it rather well.

'If we buy the drum, we can pay him a little more today, to make up for his loss. We won't tell him that, though,' Sumita says under her breath.

This time, I am the practical one: 'If we did not pay him enough and more yesterday, do you really think he would approach us again?'

'Point.'

We return to our coffee mugs. It starts to drizzle in a bit. The man gives up and walks away.

Wishing for a light snack that evening, we order cheese garlic bread. The room service man delivers little triangular sandwiches.

'But we ordered cheese garlic bread,' I tell him.

'This *is* cheese garlic bread, Ma'am. Look inside.'

I prise open the limp, sticky triangles. They have a thin layer of plain, melted cheese. Three tiny raw cloves of garlic sit strategically in the centre.

Just as the early morning bus from Pokhara to Kathmandu leaves the terminus with us, peaks of the Annapurna Himalayan Range begin to appear. From west to east, Annapurna South (23,684 ft), Hiunchuli (21,131 ft), Annapurna I (26,545 ft), Machhapuchhare (22,956 ft), Annapurna III (24,787 ft), Annapurna IV (24,688 ft) and Annapurna II (26,040 ft) reveal themselves. The most dramatic peak of them all, Machhapuchhare towers in the horizon. For the first time in 72 hours or so, I have an unobstructed view of the fish-tail that has become a magnificent obsession.

The bus picks up speed.

'Please, please tell the driver to stop for a while,' I urge Sumita.

'Stop? We've only just started. What makes you think he will listen? This is not even a tourist bus! And why *me*?'

'Your Hindi is better than mine. Please try. Try *now*.'

'The things you make me do,' Sumita sighs, getting up from her seat. I follow behind.

She goes to the driver's cabin. He and his helpers gape at her request, then at me standing behind her, camera in hand, shifting my weight from one foot to the other to keep my balance. They have never heard such an impassioned plea before.

The driver agrees to halt. 'Five minutes, only,' he says.

It will not help if the other passengers get restive. I turn to them and announce, 'Five-minute photography break.'

As expected, about eight or nine of them get off the bus with me. We spread out in a row along the busy pavement, cameras and camera phones raised like saluting bayonets towards the golden behemoths. Shopkeepers just raising their shutters gape. Pedestrians halt and stare.

'You know, we stayed at Pokhara for three days,' says a gentleman next to me, 'and did not get a single glimpse of this majestic range. Thank you.'

'Same here. You're welcome,' I reply.

It has been 15 minutes. The helpers get off the bus to shoo us back in. The wheels start rolling once more. Like Hemingway's old man, I have captured my fish and lost it again.

Loss is an integral part of loving the mountains. On the flight back home, we have a splendid, if distant, view of the Himalayas, where an avalanche has claimed the life of Chhanda Gayen five days ago. The first civilian Indian woman to have summited Everest, the young Bengali braveheart had just conquered the Kanchenjunga Main (28,166 ft) Peak, and was on her way to summit Kanchenjunga West (27,904 ft), known as Yalung Kang in Nepal.

SIKKIM

Do Not Touch
BANJHAKRI

GANGTOK

The first light has not broken through the grey mist 'that rubs its back upon the window-panes' when I thrust a foot out of the warm blanket and place it gingerly on the floor. Gingerly, for the floor, though wooden, is cold, and has a board that creaks.

Not to wake Sumita, I skirt the creaky floorboard on tiptoe and find my socks and sandals. Slip them on, then slide my arms and head through the pullover.

This moment is all mine: this quiet half hour of a summer dawn when nothing stirs, not even the second flush of flowers on the cherry tree that touches our window. The green-backed tit and the rufous sibia that live among the pink blossoms must still be curled up into puffy balls.

This chore is all mine: this ancient, calming ritual of making tea. I watch the water boiling slowly in the tall glass, bubbles that resemble little balls of mercury clinging to the silver coil of the tiny immersion heater, then rising to the surface, the light auburn hue seeping from the paper bag of fine Darjeeling tea. Fragrant steam rises above the rim and, condensed by the cold air, loops visibly, uncertainly, over it a while. Diffuses.

Pp 254-255: 'Your own village means that you're not alone, that you know there's something of you in the people and the plants and the soil, that even when you are not there it waits to welcome you': Lachen village

Facing page: 'Much of your pain is self-chosen. It is the bitter potion by which the physician within you heals your sick self': Statue of the shaman at Ban Jhakri Waterfalls, South Sikkim

The tinkling of the sugar spoon against the glass wakes Sumita. While we cradle the warm glasses in our hands, a shaft of sunlight touches the heart of the tea, changing it to liquid gold, even as the snow on the peaks turn golden.

A new day begins at Gangtok.

A peaceful hill town at 5,410 feet, Gangtok has given us a gentle initiation to altitude, and a chance at renewal after a deep, personal loss. It sends a plethora of healing colours into the cavernous, seemingly impenetrable shadows of our minds:

Little red and blue rafts braving the currents of a teal-green Teesta.

Peach and purple orchids at the annual flower festival.

The bright red cable car ferrying us over a busy town.

Red, green, blue and yellow prayer flags fluttering from every crag.

Green conifers along the uphill road we take to Enchey Monastery.

'For in the dew of little things the heart finds its morning and is refreshed': Orchids of Gangtok

'Perhaps all the dragons of our lives are princesses who are only waiting to see us once beautiful and brave': At the Directorate of Handicrafts, Gangtok

Our first brush with Buddhism, Enchey was first built by Lama Druptok Karpo, known for his levitation skill. He is said to have flown in from Maenam Hill in South Sikkim more than 200 years ago.

Marco Polo, probably the most famous Westerner to have travelled on the Silk Route and the first Westerner to formally record an encounter with the Tibetan lamas, had been a witness to the phenomenon of levitation.

Traditional Tibetan literature has many stories about Buddhist mystics who could fly. Buddha is said to have done it many a time, so had Nagarjuna and Guru Padmasambhava. The 11th-century yogi and poet Milarepa was another famous flyer.

Did they fly, or did they run? In ancient Tibet, goes the legend, there were *lung-gom-pa* runners who could run for 48 hours without rest and cover 200 miles in a single day. This was after intensive spiritual training.

Lung: air and vital energy. *Gom:* meditation or focused concentration. A *lung-gom-pa* is one who has mastered the art of harnessing spiritual energy through focused meditation and conscious breathing. He is no longer bound by the physical limits of the body.

Alexandra David-Néel, (1868-1969), the first European woman to reach Lhasa, Tibet's remote and forbidden capital, refers to a *lung-gom-pa* in her book *Magic and Mystery in Tibet*. She writes:

> *'I noticed, far away in front of us, a moving black spot which my field-glasses showed to be a man. I felt astonished. Meetings are not frequent in that region [Chang Thang in northern Tibet] ... But as I continued to observe him through the glasses, I noticed that the man proceeded at an unusual gait and, especially, with an extraordinary swiftness ... The man did not run. He seemed to lift himself from the ground, proceeding by leaps. It looked as if he had been endowed with the elasticity of a ball and rebounded each time his feet touched the ground.'*

The skill has obviously been lost to Buddhism. In one of his columns, Tibetan novelist Jamyang Norbu, also a leading campaigner for Tibet's independence, writes:

> *'I do not doubt Marco Polo when he writes with amazement that Tibetan lamas levitated the Great* (Kublai) *Khan's cup to his lips. But these days lamas are patently unable to levitate anything. When they have to fly, they do it in aeroplanes, like the rest of us. The only miraculous thing being that they do it first class.'*

With or without flying lamas, Enchey is a quaint haven, while Rumtek Monastery—a 24-km drive from Gangtok and then a breathtaking five-minute hike up a mountain road—is gorgeous. We reach just in time for the evening prayers. The sound of 30 young lamas chanting in unison in a high-ceilinged hall is something that would ring in my ears for a long time.

Without the benefit of levitation, the ride up to Tsomgo Lake (12,313 ft) and Nathu La (14,140 ft), the pass on the Indo-Tibetan border, the next morning is steep and arduous.

In its clear waters, Tsomgo mirrors the snow-covered mountains. Little shacks huddle by the shores and sell woollen caps, water-resistant gloves, earmuffs, key rings and noodles.

Hairy, huge but gentle yaks wander by the lake, their horns covered in multi-coloured wool. Their owners offer rides around the lake. Just occasionally, the yaks feel inclined to take their rider into the waters.

Driving on to Nathu La, we are caught in the midst of a traffic jam. About 15 Indian Army trucks loaded with soldiers are coming down the mountain. The soldiers insist that all upward moving vehicles wait till they have passed.

It is 10:30 am, and there are a hundred tourist cars with day permits trying to reach Nathu La before the weather turns worse, which it surely will as the day progresses. The car drivers know this and, as their patience wears thin, the possibility of a fracas looms large.

The soldiers are tall, athletic. The local drivers confronting them, short, stocky. Sumita decides to get off the car, and walk into the centre of this mismatched bunch. Surprised, the drivers make way for her, and she faces the soldiers.

'Please, bhai, do let us pass,' she says to the most aggressive of them. 'If you delay us any more, we won't be able to visit Nathu La. See the number of cars waiting? Most of us have come from distant cities. Why force us to return disappointed?'

The Army is not used to handling frail women with firm resolve. The soldiers—not much beyond their teens—look slightly sheepish. The trucks make way.

Nathu La is one of the Border Personnel Meeting points for the Indian and Chinese armies. The others are at Chushul/Spanggur and Daulat Beg Oldi in Ladakh, Bum La and Kibithu-Damai in Arunachal Pradesh.

'It is the stitch that makes a carpet wear, gives it its life and bloom':
At the Directorate of Handicrafts, Gangtok

At the high-altitude pass, we have our first brush with breathing difficulty and listlessness. We do not know about Acute Mountain Sickness (AMS) yet. Acetazolamide has not found its way into our bloodstream, to keep it from congealing so we can better use the scant supply of oxygen.

Even in early summer, the mountain pass is cold and formal interactions between soldiers guarding the Indian and Chinese borders, frosty. It is still some years to 2015. China has not opened the second land crossing in Tibet via Nathu La to allow Indian pilgrims on the arduous Kailash-Manasarovar Yatra. Moon-faced soldiers of the People's Liberation Army stand at attention on the Chinese side of the pass, while Indian soldiers try to prevent over-enthusiastic tourists from interacting with them.

The 'selfie' epidemic has not coursed through India yet, but to our annoyance, as well as that of the Indian soldiers, tourists are more inclined to have themselves photographed with the Chinese.

Just to be contrary, I get Sumita to pose with a young Captain of the Indian Army. I notice how both their faces have swollen from the altitude. Realise that mine must be swollen as well.

Two snow-covered peaks stand out on the Chinese horizon. The slate-grey and brown ranges on the Indian side have a proclamation in extra-large letters: *'Mera Bharat Mahaan'*, it says, and *'Hum Hi Jitenge.'*

With all the para-normal effort from Captain Harbhajan Singh, we should win all our skirmishes with China. In the '60s, Harbhajan Singh, then a Major with the Indian Army, was posted at the Sino-Indian border near Nathu La. On October 4, 1968, while escorting a mule caravan from the Army headquarters, he fell into a gushing stream and was washed away. The inclement weather made soldiers abandon the search for his body.

The story goes that Major Singh appeared in the dream of a soldier in his unit, and told him where his body lay. The soldier ignored the dream. Major Singh then appeared in the dream of another soldier. This time he was taken seriously, and his body was found at the spot described in the dreams.

Major Singh was cremated with full military honours, and a memorial was built for him. This is the Baba Mandir (13,123 ft), a bright, festooned temple that we visit on the way down from Nathu La.

The story does not end with the memorial, though. Soon after Singh's body was found, the Indian battalion began to talk of a uniformed man on horseback patrolling the region. Chinese soldiers claimed to have seen the ghost rider, too.

Major Harbhajan Singh was promoted to Captain after his death, posthumously awarded the Maha Vir Chakra. Captain Singh is still said to occasionally appear in soldiers' dreams: he points out the areas prone to Chinese incursion, and tells them to plug the loopholes. His findings have been accurate so far. The Indian Army believes that he would warn them of a Chinese invasion three days in advance.

Now, for the best part of the story: the Chinese Army believes likewise that Captain Singh will warn them about an Indian invasion.

Three days in advance, too. They are said to reserve a chair for Captain Singh at the Sino-Indian Border Personnel meetings.

Up on the cold mountain ranges, hostile yet haunting, a gossamer-thin line separates reason from belief.

Up on the cold mountain ranges, we learn then that life is not a certainty to be measured in months or years, but to be lived moment by moment. And living this moment, among the beautifully stark, snow-covered peaks, we are finally at peace.

GURUDONGMAR LAKE

'Hello, Ma'am, we have your permits. The car is ready, please meet us at the taxi stand,' Dinesh says over the phone.

'Taxi stand? Why can't you pick us up from our hotel?'

'We are not allowed within Gangtok, Ma'am.'

'How do you expect us to drag our entire luggage to the taxi stand? It isn't walking distance, you know that!'

'Please, Ma'am, you can call a taxi and get dropped.'

Thankfully, a taxi is available. Dinesh, our guide, meets us at the taxi stand, a mere boy in his late teens. 'Our car is from North Sikkim, Ma'am. We are allowed only till the taxi stand. Sorry about inconvenience,' he talks fast, loading our luggage into a bright red Tata Spacio. 'And this is Tsarap, Ma'am, the driver.'

Tsarap, slightly older than Dinesh and a lot quieter, nods shyly.

A visit to North Sikkim, close to the Indo-Tibetan border, must be organised through a local travel agency, which gets you a car, the mandatory permits, a guide and accommodations in the tiny hamlets of Lachen (9,900 ft) and Lachung (8,610 ft). For a hefty sum, of course.

Dinesh, Tsarap and the red Spacio are part of our package. There are more teams travelling to North Sikkim with the same travel agency, so we will have a convoy of cars following us.

Soon after we drive over a bridge with a signboard that welcomes us to North Sikkim, Dinesh urges us to get off and walk into a grove. We see three copper coloured statues, a couple and a man, on a pedestal close to several moss-draped boulders.

'Ma'am, this is Kabi Longstok,' he says. 'This is where the Lepchas and the Bhutias agreed to a blood brotherhood.'

I know the story. In the 15th century, when the Lepcha chief Thekung Tek ruled Sikkim, there was a major migration of the Tibetan Kham people into the region. Legend says that the Kham king Kye Bhumsa and his wife were childless. Lamas advised them to seek the help of Thekung Tek, who was a seer.

So Kye Bhumsa and his wife, along with some followers, crossed Yak La and Penlong mountains to reach a place near Rangpo. The couple met Thekung Tek with gifts, and Thekung Tek told them that they would have three sons. With time, Kye Bhumsa did have three sons. Thekung Tek, Kye Bhumsa and his sons then swore to be blood brothers. Thekung Tek placed nine boulders facing Mount Kanchenjunga as witnesses to this friendship. The Lepchas and the migrant Bhutias agreed to live in harmony in Sikkim.

Kye Bhumsa's second son, Mipon Rab, settled in Gangtok. There were inter-racial marriages between the Lepchas and the Bhutias. Soon, the Bhutias began to dominate the political and the religious landscape.

We have barely left the serene ambience of Kabi Longstok and hit the highway, when Dinesh gets a phone call.

'What's wrong?' he asks the caller. Then, in quick succession: 'Where?' and 'When?'

When he disconnects, and is unusually quiet, Sumita asks him what the matter is.

'Nothing serious, Ma'am. There has been a landslide. Nobody hurt. Don't worry.'

'Landslide? *Where*?'

'Behind us.' Dinesh is unwilling to divulge details, but we force him to. A massive boulder has rolled down to the road we have just traversed, probably missing our car by some minutes. It has decided to settle on the road, blocking the route completely for the cars following us. They have to find a different route, which will delay their arrival at Lachen by many hours.

The hills around us are verdant, they hide their weapons well.

We halt at Mangan (3,950 ft), the headquarters of North Sikkim, for a simple lunch, get off the car at Chungthang (5,600 ft) to see the confluence of the Lachen Chhu and the Lachung Chhu—*chhu* is the Bhutia word for river—and arrive at Lachen, the 'Big Pass', while it is still light.

Hotel Bayul has running water, electricity to run the geyser to heat the water, a generator to back up the electricity to run the geyser to heat the water.

At close to 10,000 ft, that deserves five stars.

All we need for tonight are four rotis between the two of us, and a basic curry to eat them with.

That, surprisingly, takes an eternity.

The convoy of cars has arrived at 9:00 pm, and the travellers—mostly burly men—have hit the dining hall straightaway. When we join them there, they have already been gorging on rice, but the minute they see the basket of hot rotis, they loudly lay claim to it. Many more rotis arrive in the next hour, yet none is allowed to reach our corner.

After a long, long wait, I go in search of Dinesh. 'Do something,' I tell him. 'How long do we have to starve?'

'Ma'am, I will personally make you some rotis,' he says. He gets into the kitchen where the lone cook has been struggling to meet the demonic demands, sits down with a rolling pin. Makes four perfect rotis, and hands the basket directly to me.

We finally have dinner at 11:00 pm. 'Thank you, Dinesh,' Sumita tells him. 'So you are a guide and a cook, too?'

'I can do everything, Ma'am,' the boy smiles, his eyes red with tiredness in their sunken grooves. 'Have a good night.'

We do manage to have a short, but sound night. While getting ready at 4:30 am the next morning for our trip to Gurudongmar Lake, we expect the cutting cold, even in May.

Sumita has a surprise for me.

'Take a look at this,' she says, holding up a packet of chips.

The packet is completely taut, bloated up like a dead fish.

Before this trip, we have read up articles on reduced air pressure in the atmosphere at high altitudes and the consequent health risks. We do not sense any difficulty yet, but it is obvious that our bodies too have a lot more air pressure within them than that outside.

The day has dawned cold, dull and grey. At 5:30 am, we clamber into the Tata Spacio. The steady drizzle adds the last dampener. But our destination this morning is much higher than the rain clouds. At 17,100 ft, Gurudongmar is the highest lake in North Sikkim, on the Indo-China border.

By 7:30 am, we are above the rain clouds and at Thangu (13,000 ft), our first halt. Shivering with cold, we walk into the dark but warm interiors of a fog-wrapped wooden cabin, its walls adorned by posters of Shahid Kapoor and John Abraham. It is time for breakfast: a welcome mélange of steaming, soft bread, bananas and apples, tomato soup and coffee. Almost in that order, since the friendly locals serving the food are few, and several carloads of hungry, demanding tourists appear out of thin air.

'Buy popcorn packets,' advises Dinesh, back to being a powerhouse of energy. 'And this,' he dangles a garland of solid yak-cheese chunks before me. 'If you chew on them, you won't feel the effect of the high altitude.'

Chewing on a single rock-strong chunk gives me serious jaw ache, but then, I am neither a local nor a yak calf.

My watch says it is almost 9:00 am. A herd of yaks scurries off the winding dirt road and up the mountainside to make way for our SUV. A rugged terrain bereft of vegetation leads us up to Café 15,000. Rows of Indian Army bunkers stand formidably behind the café. On the other side, snow-laden mountain ranges tower like natural sentries at the frontier.

A counter at Café 15,000 run by Army Wives Welfare Association and manned by soldiers sells handicrafts. We pick up copper keychains that say 'Gurudongmar Lake, 17,100 ft' and a Certificate of Visit signed by the garrison commander. The certificate comes in a folder with photographs of the local flora and fauna, and a cover image of the Kanchengyao Peak (22,964 ft). A portion of the snow on the peak, the caption points out, looks like the map of India. It does.

At 15,000 ft, the air is thin. The slightest activity is making us gasp. But Dinesh has warned us that if we display any fatigue, the Army unit would summarily send us back.

Sure enough, a hawk-eyed young soldier peers at us through our driver Tsarap's window, the only one with its pane lowered. We fake huge smiles. Reassured, he says in the gentlest of tones, 'If you have any feeling of nausea or think you will collapse, please return immediately.'

Soon, the dirt road gives way to a stony plain dotted with landmines. Even where there is the semblance of a dirt track, Dinesh coaxes Tsarap into shorter, bumpier routes. Confident of skirting the landmines as if he has laid them himself, our young guide points out well-camouflaged Army bunkers on the distant mountain ranges, and the remnants of a brick-n-kiln check post built by the British.

We sense we are almost there when on the horizon to our right appears a stunningly beautiful snow-covered range. The brilliant sun lends its radiance to the mountain peaks against the azure sky.

Around 9:45 am, the road ahead widens into a barren patch of land that, in turn, falls away into nothingness.

We get off the car and go to the edge of the patch. Quite a distance below us lies the placid blue-green Gurudongmar Lake, surrounded by the Tibetan plateau on one side, and the Kangchengyao Range with the Raja-Rani peaks on the other.

A steep flight of steps leads down to the lake. Colourful prayer flags flutter in the gentle morning breeze.

The water of the lake is considered sacred by Hindus and Buddhists. Even in winter, a portion of the lake does not freeze. It is believed that, when the locals prayed to Guru Dongmar or Padmasambhava to end their water scarcity, the Guru had touched and blessed this portion.

The prevailing calm is deceptive, Dinesh tells us. As the day progresses, the wind turns fierce. By noon, it can lift stones off the ground, and even cars.

Tourists are advised not to spend more than 10 minutes by the lake, because the lack of oxygen causes Acute Mountain Sickness (AMS). AMS begins with nausea, headache, irritability, sluggishness, and may lead to cerebral or pulmonary oedema, which is usually fatal.

We already feel sluggish. There is this immense sense of tiredness. I remember what Eric Shipton, team member on all four Everest expeditions during the 1930s, had said in *Upon That Mountain*:

> *'I doubt if anyone would claim to enjoy life at high. There is a certain grim satisfaction derived from struggling upwards…but altitude has the same effect on the mind as on the body, one's intellect becomes dull and unresponsive.'*

Physical unease notwithstanding, we are mesmerised. I take some photographs, totter to the SUV with its window panes drawn up, and sink into my seat for five minutes. There is more oxygen in the car than outside it, and this helps me recover. I get out again, take some more photos. After about 40 minutes of this, Dinesh insists we return. Smoky clouds have already begun to loom over the ranges.

On the return journey, Dinesh slips into the driver's seat.

'What happened to Tsarap? Where is he?' Sumita asks.

'Ma'am, one of the other drivers has fallen ill from the altitude. Tsarap will drive his car. I will drive you.'

'You can drive, too? Do you have a licence?'

'Yes, Ma'am. Don't worry,' says Dinesh.

He drives well, takes the bends too fast. But Sumita has something else to worry about.

Me.

I have a headache. A million, no, a billion times stronger than the migraines I generally have. Every two minutes, I feel a giant palm thrusting my head into a body of water. I suffocate, and come up gasping. Through a haze, I see Sumita's face, barely hear her asking me: 'What's wrong? Are you all right? Do you want a medicine?'

Her voice sounds strange, miles away. I want her to stop talking, to let me drown in peace.

I recover from the 'sinking feeling' only after we reach Lachung. The headache remains. Despite a tremendous nausea, I force myself to eat, just so I can have the painkillers.

Postscript: The chips are no worse for the climb.

YUMTHANG VALLEY

Lachung, at 8,610 feet, is the 'Small Pass': a random cluster of village houses sprawled on either side of the Lachung Chhu. Our hotel has a power cut at dusk, and the electricity does not return all night. Still exhausted from my AMS attack at Gurudongmar Lake, I lie awake most of the night listening to Sumita's shallow breathing.

She takes a few deep breaths, then some very short ones. Then she does not seem to breathe at all for a few seconds. Just when I think of getting up to check her pulse, she stirs, starts breathing again.

If I did not know about periodic breathing at high altitudes, I would be scared out of my wits.

At sea level, the amount of carbon dioxide in our blood controls our breathing. When the carbon dioxide level rises, it creates the urge to breathe. At high altitude, the body can feel the low oxygen level in the air, so we breathe faster and deeper. This, however, leads to a deep reduction in the carbon dioxide levels in the blood.

During our sleep at high altitude, the levels of carbon dioxide in our bloodstream can dip very low and this can totally switch off the urge to breathe. It is only after the body senses a further drop in oxygen levels that we start breathing again.

Sumita does not show any effects of shallow breathing in the morning as she leans out of the window to take a look at our Tata Spacio parked under it. There are a row of SUVs in the small parking space.

'Look at all the cars,' she tells me, 'see any difference?'

I look. 'Not really, what?'

'All the other SUVs have a spare tyre on the roof. Ours doesn't,' she points out.

'I am sure Tsarap has one inside the car,' I assure her. 'They drive on the hills every day, they shouldn't make these mistakes.'

Nevertheless, before we drive to Yumthang Valley at 11,800 feet, Sumita checks with Tsarap. 'Yes, Ma'am, I have a spare,' he says. For good measure, Sumita bends to take a good look at the fitted tyres, only then gets into the Spacio.

Silver firs and rhododendron shrubs mark our entry into the Shingba Rhododendron Sanctuary. This is the rhododendron season. I count 6 of the 24 species that grow in the sanctuary: white, cream, yellow, pink, mauve, and red. Primulas have taken over the open grassy patches, and in places the tall trees part to reveal snow-topped blue mountains.

In one such verdant patch, a lone black yak, its hump marked by a thatch of snowy hair, has its nose in the grass. Just before it, a clump of scarlet rhododendrons sways in the wind. I get off the car to take a photograph.

For a better angle, I inch closer to the yak and get down to my knees. The yak looks up from the grass, and does not like what he sees. He lowers his head and moves it from side to side, rolling his red eyes at the same time.

I do not know whether I should move right then, or hold my stance. Behind me, in the car, Sumita senses trouble. 'Go help her,' she goads Dinesh and Tsarap in an urgent whisper, 'do something.'

The yak is now pawing the ground with its right hoof. It is sure to charge. I get ready to make a dash to the SUV.

Tsarap gets off the car, coolly walks up behind me, and says 'Shoo, shoo.' The yak looks at him, scampers off.

Tsarap throws me a gentle smile: 'Very scared animals, yaks.'

The alpine meadows of Yumthang Valley, flanked on the east by the Chuba-Sagochen mountain ranges and on the west by Chomzomei Tso, are uncomfortably cold and misty. Not too many blossoms have come up on this 'valley of flowers' yet, and the snow-covered mountain

'The clearest way into the Universe is through a forest wilderness':
Yak, Yumthang Valley, Sikkim

ranges within touching distance from the road have their heads in low-floating clouds.

'Feeling cold?' Dinesh asks Sumita. 'We can hire jackets.'

We do, for ₹ 50 an hour. From a tea shack that has a low, rusted tin-roof, I choose a sober, navy blue jacket. Sumita goes for a bright orange, mostly for the hood lined with faux fur. The jackets are oversized. Sumita looks lost in hers, like a tanned baby Eskimo.

A brightly-dressed Sikkimese woman offers us tea in small green mugs. To shelter from the cutting wind, we take our mugs into a bare, one-roomed wooden hut with a window. Imagine for a while that we live in it.

The Yumthang Chhu winds its way through matte orange shingles, and pine trees rise from the river valley to layer the slope next to it. Tsarap drives us towards Yumesamdong (15,000 ft), better known as Zero Point since that is where the civilian road ends, close to the country's border. The views should be great.

Nature has other plans. It starts snowing hard. The road ahead, we discover, is lost in a deep layer of snow. After a snowball fight, it is time to return to Lachung.

On our drive to Gangtok the next morning, we have a tyre puncture. Tsarap gets off to change it. Dinesh, Sumita and I get off to straighten our legs. When the tyre is replaced, Dinesh and I climb into the car. Before Sumita can get in, Tsarap starts the engine, almost drives off.

'*Hey*, wait for Sumita, she hasn't got in yet,' I exclaim. Tsarap hits the brakes without turning to look.

'Were you planning to go without me?' Sumita asks Tsarap.

'All these years of driving, I never get a punctured tyre,' Tsarap mumbles. 'Yesterday morning, you look at my tyres, talk about puncture, and it happens today.'

The poor, superstitious man was actually trying to leave her behind.

For the rest of our journey, we speak with caution. Tsarap has used up his only spare, and another puncture—for whatever reason—would have us out on the lonely road.

'Ma'am, remember the boulder that just missed our car while we were going to Lachen?' Dinesh asks suddenly.

We see it the same instant. The Border Roads Organisation must have tried to clear the road for traffic. The boulder now sits a little closer to the mountain range, leaving just about enough space for a single car to pass.

Shaped like a giant gaming dice rounded at the corners from use, it has the dimensions of four overloaded trucks stacked up in pairs.

PELLING

The 100-minute narrative of Satyajit Ray's first colour film evolves around a mountain peak. To Andrew Robinson, his biographer, Ray had said:

> *'The idea was to have the film starting with sunlight. Then clouds coming, then mist rising, and then mist disappearing, the cloud disappearing, and then the sun shining on the snow-peaks.'*

Ray had named that movie *Kanchenjungha*, after Kanchenjunga (28,169 ft), the third highest mountain in the world.

Kanchenjunga gets its name from four Tibetan words: Kang-chen-dzo-nga or Yang-chhen-dzö-nga. It is interpreted in Sikkim as the 'Five Treasuries of the Great Snow'. Four of the mountain's five peaks are over 27,000 ft. The treasures represent the five repositories of God: gold, silver, gems, grain, and holy books.

Pelling, at 6,690 feet in West Sikkim, is said to offer the closest view of Kanchenjunga from India. This mid-summer morning, however, the peak decides to be completely elusive, hiding behind a thick fog. Let alone a 100 minutes, it seems that our entire stay would be spent moping about the no-show.

If not the snow-laden Kanchenjunga, Pelling presents us a copper-coloured mountain, the Zangdok Palri. Or at least a seven-tier intricately carved and painted wooden version of it, at the Pemayangtse Monastery founded by Lama Lhatsun Chenpo.

The heavenly palace of Guru Rinpoche or Padmasambhava—the 'Second Buddha' of Tibetan Buddhism, also the tantric master who carried Buddhism from India to Tibet—is said to be atop Zangdok Palri. As its base, the palace has an eight-sided jewel and a thousand-petalled lotus. There are four gates, four arches and eight pillars. The walls are made of precious stones: crystal in the east, lapis lazuli in the south, ruby in the west and sapphire in the north.

It has taken a lot of imagination to craft this little heaven in timber.

Royal palaces for mortals are not as everlasting. A two-km trek through a thick forest close to Pemayangtse leads to the ruins of Rabdentse, the second capital of the kingdom of Sikkim. In 1814, the capital was destroyed in an invasion. The ruins, declared a monument of national importance by the Archaeological Survey of India, seem a popular picnic venue.

The weather turns worse. There is a depressing drizzle over the Khecheopalri Lake, 24 kilometres from Pemayangtse. This holy lake is also called Wishing Lake, Kha-Chot-Palri and Sho Dzo Sho (meaning, 'Oh lady, sit here').

The 'history' of the lake is painted on a signboard put up by the Department of Ecclesiastical Affairs, Government of Sikkim. A long time ago, this area was a grazing ground filled with nettle. The tribal inhabitants had various uses for the nettle. One day, even as a Lepcha couple was peeling off the bark of the nettle, they saw a pair of conch shells fall from the sky and go into the ground. The earth shook severely, and water spouted from it, forming the lake.

An oral lore says that birds keep the lake litter free, regularly picking up dead leaves and twigs from the water. This is believable: the water is crystal clear. Orange fishes swim merrily in it, and a few candles hold on to their light by the shore.

Sumita tries to turn the enormous red-gold prayer wheel at the tiny Buddhist monastery near the lake. The wheel does not budge. Both of us grab the circular iron handle at its base, and break into a brisk trot around it. This time, the wheel moves. At its touch, a bell hanging just above its upper rim starts to chime. It has a deep, resonating sound.

Buddhism made inroads into Sikkim in the 17th century. Lama Lhatsun Chenpo, from the Red Hat sect of Tibet, had wandered into Sikkim with a dream to establish a Buddhist monarchy, and to bring all the Lepcha clans under it. At Norbugang in Sikkim, Lhatsun Chenpo met two learned men—Sempa Chenpo and Rinzing Chenpo. The venue of this meeting came to be known as Yuksom: 'meeting place of the three learned monks'.

The three monks selected Phuntshog Namgyal, the grandson of Kye Bumsa, and the son of Mipon Rab, as the first King of Sikkim and conferred on him the title Chogyal: 'the king who rules with righteousness'. They crowned him at Norbugang on a stone pedestal, now known as the Norbugang Throne or the Coronation Throne.

Phuntshog Namgyal ruled Sikkim from 1642-1670 AD. He was succeeded by 11 more rulers. Chogyal Palden Thondup Namgyal was the last of them, and it was during his reign that the kingdom merged with India, becoming its 22nd state in 1975.

With its ancient inscriptions, the Coronation Throne still stands under an equally ancient pine heavy with dew. Yuksom today is a starting point for mountain treks.

Near a tea shack, we meet a grey, furry, palm-sized pup with beautiful grey eyes and the serene air of a philosopher. Sumita lifts him up into her arms, and does not wish to put him down ever again.

'Let's take him home,' she says.

'I would love to. But he was born in this very cold clime. He won't survive the muggy heat of Kolkata.'

'He will adjust. He is so young he won't remember the cold climate.'

'We are going back by train. All that noise, the crowds... his little heart will fail from fright.'

It breaks Sumita's heart to put the pup down and walk away. It breaks mine, too.

We return to the hotel for the night, hoping to wake up to a brilliant view of the Kanchenjunga. But the second day dawns foggy again. So we splash about at the Changay Falls 10 kms away, walk the Singshore Suspension Bridge, considered the second highest in Asia, and visit the Alpine Cheese Factory. It is an Indo-Swiss collaborative effort.

We believe in contributing to the local economy wherever we go. I come away clutching an oval mound of light golden Gouda cheese. Since Sumita is not fond of cheese, this innocuous mound of fat will generously contribute to my contours.

I feel quite the martyr.

Third morning's weather report: Foggy, get used to it.

Partly to make space for the cheese, and mostly because it is a day to go exploring, we get on a route leading to a small white speck high up on a mountain. A couple of horses graze by the roadside. A furry black dog follows us. Soon, in a subtle reversal of roles, the dog begins to lead us on the steep climb, pausing patiently every time we stop to regain our breath.

Mist comes in like large rings of blue cigarette smoke, cutting us off from the world. We are now above the canopies of trees. At every turn, we expect to see the white structure, but find another slope.

The dog takes us four kilometres uphill to the quaint Sanga Choeling Monastery. Established by Lhatsun Chempo in 1697, it is highly revered among the Nyingmapa sect. Once we reach the monastery he leaves us abruptly. On our way down, however, we see him again—this time leading a couple of foreign tourists up the same path.

We would like to feed him to show our gratitude, but do not even know where he lives. Sumita and I go from shop to shop asking for the whereabouts of a black dog.

'You are looking for Kalua?' says one of the shop-owners. 'He must have gone with the tourists again. He does the Sanga Choeling trip 12-13 times every morning. You will find him here at noon.'

True to routine, Kalua is back in front of the shop at noon. Tired, dozing. I run my palm down his dusty back and offer him biscuits. Not accustomed to gratitude—or biscuits—Kalua takes his time to sniff at them, then gently picks them off my palm.

Waiting has its rewards. On our last morning at Pelling, the mist clears like it has been touched by a magician's wand, and Mount Kanchenjunga appears in shining armour of white snow. A plume of white clouds rises from its crown.

> *'I see skies of blue and clouds of white*
> *The bright blessed day, the dark sacred night*
> *And I think to myself what a wonderful world…'*

Ray had built a 100-minute movie around it, but right now we wish to build the rest of our lives around this majestic peak.

RAVANGLA

The three-hour journey from Pelling has been pleasant enough, with fruit-laden orange trees waving their bounty at us every now and then. A kilometre from our destination, our Maruti van turns right from the tar road and bravely scrambles up a winding, pebbled path, its poker-faced driver grabbing the steering wheel just a fraction tighter than usual.

Probably, a lot tighter than usual.

A minute later, we are back at the base of the path, the car wheels skidding fast in reverse.

After a couple of retakes in this travel documentary threatening to turn into a horror movie, the driver gives up. The path is too circuitous, too steep, too narrow and too pebbled for a Maruti van. There is no way he can take us to the top of the hill, where one of the cottages of Mt Narsing Resort has already been booked for us.

Before we toss our accommodation receipt out of the window and go back to Ravangla bazaar to search afresh for hotels, an empty Indica cruises up. Two 100-rupee notes change hands. We change cars.

This time, we manage to reach the top.

Ravangla in south Sikkim gets its name from Rabong, which means a wet goat. It sits at an altitude of 7,000 ft, on a ridge between the Teesta and the Rangit River valleys, and offers remarkable, if somewhat distant, views of Kanchenjunga, Pandim, Kabru, Siniolchu, and Mt Narsing. The last peak has lent its name to the quaint set of log cottages we are at.

'I believe that what people call God is something in all of us': Guru Padmasambhava at the Old Ralong Monastery, Ravangla

Each single-roomed cottage is, again, named after a peak. Ours is K2, and has a framed photograph of the peak, two sturdy beds made entirely of logs, a typical ornately painted Sikkimese side-table, and one hanging light bulb. Since this is November, we take in the presence of thick blankets and the geyser in the attached washroom with relief, and that of the candles on the side-table with apprehension.

But it is just mid-morning, and the large dining cottage is warm, inviting and strange.

Warm, from the colourful carpets thrown over the log seats.

Inviting, with its collection of old books and magazines left behind by thoughtful travellers.

Strange, for its assortment of buffalo or yak skulls, masks, wooden pots and pans. A whole armadillo skin.

Post a very basic lunch and the forecast of a more basic dinner—most of the eggs, chicken and vegetables at the bazaar below have not found their way up, and seldom do—we set out to visit the new and old Ralong monasteries.

Ralong Palchen Choling, the new and larger monastery built in 1995, belongs to the Kagyupa Lineage, and was established by Goshir Gyaltsab Rinpoche.

The monastery porch is sprawling and clean. Just where the porch falls off the edge of the hill, lamas sit on their haunches facing the precipice, their backs warmed by the afternoon sun. The same warm glow bathes the building they live and meditate in. The golden Buddha inside the monastery glows too.

Ralong Karma Rabtenling, or the older and much smaller monastery, was built by Sikkim's fourth ruler Chhogyal Gyurmed Namgyal in 1730. History has it that internal strife in his kingdom forced the ruler to travel to Tibet in the guise of a mendicant, where he was recognised by the 12th Karmapa, or head of the Karma Kagyu sect, and given a warm welcome.

The two monks playing at the ancient monastery are barely into their double digits, and the only adult around sits on a platform 10 feet from the ground, painting the monastery walls with an army of red-robed little Buddhas. A shining and impressive statue of Guru Padmasambhava stares at us from the main altar.

I have this impulse to be photographed with the boy lamas. A smile and some sign language get them on either side of me. I place a palm on each of their bony backs. We pose.

Sumita composes the shot. The boys patiently hold their smiles. I find it difficult to hold mine: I am overwhelmed by the odours oozing off their thick maroon robes:

Sweat.

Unwashed blankets.

Burnt oil.

Grass dotted with cowpat.

The photograph comes out well.

Back at the resort after sundown, we find that the temperature has suffered a huge fall. There is no electricity. We come into the dining hall to the sound of rattling. It is our teeth.

A fire has been lit in the hall. A bald gentleman with a goatee stands by the fire, and says hello. It is embarrassing to respond, for we cannot yet keep our voices from quivering with the cold. But if he senses how cold we are, and there is no way he cannot, he does not show it. KK and his wife have checked in at the cottage next to us.

Later that evening, KK sits by the fireplace, strumming a guitar he has managed to lay his hands on, and breaks into the Eagles' song, *Hotel California:*

'On a dark desert highway, cool wind in my hair
Warm smell of colitas, rising up through the air
Up ahead in the distance, I saw a shimmering light
My head grew heavy and my sight grew dim
I had to stop for the night...'

KK has a good voice and the song echoes in the dining hall, punctuated by the crackle of logs in the fire that only creates a small pool of light around KK, his wife, and the two of us. A warm pool of comfort and camaraderie envelopes strangers.

The yak skull and horns throw long shadows on the walls, and the freezing wind howls over the mountain-top now lit by numerous fireflies. It is an unreal evening.

When the fire starts dying, we think of returning to our cottage to wait for the call for dinner. Two arching steps lead out from the near-dark dining hall, and the second one throws a shadow that looks like a third step. Sumita misjudges and has a fall, landing the weight of her body on her fingers. Thankfully, she hasn't hurt herself much.

Things take a serious turn post dinner. While leaving for our cottage, Sumita misjudges the dining hall steps again, has another fall. Lands on all fours, most of her body weight shifting, again, to her curled up fingers.

This time, the pain is excruciating. She stops talking. The torch falls from her hands, yet she does not even look at it, let alone make an attempt at retrieval. The dining room attendant picks it up and switches it on, accompanying us as I rush her to our cottage.

'Ma'am, are you all right? Ma'am?'

Ma'am does not answer. Once in the room, I make Sumita sit down on the log bed, run into the washroom to grab a mug of hot, very hot water, and stuff her palms into the mug.

On the plains, where it is never this cold, I would use ice cubes for such an injury. But somehow, my quack treatment works like magic. Sumita lets out the breath she was holding, relaxes.

'I think I may have broken my fingers,' she says.

We do not have a car. In any case, there is no way we can drive down the hill in search of medical aid. It is too dark, and the road downhill cobbled and winding and treacherous. She will have to live with the injury. She finds the pain slightly bearable now. A painkiller manages the rest.

Years later, Sumita would remember the hundred fireflies in the garden that night. Her knuckles would forever remember the pain.

The electricity does return. But the night is bone chilling, more so because of a long, untimely shower. We lie awake a long while, listening to rain drops tap dancing on the tin roof. Then daybreak is upon us, clear and crisp with the promise of a great mountain view. In minutes, we are out on the grassy, dewy lawn watching the peaks turning pink to gold to white.

Sumita is overjoyed with the golden ranges. '*Yehi hai, yehi hai, yehi hai mera pyar*,' she sings. It is a '70s film song.

'Why *that*, of all tunes?'

'I don't know. I am so happy, I have to sing something. That's what came to my mind.'

The rain-drenched zephyr seems to have brought in a little madness on its wings. That old tune will now play on in our heads all day.

As I frantically fill my camera frame, a leech in my right shoe has its first taste of my blood.

ARITAR

'Sikkim? Again?' Sumita could not help asking.

'Well, it is just an overnight journey, and you don't think we can afford to take too many days off work,' I said.

'Won't this be the fifth time? I thought we had seen most of it?'

'This time, we will do what the locals do. After all, that's the best way to understand a state.'

Two months post the conversation, we are hanging out at Ban Jhakri Waterfalls Park a few kilometres from Gangtok: Lots of trees; a 100-ft waterfall; an artificial green lake with a brightly painted dragon statue at its centre; strange, life-sized male and female figures with drums, sickles and feathered headgear; local children laughing on a bench under a colourful cement awning. A lone whitecapped water redstart.

No tourists.

In an enclosure, statues labelled Phedangma and Mangma stand over a supine figure with bulging eyes and a frothing mouth. '*Jhakri*s in healing ritual of sick person' says another label.

'What's a *jhakri*?' Sumita asks. 'Some kind of a doctor?'

'*Jhakri* is the Nepali word for a shaman,' I tell her. 'In Lepcha language, they are called Bóngthíngs. Lepchas, or the Mútunci róngkup rumkup, are a Sino-Tibetan ethnic group, and probably the earliest inhabitants of Sikkim. They believe in spirits, and to them, illness means that an evil spirit is trying to cause them harm. The Bóngthíngs or the shamans know how to get rid of evil spirits.'

'How do the Bóngthíngs have special powers?' Sumita persists.

'Let's find a bench,' I tell her, 'it is a long story. The Bóngthíngs come alive in *lúngten sung*, an oral lore with different narrative strands intertwined. The narrator has the freedom to travel down a different path at crossroads, and highlight any aspect of Lepcha culture.'

'A never-ending web of stories... sounds like our *Panchatantra*, doesn't it?' Sumita says.

'From the little I have gathered about *lúngten sung*, it sure does,' I reply. 'Now listen to the story.

'Long, long ago, goes the *lúngten sung*, God *Ítbú debú rum* took fresh snow from Mount Kanchenjunga and created Fadróng thing, the first man, and Nazóng nyú, the first woman. God made them immortal, and told them they should live as siblings.

'Fadróng thíng and Nazóng nyú, however, had a physical relationship and their first son Láso múng was born. Ashamed of what they had done, the couple abandoned their son in the forest.

'They continued the relationship, though, and abandoned six more children. The eighth time, Nazóng nyú gave birth to twins: Ralbu the girl, and Singbu the boy. She decided to feed them and bring them up with care.

'The other seven children, led by the eldest Láso múng, had meanwhile turned into demons. Jealous of Ralbu and Singbu, they directed their evil energies towards the twins. The twins fell ill, and died.'

'So that is how they connected negative energy with illness?' Sumita asks.

'I guess. The story isn't over yet,' I say.

'Go on, I'm listening.'

'Fadróng thíng and Nazóng nyú gave birth to more children, who became the Lepcha race. The demons continued to torment them, and they, too, began to die. This was how the Lepchas became mortal.

'God *Ítbú debú rum* saw the sufferings of the Lepchas. He took the purest snowflakes from Mount Pandim, and created the first priest, Jor bóngthíng. Bóngthíng was given immense powers and knowledge.

'Bóngthíng fought Láso múng for 12 years. Every year, Láso múng evaded Bóngthíng by changing into a different animal: mouse, ox, tiger, eagle, dragon, snake, horse, sheep, monkey, bird, dog and pig. Ultimately, Bóngthíng killed him.'

'Mouse, ox, monkey, pig... why do they sound familiar?'

'The Lepcha calendar has a cycle of 12 years, each year named after these animals.'

'I remember now, the Tibetan calendar,' Sumita says.

'Quite close. With one exception, the sequence of animal names is the same as in the Tibetan calendar. We are now in the year of the Ox.'

I do not feel as strong as an ox, though.

Driving down from Gangtok to Aritar the next day, we are met by a wide staircase rising next to Lampokhari (4,600 ft)—one of the oldest natural lakes in Sikkim—and loping in and out of a fairly dense, lush green forest, all the way to Mankhim Dara, the mountain top. The steps are steep, but Nandu, our driver, and Sumita find no real difficulty in negotiating them.

For me, out on my first trip after a surgery, it is a different story altogether. After every 10 steps, I hunker down and gather my breath. And at every such halt, we see more and more of the jade-green Lampokhari, or Ghati Tso or Aritar Lake, below us until the entire lake lies shining in the November sun. It is shaped like a sock.

Aritar in East Sikkim hardly sees tourists. It is a spot where the locals hang out on their holidays, driving down from Gangtok for a picnic by the lake, riding paddle boats or ponies, or trekking up to Mankhim Dara.

We climb around 2,000 ft, and are finally at Mankhim Dara. Had we reached at sunrise, the Kanchenjunga, Makalu, Pandim and Siniolchu peaks would have revealed themselves in full glory against the azure horizon, but their absence helps us appreciate the 360-degree view of the golden, terraced paddy fields. Brilliant white orchids speckled with pink sway around us in the cooling breeze.

Mankhim, or *mangkhim*, in Sikkimese, means a temple. The small temple on the mountain top belongs to the Rai community. Of Nepali origin, the Rais are worshippers of nature and believers of shamanism. The temple sanctum has just a couple of tridents and an array of small, shining copper pots.

'In spring,' Nandu says, 'the Rais hold the Sakewa festival here to celebrate the growth of plants. The *mangma* (priest) dances to the beat of drums. Chasum Sili, a popular dance, enacts the sowing of paddy, harvesting, husking, cooking and then eating rice.'

From Mankhim Dara, we walk a sun-dappled path through the shady forest to the Aritar Monastery, one of the oldest monasteries in Sikkim under the Karma Kagyu lineage of Tibetan Buddhism.

Local ladies sit twirling their rosaries and prayer wheels inside a quaint prayer room, their eyes on us, but minds far away. At the feet of a six-headed Avalokiteśvara lies a pile of everyday offerings: bananas, loaves of bread, and biscuit rolls. Copper lamps glow in a corner untouched by the morning sun. Outside, boy lamas idle on a wooden balcony and look at us with incurious eyes.

Under a temporary colourful canopy close by, a Sikkimese family has just held worship. Bejewelled human femur bones speak of their Tantric Buddhist beliefs. The family welcomes our presence in their private affair, and insists that we take some of the offerings. Embarrassed, but not wishing to hurt their sentiments, we accept carry-bags loaded with packets of biscuits, chips and fruits and begin our trek down to the lake.

On our way down, we pause to admire a pinewood dak bungalow, with white-washed walls and a green roof. Popularly called Ari-Bangla, it was built in 1895 by Sir James Claude White, the first political officer of Sikkim during the British rule in India. It had held Sikkim's first treasury, and served as the first Sikkim Police outpost. With sprawling lawns and a fabulous view of the Sikkim mountain range, it would soon become a tourist accommodation.

'Ari-Bangla is said to be haunted, you know?' I tell Sumita.

'Please, I have had enough of evil spirits for one trip,' she says.

While we lunch at a resort by the shores of Lampokhari, ducks and swans swim busily on the glassy, green water, picking at their food. White prayer flags flutter all round the lake, their reflections blending with that of the cottony clouds floating across the sky. A genial Sikkimese gentleman paddles a boat while his three young sons sit back and enjoy the ride.

It is family time at Aritar.

Back at the Gangtok guest house, the caretaker's family offers us a special vegetable curry for dinner. We cannot identify the creamy green vegetable in the soup-light gravy.

'Did you like the curry?' the caretaker's wife asks post lunch.

'Sure. It tasted a bit like cabbage, slightly sweeter. What was it?'

'Bamboo shoots,' she replies. 'We also make pickle with it.'

Since we like the curry, we boldly buy a bottle of bamboo-chilli pickle from the market.

The chillies—locally called *dalle*—are round, bright red, and fiery. The bamboo smells fermented. Eaten in fair amounts, I think the pickle might even make us tipsy.

After a spoonful, Sumita refuses to touch it again.

Facing page: 'What we lose in flowers we more than gain in fruits.' West Sikkim

BENGAL

DARJEELING

It is strange what the mind remembers of childhood: a warped collage of the sights and sounds and smells, a collage that may highlight the insignificant and completely ignore the serious.

My first memories of Darjeeling (6,700 ft)—on the Mahabharata Range of the Lesser Himalayas—are a collage of the insignificant: the first very cold night; the loss of a milk tooth; the lavatory's wooden bench with a hole in its centre and an enamel chamber pot under the hole; the *chhurpi* or the hard yak cheese I chewed on for three days, wrapping it carefully in a clean handkerchief when I went to bed. And yes, the snot-nosed schoolchildren in maroon coats with streaks of dirt on their rosy round cheeks coming up the hill to their school next door.

The Kanchenjunga figures—barely—on the sidelines of that memory, a flash of gold behind the light blue dome of the Raj Bhavan, seen once in passing.

Sumita, in her teens when she first visited Darjeeling, remembers the sense of waiting for the mountain to appear in the horizon, the excitement among the elders when it finally did.

Pp 292-293: 'You have to be very strong to live close to God or a mountain, or you'll turn a little mad': Kanchenjunga Peak at sunset

Facing page: 'I thought the most beautiful thing in the world must be shadow': A cable car passes over the Takvar Valley Tea Estate, Darjeeling

Decades later, we arrive at Darjeeling in pursuit of our unreliable memories, and find myriad options to fashion new ones. With time to call our own, we:

Idle away the hours under the tall maples of the Mall, while pigeons pad about and ponies swat flies with a swish of their long tails.

Munch on sandwiches at Keventer's, lunch at Glenary's.

Zoom down from North Point to Takvar Valley in a cable car, with rolling green tea estates below, and the snow-covered Kanchenjunga in the horizon.

Pick up oranges from the ladies who sit by the station with their loaded cane baskets.

Chug through markets and narrow, curved lanes on the toy train ride to Ghoom.

The toy train halts at the Ghoom Railway Station for a while before resuming its return journey. A visit to the Ghoom Railway Museum is rewarding, with interesting bytes about the construction of the Darjeeling Himalayan Railway on such a difficult terrain.

'Deep in their roots, all flowers keep the light': Dahlia imperialis, near Darjeeling

'Orange is the happiest color': Fruit sellers near a toy-train station

Mark Twain (1835-1910), in his travelogue *Following the Equator,* mentions his ride over the same tracks:

> *'After a while we stopped at a little wooden coop of a station just within the curtain of the sombre jungle, a place with a deep and dense forest of great trees and scrub and vines all about it. The royal Bengal tiger is in great force there, and is very bold and unconventional. From this lonely little station a message once went to the railway manager in Calcutta: "Tiger eating station-master on front porch; telegraph instructions." '*

In the same humorous breath, Mark Twain claims that this is where he had his first tiger hunt: he killed 13.

Eats shoots and leaves: Red panda, Darjeeling

Tiger hunting—only officially—is a thing of the past, and we see a fine specimen of the Royal Bengal at the Padmaja Naidu Himalayan Zoological Park. The Himalayan Black Bear gorges on pink radish and the pair of flame-red pandas devour bamboo shoots as if it were the last bunch of bamboo in the world. The stuffed animals and birds at the well-stocked and maintained Bengal Natural History Museum are a poor second.

We think we have really earned our stripes by covering the 4.4 kilometres between the zoo and the museum on foot.

Having managed to shake off our indolence thus, we drive down to the Lebong Racecourse. In a flash, I remember beautiful stallions galloping by, and my father—who had never won a game of luck in his entire life—betting and promptly losing ₹ 10. The racecourse had first hosted the Darjeeling Gymkhana Club races in 1925. It shut down in 1984, the day Indira Gandhi was assassinated, and is now an Army camp. Villagers sit outside it, playing 'parsao', an old game of dice.

A climb to the Mahakal Temple Complex atop the Observatory Hill the next day is invigorating. The morning sun highlights the moss-covered boughs of trees along the path, the wing feathers of a sleepy hawk, and the red-brown back of a large flying squirrel. Within the temple, Buddha and Shiva share the same altar. It is a lesson in harmony.

It is also the first time we see an idol of Shiva with a snub nose.

A lesson in grit awaits us at the Himalayan Mountaineering Institute, where a glass case exhibits a pair of mountaineering shoes that are too small for any adult. These belonged to Reinhold Messner. Messner believes in 'alpine style' mountaineering, which means the use of minimal gear (no satellite phones, or pre-fixed ropes, or established camps). In 1978, Messner and Peter Habeler became the first people to climb Everest without bottled oxygen. Messner was also the first person to summit Everest solo, in 1980. He lugged everything he needed on his back and climbed up and back in four days.

'Why are Messner's boots so small?' Sumita asks.

'He lost seven toes and several fingertips to frostbite during his climb up Nanga Parbat, the ninth tallest mountain in the world at 27,000 ft. It is in Pakistan, a part of the Karakoram Range, at the western end of the Himalayas,' I tell her. 'This was in 1970, but it did not end Messner's climbing career, just that his boots had to be made to order afterwards.'

'That climb must have been quite an ordeal,' Sumita says.

'Well, Messner lost more than his toes and fingers on that climb,' I reply. 'Reinhold Messner and his brother Günther were climbing Nanga Parbat together. The Messner brothers managed to reach the summit, exhausted and with no food and water left. Günther had altitude sickness, too.

'When the two were coming down the mountain, Günther, lagging behind, was swept away by an avalanche.

'As if this were not enough, Reinhold was blamed by two fellow mountaineers for callously leaving his brother to die on the highly dangerous Rupal face of the mountain, while he himself came down an unknown route on the western Diamar face, in order to be the first to do so. For 35 years, Reinhold Messner lived with that allegation. Then, in 2005, his brother's remains were found on the western Diamar

'Those who deny freedom to others deserve it not for themselves':
Refugee at the Tibetan Handicrafts Centre, Darjeeling

route, confirming Messner's claim that Günther had indeed been swept away.' Messner has attributed his successes to his 'willpower to fail, and to try it again, again and again'.

Such endurance also defines the refugees from Tibet. The window panes of the Tibetan Refugee Help Centre are full of slogans: 'Free Tibet. Tibet is not part of China'. But the women who work at their looms and the men who make pincushions for a living are old. The flight from their lost land has etched deep, craggy lines on their face. They smile at us, but their eyes are sad.

As we walk uphill to our hotel past the Darjeeling Gymkhana Club after nightfall, two men sit by a fire in the compound of the club. Renovations are on: old wooden doors and windows have been taken down and hacked into logs. As they burn in the fire, the fragrance of juniper fills the night air. We pause to take a deep breath.

'Most houses used to be built out of juniper logs,' explain the men, 'it kept the interiors warm.'

The 'old order changeth'...

MIRIK

The SUV we are in is officially meant to accommodate 10 passengers and a driver. And since this is our first ride in a shared vehicle on the hills, we book four seats for the two of us. Just for that extra elbow room.

So, logically, there should be six more passengers besides us and the driver.

When we start out, however, there are 13 more, all local men and women, not counting a 10-month-old baby. We are like chickens stuffed in wooden crates on their way to the slaughterhouse. Despite the obvious discomfort generally experienced in such situations, we hear constant munching noises from the seats behind us, punctuated by peals of laughter. And this is when we make a late discovery: None of the door locks works, and the driver's door is fastened with a crude hair pin.

This journey from Darjeeling to Mirik is already becoming memorable, for all the wrong reasons.

Close to Gopaldhara, our vehicle is flagged down by soldiers at an Army outpost. The local women are made to get off and bring down their wares from the car roof.

It is a search for smuggled goods.

In the manner of indignant hens, the women puff up their chests and produce authentic goods receipts issued in Darjeeling. The ones without cargo share with us the real reason behind the search: soldiers usually look for heaters and Korean caps that they can confiscate—for personal use, of course.

The ride through green tea estates and crucial bends in the mountain road has one other halt: lunch break for the driver at Pashupati Fatak. We reach Mirik around 3 pm.

A hill resort at an altitude of 5,797 ft, Mirik is 49 kilometres from Darjeeling and 52 kilometres from Siliguri. The 1.25 km-long Samendu Lake, fed by perennial streams, is Mirik's claim to fame. A deep-green forest of conifer, chestnut, oak and maple trees covers the western slopes. A footbridge connects the open ground on the east with the woods on the west. Tourists usually go for a stroll on the 3.5-km path along the lake, ride a boat or a horse.

After a bowl of hot but expensive *thukpa* at one of the eateries surrounding the lake, we amble over to a nursery of exotic plants. For Tsangdup Tamang, the teenager in charge of Moktan Nursery, every flower in his little Eden is special, be it an orchid, a camellia or an azalea, or even a bright purple plant of the spinach family.

The Mirik Tourist Lodge, run by the Gorkhaland Territorial Administration (GTA), is still receiving finishing touches. We have a large, wood-panelled room with a great view of the lake, but no water in the washroom. There is a large dining hall, but no functional kitchen.

'No problem, Ma'am,' says the waiter, after he has knocked and sucked on several taps in the washroom to coax the water to flow. 'You order, I get food from Thuling Restaurant.'

We order dinner, but choose to walk down to Thuling Restaurant—a tiny joint at the base of a winding flight of steps from the lodge—for breakfast the next day.

While we are at breakfast, a Gorkha youth with a black anti-pollution mask over his nose and mouth walks up.

'You are journalist?' he asks, pointing to my camera on the table.

'I freelance as one.'

'I take you around Mirik.'

Sumita and I look at each other. We are a little uncertain about trusting strangers. A stranger with half his face covered, that makes it worse.

'Earth laughs in flowers': Cherry blossoms by the wayside

'I am Prabhat. My name easy to remember, just think "good morning", *prabhat* means morning.'

'Yes, I know,' I tell him. 'But we are just here for the morning, and have to leave for Kurseong after lunch.'

'You give me one hour, that is enough,' he insists. 'I take you free.'

'Okay, let's go,' I tell him.

For the next two hours, we walk with Prabhat: up steep steps; past pea bushes heavy with mildly fragrant, greenish white flowers; through people's backyards in Krishnanagar with a halt at the little Krishna Temple (established: 1962) that gives the village its name.

On a lonely uphill stretch, Prabhat stops once to talk to four men. Immediately tense, we try to look away, be casual. 'They are my friends,' Prabhat says. After a while, the friends move on.

'Just living is not enough... one must have sunshine, freedom, and a little flower': Bird of Paradise, near Darjeeling

We arrive at the Bokar Ngedhon Choekhor Ling Institute and Monastery on a hilltop that has a fabulous aerial view of Samendu Lake. Prabhat takes us into the sunny and squeaky-clean monastery library. Polished wooden racks hold old *thangka*s, books handwritten on parchment and bound in bright satin or silk. Inexplicably, books on the French Riviera. There is a computer corner, too. In the courtyard below the large glass windows, a little monk is at play, occasionally ploughing his spoon into a breakfast bowl of *chao mian*, better known in its corrupt avatar of chowmein.

Prabhat talks of clear days when a five-minute uphill walk from our lodge would have given us a good view of the Kanchenjunga. But today is not such a day.

'Have lunch, and check out,' Prabhat says. 'I put you in shared jeep.'

At the shared taxi stand, he waits till we get our tickets, helps us get our luggage into the waiting SUV.

'Thank you, Prabhat,' I tell him. 'You gave us a good trip.'

I extend my hand to shake his, slip in a 100-rupee note.

Prabhat is suddenly overcome with emotion. He takes my hand again, plants a kiss. Walks away, fast.

This time, the passenger strength in our SUV is 18: some of them ride the luggage rack on the roof; three hang from the back door. The driver practically sits on a passenger's lap.

Close to sunset, the vehicle stops suddenly at Garidhura. It is a Saturday, and the locals have gathered at a village haat. The driver and several passengers get off to buy their weekly vegetables at this makeshift market.

I get off too, but to stretch my cramped legs. Kurseong is still half an hour and several sharp, hairpin bends away.

KURSEONG

If Sumita and I were to mention a few of the things that really bother us on the hills, the 'hotel pillow' would definitely make the list. Even the best of hotel rooms have often offered us pillows as hard and lumpy as a sack of potatoes.

Kurseong's tourist lodge is no different. I leave the bed massaging a crick in my neck, and think how little the pillow has changed since Mark Twain's visit to these hills in 1896. This is how he cheekily described it:

> *'In India from the beginning, in time of war breastworks have been built of hotel pillows. It was found that a cannon ball could go thro' earth or sandbag, but when it hit a pillow it hit with a dull thud and dropped to the ground.'*

It has been daylight for some time now, yet there is a nip in the air. I cannot wait to dress for the chilly wind, for I am running late.

A short while later, I am at my post. My feet in bedroom slippers are freezing, and I regret not changing into my regulation sneakers. Behind me and at a lower level, the tourist lodge registers faint stirrings. Beyond the lodge and far away in the horizon, the Kanchenjunga, Kabru and Kumbhakarna peaks are awash with the first sunlight.

Inside the St Paul's Church I face, people have gathered for the morning prayer. I can hear the church bells ring. And then, another

'In truth, there was only one Christian and he died on the cross':
St Mary's Grotto, Kurseong

sound blends with the bells, the faint echoing sound of metal clanging against metal in a familiar rhythmic beat.

Soon, from the right of the tree-edged, elevated corridor I am standing on, the toy train's blue coaches loom into view. As I step back from the tracks to take my shot, the train chugs past with its handful of local passengers smiling indulgently at me.

At 4,864 ft, Kurseong would have been just right for Goldilocks and the Baby Bear. The winters here are neither too warm nor too cold, the mountain ranges are neither too close nor too formidable, and this hill town is neither too touristy nor too mundane.

The active tourist can hike up the narrow uphill road past the railway station to visit Eagle's Crag for a bird's eye view of the distant Teesta River and the entire township, drive down to Giddhapahar for a picnic and a tour of a historic bungalow, or ride the toy train to Ghoom or Darjeeling. The visitor wishing to rest and recuperate from the daily grind of his job in the city can simply laze on the hotel balcony and watch the mountains over a good book and a cup of tea.

Kurseong is a part of West Bengal's 'chai county'. For tea lovers like Sumita, a trip to the rolling fields of green bushes in one of Kurseong's tea gardens is a must. At the Makaibari Tea Estate, store manager Om Shastri takes us around, proudly briefing us about pruning and plucking processes, and tea auctions. Makaibari, he says, is the only tea estate which does not auction its tea. The produce is sold under its own brand name. Other tea estates auction their tea leaves, which might be blended with other varieties, named after the buyer company, and then sold.

Giddhapahar has its tea estate too, but we are drawn to the picturesque bungalow of Sarat Chandra Bose, elder brother of Bengal's firebrand freedom fighter Netaji Subhas Chandra Bose.

Netaji was interned here by the British, and this was where he wrote the speech he would deliver at the Haripura Congress in 1938.

A Camellia tree planted by Sarat Bose in 1934 is in full bloom next to the bungalow. The house now serves as the Netaji Museum and Centre

'One individual may die for an idea; but that idea will, after his death, incarnate itself in a thousand lives': Netaji Institute for Asian Studies, Giddhapahar, Kurseong

for Studies in Himalayan Languages, Society and Culture. Inside, the reclining chairs, writing desks and carved wood tables once used by the Boses gleam with polish. Glass cases hold photographs of the Bose family, often with well known personalities of the times. There are copies of letters exchanged between Netaji and Rabindranath Tagore, Jawaharlal Nehru and Netaji's wife, Emilie Schenkl. The visitors' book gushes about the museum's collection.

The Forest Museum close to the Dow Hill and Victoria School is closed for renovation, but we do not regret the journey through cool avenues canopied with huge, Mexican weeping pines.

'Four of my father's cousins studied here,' I tell Sumita. 'My uncles were in Dow Hill, the aunt, at Victoria.'

'It's a lovely place to grow up in,' she says.

It sure is. White orchids that give Kurseong its name—*kharsang* in Lepcha language means Land of the White Orchids—bloom on the Dow Hill School campus. The Victoria School building and the old

'I am so fond of tea that I could write a whole dissertation on its virtues': Flowers bloom on a tea-bush

church next to the school seem straight out of an Enid Blyton book. Schools are closed, and the basketball court is silent.

Silence is broken only by bird call at the St Mary's Hill and grotto. A blue-eyed statue of Virgin Mary stands inside an alcove cut into the hill, her face tilted upwards in prayer. In a bigger alcove, water from a hidden rivulet drips into a stone bowl, and is labelled as Holy Water. A lone blue redstart hops next to it.

I scramble up the steep, near-vertical surface of a tree-loaded hillock close by to reach a statue of Jesus on a pedestal. Long, exposed roots of giant trees clutch onto the hillock like gnarled, monstrous fingers. Worried that I might trip on them, Sumita makes the driver follow me.

Venite ad me omnes, reads the pedestal, the first part of a Biblical quote that goes 'Come unto me, all you who are troubled, and I will give you rest'. The place is indeed a sanctuary for the troubled soul.

For young lovers, too.

Eagle's Crag viewpoint is also teeming with lovers when we hike there the next day. Eagle's Crag offers a somewhat misty view of river

Teesta on one side, and a crystal clear view of Kurseong town on the other. Sumita and I choose a narrow ledge amid tea bushes growing on the sloping hillside and sit down to watch the town far below.

The toy train's chugging reaches our ears long before its blue coaches make an appearance through the town's busy lanes. After it has gone by, we come down the cliff and walk like locals along the tapering hill roads. Built at different levels, they are all connected to one another by narrow stone staircases.

We discover the Sakya Kunga Shedupling Monastery, where teenage lamas are attending a class. Closer to the bustling market, the Tamang Buddhist Association Monastery established in 1925 is undergoing a major renovation. The association elders sit in a circle and discuss an upcoming festival. 'Their ancient, glittering eyes, are gay.'

Coming out of an alley and directly upon the market, we try our hand at bargaining like locals over a pair of woollen caps. Fail miserably. Buy them anyway, and then try wearing them.

The caps are warm, hand-knitted triangles of thick, bright, multi-coloured wool. Each cap comes with three six-inch plaits: one falling on either side of the face, and a third rising from the peak.

I find that I can tie the plaits on the side together under my chin: they have a purpose.

I can do nothing to the plait on the top of my head: it keeps bobbing with every step I take.

It is a silly cap, more suited for children. But the local adults—labourers, fashionable teenagers—wear it casually, even to work.

We walk on the toy train's tracks back to the Kurseong Tourist Lodge. A big furry dog trots ahead of us, occasionally sniffing for rats.

Sunflower bushes growing on the hilly slopes next to the road are bursting with flowers. But the late morning sun has wilted most of them; the petals are folding up.

I have always wondered why Van Gogh's sunflowers looked so lifeless. Now, I know.

BHUTAN

PARO

January 14, 1983. Even as the first airplane—a Dornier Do-228 aircraft from Calcutta (now Kolkata)—lands at Paro Airport to the chanting of prayers, clanging of cymbals, and the blowing of conches, a schoolboy on vacation chases away the cows grazing around the runway.

It is considered one of the most dangerous runways in the world.

Almost 33 years later, KB-151 of the Royal Bhutan Airlines takes off on time from Kolkata. About an hour into the flight, Mount Everest appears on the horizon, the regular plume of snow at its crest. In the foreground, tree-covered mountain ranges cradle trellised fields, and the Paro Chhu rushes by at their base.

I am absorbed in photographing the white dragon on the bright orange-yellow tip of the plane's wing, when the plane almost brushes the tin roofs of a row of buildings. Makes a landing.

It seems to me the runway has appeared out of nothing.

Aviation Stack Exchange, an online forum for aircraft pilots, mechanics, and enthusiasts, says that to fly into Paro Airport (7,333 ft), a pilot needs a special certification. Here is why:

Given the altitude, the air is less dense, and a higher ground speed is required on landing.

Pp 312-313: 'It's always further than it looks. It's always taller than it looks. And it's always harder than it looks': Mt Jomolhari from Pele La

Facing page: 'The fewer the words, the better the prayer':
Boy with offerings for the Buddha, at the Khamsum Yulley Namgyal Chorten

Often, there are unpredictable and gusty crosswinds.

The runway—considering the terrain—is short, which increases the chance of the plane needing to go around. For that, the pilot has to know exactly where he is flying.

The airport nestles among mountains over 15,000 ft, with village homes on their slopes. This seriously limits approach or escape options.

All approaches and departures have to be flown according to visual flight rules: the pilot must make his judgements by familiar landmarks. He cannot rely on instruments.

Only 10 pilots in the world are allowed to fly to Paro Airport.

It is good neither Sumita nor I know any of the above *before* KB-151 flies us into Paro.

City of stars: Paro and its dzong

The airport is quaint; the terminal building we walk into looks a monastery, and the queue for immigration long and winding. I notice:

A predominance of Caucasians in the immigration queue.

A predominance of grey hair among the Caucasians.

Once we step outside the airport, Ugyen Drukpa, our guide in Bhutan, approaches us, his face creasing up with a smile. He is a big man in his 50s, with very short hair.

'*Kuzu Zangpola,*' I say to him, the Bhutanese for hello.

'*Kuzu Zangpola* and good morning,' he replies, placing a white scarf around my neck. 'In Bhutan we welcome visitors with this traditional scarf or *khada*.' He places one around Sumita's neck. I step back to take a photograph and notice Tandin, our driver, smiling widely. Tandin

(pronounced Tandi) is much younger, fairer, and readier with his smile than Ugyen. His hair is as short as Ugyen's, but upturned in the boy-band—or a hoopoe—style.

Both Ugyen and Tandin are dressed in *gho*s. *Gho*, the Bhutanese national attire for men, is a long robe pulled up to knee length and fastened with a woven cloth belt called *kera*. The belt is tied very tight, and the pouch formed by the extra cloth above it serves as a deep pocket.

Ugyen's *gho* has a *marthra*—a plaid weave on a red ground typical of textiles from Bumthang. He wears it over long black socks and sneakers. The folded cuffs of his *gho* are white. He has a guide's ID card on an orange-yellow ribbon round his neck and a round badge with photos of the current and the previous kings on his chest.

Tandin wears a plain grey *gho*—the cloth made in Gasa—with white cuffs, black socks and sneakers. He sometimes wears the *gho* over a pair of jeans and a full sleeved shirt. There was a time when, under the *gho*, the Bhutanese wore what a true Scotsman wears under his kilt. But for Tandin's 'jeanatic' deviation, only occasionally at that, we would always see them dressed according to the *driglam namzha*.

Driglam stands for discipline, custom, rules, and regimen. *Namzha* means system. *Driglam namzha* is the official code that governs how Bhutanese nationals should dress in public and how they should behave in a formal ambience. It traces its roots to the 17th-century rule of Ngawang Namgyal, the first Zhabdrung Rinpoche, Tibetan lama and military leader who sought to unite Bhutan both politically and culturally.

Since 1989, it has been mandatory for all citizens to observe the dress code in public during business hours.

The landlocked kingdom of Bhutan had no roads or currency until the 1960s. Until 1974, it allowed no tourists. Even today, the tiny nation has a strict policy of 'High Value, Low Impact Tourism'. The Tourism Council of Bhutan defines this as a policy to attract 'discerning tourists that will respect the unique culture and values of the Bhutanese people while also providing the visitors with an unforgettable one of a kind experience.' Government regulations state that a visit to Bhutan has to be planned through a Bhutanese Tour Operator.

I have made some changes to the suggested itinerary and the accommodations booked for us by the local operator. But, from this moment onward, we will be tagged with a guide, a driver, and a Hyundai Santa Fe to ensure that our tour of Bhutan is 'one of a kind'.

Ugyen Drukpa—UD as he would like to be addressed—is the schoolboy from 1983: the one who chased the cows off the runway. 'Some of my aunt's land was taken to build the runway,' Ugyen says as we drive away from the airport, 'she was given a plot in Thimphu as compensation.'

The growing up years of Ugyen also witnessed the growth of Bhutan. 'Twenty-five years ago, Bhutan did not have a bank, but used the services of State Bank of India. Delhi University was where Bhutanese students went to study.'

Ugyen gives us an overview of Bhutan, the number of its districts, its 18 languages and the dialects within each language. We are passing Paro or Pa Chhu, the river named after Paro. Ugyen points to its shores: 'People living on one shore may not understand the dialect spoken by those living on the other.'

'So you have an official language?'

'Yes, that's Dzongkha. All schools teach in Dzongkha and English.' He says it with pride.

There is a downside to this uniformity, feel some locals. In the Bhutanese newspaper *Kuensel*, Saacha Dorji, a teacher of Darla Middle Secondary School writes:

> *'....our mother tongue dialects like Khengkha, Kurtoep, Sharchop are vulnerable as most children speak English... Now local languages are mostly used by grandparents and older generations and even if our younger generations speak it, they speak the language partially and infrequently.*
>
> *'In schools, I remember we were punished for speaking our own mother tongue.... We had to wear the tag labeled 'Speak English,' for*

> *speaking Sharchop or we were made to cut grass or even beaten badly just for speaking the native language... English has become the measure of intelligence. We have been rewarding any achievement in spoken or written English.'*

This, Saacha Dorji fears, will lead to a loss of unique cultural, historical, spiritual and ecological knowledge. The oral lores of Bhutan passed down through its different languages will be lost. Without their specific dialect or language, communities will merge into one another and lose their identity.

The grey-green Paro Chhu speaks its own language. The river's gurgling waters lead us to the Tshenden Incense Factory, a spot I have wished to include in our itinerary.

Tsenden in Dzongkha means cypress. The one-storeyed factory in Bondey is just across the road from Pa Chhu. On the factory porch, incense sticks dry on square boards placed on rows of wooden benches. Four women tie up the dried sticks into neat bundles.

Ingredients from flowers and trees go into the incense mix, says the lady explaining the incense-making process. Inside the factory, one woman stuffs maroon lumps of the mix into a machine. Long noodles ooze out of the machine four threads at a time and fall on a stone slab in four heaps. Five women cut the noodles into eight-inch pieces. Bent over their wooden boards, they work fast, with skilful fingers.

Unparalleled skill and innovation define Thangtong Gyalpo (born: 1385). Gyalpo was a busy man: master of the Vajrayana teachings, architect, blacksmith, civil engineer, artist and inventor of Tibetan lhamo opera. He could even dispel epidemics.

It is said that when a boatman refused to ferry him across water to a holy site because he looked like a mad man, Gyalpo had a vision of iron-chain suspension bridges that any pilgrim could cross. To build a bridge like that, he taught himself metallurgy to create durable links, and engineering, to span unpredictable rivers and gorges. To collect the money to buy the iron ore and pay for labour, Gyalpo staged operas.

Thangtong Gyalpo—his first name sounds to me like the clang of metal—developed a method of smelting iron to create enormous chain links that are untarnished to this day. He went on to construct 58 suspension bridges, 60 wooden bridges, 118 ferries, 111 stupas, and countless monasteries in Tibet and Bhutan.

Five kilometres before the confluence of Paro Chhu and Wang Chhu, Ugyen makes us walk across a traditional bridge over Paro Chhu. Built in 2005, the bridge uses some of Thangtong's original chain links brought from Duksum in eastern Bhutan, and thick steel meshes.

It is a challenge crossing the swaying, boat-shaped bridge, the sides heaped with prayer flags. We look down through the mesh under our feet at the river surging and frothing beneath us, and claw at the meshes on the side for a grip. Though rusted, Gyalpo's chains look tough enough to last another century.

The far end of the bridge has a two-storeyed structure. Numerous *tsha-tshas*—droplet-shaped lumps of clay at times blended with the ashes of the dead—sit by a window on the ground floor. Small enough to fit in the palm of my hand, these have bas-relief images of Buddha and other holy beings stamped on them.

A small room on the first floor has a portrait of Gyalpo painted on the wall. The Lama Chakzampa or the Iron Bridge Lama is seen with: curly grey hair in a topknot, a beard, a pot belly, and a piece of a chain in his right hand.

Ugyen shows us a cave beyond this tiny *lhakhang*, or temple. 'When leprosy touched Bhutan, this is where the afflicted were kept in isolation,' he says.

On the neighbouring slopes, the blue Griffith's plumbago blooms at random. Carpets of red chillies dry in the sun at the base of the Tamchogang Lhakhang, a private temple owned by Gyalpo's descendants.

Ugyen does not encourage us to visit Tamchogang Lhakhang. 'You will see many such temples during your trip.'

Back from the bridge, he suddenly makes us climb a steep rock face—a shortcut to the road where the car waits. 'Let me see how fit you both are,' Ugyen says.

'So, what do you think, UD? Will we be able to climb up to the Tiger's Nest?' Sumita asks after we have scrambled up the dry grass-covered slope.

'You may take a while longer than others, but I think you will be able to complete the trek,' Ugyen replies.

A winding, uphill drive takes us to Bhutan Mandala Resort.

Below the balcony of our first floor room, we have widespread farmland: separated by elevated aisles, the fields now completely shorn of their crop. Multi-storeyed homes with tin roofs hem the fields. They have sloping roofs, but not the many-coloured wood frontages and small arched windows with trefoil motif that characterise the architectural uniformity dictated by the *driglam namzha*.

Beyond the houses runs the road. Beyond the road flows the Paro Chhu, and beyond its shores, the blue mountains rise and fall and rise and fall until they are cut off by a now orange sky.

The balcony offers a distant view of Rinchen Pung Dzong, Paro's 'Fortress on a Heap of Jewels'. A *dzong* in Bhutan serves as a fortress, a temple, and a seat of government.

As the November night wraps the valley in its cold, dark mantle, red-gold lights come on in the long row of houses; only the buttressed walls of the *dzong* shine white, transforming it into a large solitaire on a ring of flame.

Our meals are pre-decided by the hotels and paid for by our travel agent on this 'one of a kind' tour to Bhutan. For the first time on our trips, I have no choices to make. While we wait for dinner to arrive at our table, Sumita and I look around the large dining hall. We see: one large team of Europeans and Far-Easterners in an animated yet low-voiced conversation; a smaller, far more boisterous, team of Bangladeshi businessmen, their conversational volume rising by the peg.

It is good to retire to warm beds, with the room heater thoughtfully switched on in our absence by an invisible housekeeping team.

Ugyen is ready sharp at 9:00 am the next morning. Staying at the same hotels as us, he and Tandin will meet us at nine every morning through our entire trip. There will be days when I will beg him to start early: 'Please, I want to see the sunrise over the snow peaks, UD.' He, forever calm, will always say, 'Mornings are foggy in Bhutan, the views will clear only after nine.'

Sumita and I do not appreciate inflexibility. In Bhutan, we will never have it our way.

It is a clear day, and the sun warm on our backs as we climb the short flight of stairs from the car park to the National Museum. The watchtower that houses the museum is under renovation, so the exhibits are on display at an annexe.

The mask gallery has an impressive collection of brightly coloured wooden or papier mâché masks, neatly labelled.

One of the labels has my attention: 'What's a Bardo dance, UD?'

'The soul goes through an intermediary stage between death and rebirth,' explains Ugyen. 'This stage lasts 49 days, and is called Bardo. Both peaceful and wrathful gods appear to the soul in this stage. How we behave during these 49 days decides the form we will take in our next birth.'

Guru Rinpoche (Rinpoche: Precious Teacher) or Padmasambhava, a great Indian Tantric Buddhist most likely from the Swat Valley in modern-day Pakistan, had initiated a very vibrant mask culture in the Himalayas. The gallery has a mask for each of his eight manifestations, and those from the Ging Toling dance that the Guru performed to subdue demons preventing the construction of Samye Monastery in Tibet. There are also masks of the sluggish *yeti*, the 'abominable snowman'.

We settle down to watch a looping video on the dances of Bhutan. A couple and their children join us on the narrow bench in front of a large television screen. The gentleman has an ankle bandaged with crepe. He is walking with a noticeable limp and an equally noticeable grimace.

'How did you hurt yourself?' I ask him.

'While trekking up to the Tiger's Nest,' he smiles ruefully.

It is an informative video. Virtually all masked dances dramatise moral lessons, promote Buddhist teachings, or commemorate the life of Guru Rinpoche. These are believed to purify and protect places from demonic spirits. The dancers turn out in spectacular costumes. Most masks are wooden and very heavy. The dancers first bind their heads with strips of cloth to protect them from the weight of the masks, and to keep the masks from slipping off during their energetic dances.

We walk through the gallery of ancient *thangka*s depicting Buddha, Tara Devi, and the arhats in intricate detail. The Heritage Gallery displays arms and weapons, household utensils, a rare tea kettle with a lotus-shaped opening, poisoned darts, headgear made entirely out of fish scales, ingredients for making butter tea, and *ja-sum*, the tea churner to make it with.

The egg laid by a mule does necessitate a suspension of disbelief.

Bhutan's flora and fauna come alive in the Natural History Gallery. We get to see as well as listen to 85 birds in an audio-visual presentation. It is quite impossible to remember their names, something I will regret many a time through our journey in Bhutan.

Ta Dzong, the watchtower under renovation, was built in 1649 to protect Paro Dzong. It is a beautiful round building that seems to rise in spirals like a conch, with ornate wooden windows that lighten the formidability of its 2.5m-thick stone walls.

Tall prayer flags, called *darpa* or *chopen*, flutter before the watchtower, each of their long posts topped by a wooden sword. It is the *sherab redri*, or the *prajna khadga*, the sword of wisdom that cuts through ignorance and delusion. The sword is associated with Jampelyang, the Bodhisattva of Wisdom.

We linger a while near the watchtower under the pines, conifers and the cypress, gazing at the valley at our feet. Ugyen Pelri—the palace of the queen mother designed in the image of the celestial Zangto Pelri (known as Zangdok Palri in Sikkim)—and the red-gold roof of the Paro Dzong shimmer in the sun.

Paro Dzong was built in 1644, by the order of Zhabdrung Ngawang Namgyal. Through the years, the fort has defended the Paro valley from Tibetan invasions. British political officer John Claude White—we admired his bungalow in Aritar, Sikkim—had said that in 1905 the rafters of the *dzong*'s balcony had old catapults that could be used to throw large stones at the enemy. Paro Dzong survived an earthquake in 1897, to be severely damaged by fire in 1907.

Bearded figures and a couple of black-necked cranes painted on the narrow passage walls lead us to the main *dochey*, the stone-paved courtyard of the Paro Dzong. On either side of the door, there are paintings of Gesar of Ling, the superhuman warrior ruler of the legendary kingdom of Ling. Ugyen explains the images: 'This one is Gesar and his pet tiger on his visit to Russia, and that is Gesar with a buffalo on his visit to Mongolia.'

The main temple within the *dzong* is closed. 'It is a Ganesh temple,' says Ugyen, 'worship is held in the morning, and only the king and Je Khenpo, the chief abbot, go in.' The outer wall of the temple has the Circle of Life painted on it.

The other sanctum in the *dzong* has a central statue of Tshepamey or Amitayus, the Buddha of Long Life: he wears a crown, large earrings and a necklace.

Every bit of the woodwork around us—the pillars, the arcades, the balusters, the eaves—is exquisitely detailed, and the colour theme vibrant with a blend of black, maroon, gold and terracotta.

In the administrative section, ladies are arriving to work. Under a board proclaiming Royal Court of Justice, appellants wait in the shade of the ornate wooden arches. Some ladies nestle children in their arms.

We walk out to the Nyamai Zam, the covered wooden bridge that goes across Paro Chhu. The original bridge was washed away by a flood in 1969. In the earlier war times, the bridge would be removed to protect the *dzong*.

'This is one of the last *bazam*s in Bhutan,' says Ugyen. *Bazam*: traditional wooden cantilever bridge.

It is good to loiter a while on the *bazam* and watch the green river dance past a bed of cream, rounded pebbles warm with the sun.

By noon, long, parallel rows of two-storeyed shops provide the only shade on Paro's market street. Colourful banners and large photographs of the Fourth King adorn the maroon-and-white shop fronts. The ornate wooden window frames on the upper floor have strips of meat drying on strings.

While we look for souvenirs, Ugyen poses with an *atsara* or a clown mask in one shop, and a black, sombrero-shaped woollen hat in another.

He looks at home in both.

Post lunch, we drive down to the north-western end of the Paro Valley. 'I think I will have a surprise for you,' says Ugyen, and he does. Against a clear blue sky, Mount Jomolhari (23,930 ft) rises above the valley like a butterscotch ice-cream cone.

The golden light of this early afternoon shines on the red-leafed maple, the yellow-leafed weeping willows and the ancient cypress guarding Kyichu Lhakhang. The *khemar*—a broad maroon band across the white walls—and the golden spire of the chorten in the compound are aglow with the same magical light.

One of Bhutan's oldest and most beautiful temples built in 659 AD by Tibetan king Songtsen Gampo, this *lhakhang* is said to pin down the left foot of a demoness who had tried to prevent the establishment of Buddhism in Tibet.

The sanctum's central image is that of Guru Rinpoche. The five-metre high statue has very compassionate eyes. On his right sits the idol of Dilgo Khyentse Rinpoche, a Nyingma Buddhist teacher. 'He died, and has been reborn since. The one behind him is Dorje Drolo,' says Ugyen. 'On our right, you have Goddess Kurukulla or the Red Tara.' She holds a bow and arrow made of flowers.

Ugyen has reserved the most dramatic monastery till the last: the Dungtse Lhakhang, or the Circular Stacked Stupa, built by Thangtong Gyalpo in 1433.

A chorten-shaped structure differentiates this monastery in Jangsa village from all the others we have seen so far. The temple is said to have been built over the head of a demoness, and is literally chained down to the ground.

Dungtse means a conch. The *lhakhang* was conceived as a mandala, with three storeys that correspond to the different levels of initiation. The three floors are said to represent hell, earth and heaven.

'You laugh because what's fearful and unknown is also what's funny':
The *atsara* or clown mask of Bhutan

Electricity has not been allowed into the *lhakhang* so that the original colour of its murals may be preserved. We leave our shoes outside and step into the very dark interiors, moving more by feel than by sight. Frescoes and murals on Lord Buddha's life, Zangto Pelri and Thangtong Gyalpo cover the walls. Narrow ladders lead to the upper floors.

'I don't think I can go up those ladders,' Sumita says. She hands me our torch, choosing to wait by the butter-lamp lit altar on the ground floor.

'I'll go ahead of you,' Ugyen tells me, and starts to climb. The steps are smooth, worn out at the centre, and slippery under my socks. I drag myself up the rungs, clutching onto the sides of the absolutely vertical wooden ladder with all my might.

If I do not keep my distance from Ugyen, my head will hit his feet.

In the near-total darkness, I look up once to check how far ahead he is, forgetting that he wears the *gho*. I do not look up again.

It feels good to come out of the monastery and into a golden dusk. We are not through with the ambient eeriness, though. Ugyen takes us circumambulating the building. He points to a spot covered with *tshas-tshas,* and asks us to hurry: 'Don't linger here, you will fall ill. There is a lot of evil energy.'

He says that a *National Geographic* team with members from the UK and the US had visited this *lhakhang*. 'The team admitted that there was negative energy at this point. The members said that somehow, the lamas have built all of Bhutan's monasteries at the right spots.'

The next morning finds us at the crossroads leading to Thimphu, Haa and Phuntshoeling. It is also the confluence of Paro Chhu and Wang Chhu.

Evil energy prevails at the confluences of rivers, too, believe the Bhutanese. So, to ward off any negative vibes, three chortens—Nepali, Tibetan and Bhutanese—protect the site.

To us, the *chhuzom (chhu*: river, *zom*: join) is just the unceasing, exultant, wildly musical surge of two teal-green rivers blending into one. We walk across the bridge over the confluence—an Indo-Bhutan friendship project—through the ornate gateway with its two golden dragons and a three-tiered, pagoda style roof, and drive towards Thimphu.

THIMPHU

Once upon a time, there was a kingdom. It had lush green forests. Snow-covered mountains in the north protected the kingdom from invasions. Monasteries guarded the kingdom from all the evil spirits within. The king was well-loved by his subjects. A good king, he wanted his subjects to be happy, too, and he measured the success of his reign by the happiness of his people.

The king lived in his large, beautiful, ornate wood-and-stone palaces with his four wives. He had sent his eldest son, the crown prince, to a distant land to study. The king's subjects lived in small, beautiful wood-and-stone houses which looked very alike.

After ruling his kingdom for 34 long years, the king gave the throne to the crown prince. The subjects were very happy to have two kings. They called them the Fourth King and the Fifth King.

Two years into the new king's reign, he decided that the people should rule themselves, even while he stayed on as their king. The people did not see any need for this, but they obeyed the king's wishes, and formed a body to govern the kingdom.

The Fifth King married, and soon, his wife was expecting a child. The whole kingdom waited to welcome the child. They had something else to celebrate meanwhile: the birthday of their Fourth King who would soon turn 60.

Entering Thimphu, it feels as if we have returned to the three-dimensional fairy-tale books of our childhood, where, at every turn of the page, cut-outs of castles, trees, mountains and people would pop up from the centre of the book and bring the tale to life. This miniature capital of a miniature nation has all the elements of a fairy tale: kings and their queens, the hills and the dales, the palaces and the temples, the evil demons and their destroyers.

Even the traffic policeman at the crossroads—there are no traffic lights in this kingdom—gracefully waving at the cars with white-gloved hands seems less a guard and more a member of a philharmonic.

Life seems simple in Bhutan, and thus, unreal.

At Simply Bhutan: A Living Museum, we meet Zimpa, a shy young thing in a fluorescent green silk jacket with golden cuffs over her *kira*—the formal attire for Bhutanese women. She welcomes us with tiny wooden bowls of chilled *ara*, or rice-wine, the local brew. I take an apprehensive sip, and am surprised by its punch.

Simply Bhutan is an offshoot of the Bhutan Youth Development Fund started by the queen mother Ashi Tshering Pem Wangchuck. Zimpa takes us on a tour of the campus.

Silk scarves adorn framed photographs of Bhutan's five kings. 'For the dead, we place the *khadas* on the top frame,' Zimpa explains, 'for those alive, we fix the scarves on the bottom frame.'

Two teenagers in *ghos* play a little tune for us on the *yang-chin* or the dulcimer and a *dranyen*, the ornate local guitar that has the curling head of a dragon at its narrow end.

Zimpa shows us how village women ram earth to build their mud houses and the vessels used to distil wine. A red chilli boils in water to ward off evil spirits. Phalluses have the same function, she says. These are everywhere: gigantic pink ones upright in a grassy patch on the courtyard, smaller models hanging from the eaves.

Gyanden, in-charge of our traditional lunch, offers butter tea with roasted rice first. Soup, red rice, vegetable curry, omelettes and *ema datse* follow. This is our first of many encounters with *ema datse*, the chilli-and-local cheese staple dish of Bhutan.

'Would you like some more butter tea?' Gyanden asks us after we are through with lunch.

'Thank you, but no,' I reply, 'with all that butter, it is quite a loaded drink.'

'I have it many times a day,' she laughs. 'Many of us Bhutanese people have butter tea with all our meals.'

While we digest the food, the staff of Simply Bhutan presents an impromptu local dance. The steps are simple, and the men and women perform them in sync, manoeuvring deftly past the long, low dining tables and benches.

In one of the shops around the courtyard, Yeshi, a differently-abled youth, sits among colourful souvenirs well-crafted from wood. He has fashioned them all: with his feet. The queen mother had come across this differently-abled baby in eastern Bhutan and brought him to Thimphu. She had enrolled him at Zorig Chusum, the Traditional Arts and Crafts Centre for a seven-year course.

Yeshi laps up the admiration of tourists, his smile and his skills more than making up for his incoherent speech. We buy a couple of souvenirs, but not before he has put his stamp and signature on them.

With his foot, of course.

Garlic cloves, corn cobs and red chillies have been hung out to dry across a kitchen window. 'Earlier, we did not have any means of preservation,' Zimpa tells us, 'so we had to dry vegetables and store them for the winter months. Now there are many ways to preserve food, but somehow we Bhutanese still prefer the taste of dried vegetables.'

In one corner, women weave cane baskets and woollen shawls. Next to them stands a bull's eye.

'Would you like to try your hand at archery?' Zimpa asks. I am handed a bamboo bow and some arrows.

Archery was declared the national sport in 1971, the year Bhutan became a member of the United Nations. A team of archers represents Bhutan in the Olympics.

I do not make it to the Olympics team.

At the Changlimithang Archery Ground opposite our hotel, men hone their skills on compound bows. Women stand on the side in a row, cheering their team, and jeering at the opponents. There is a lot of laughter. In the Changlimithang Stadium next to the archery ground, a large team of senior citizens rehearse their dance for the approaching birthday of the Fourth King, Jigme Singye Wangchuck.

'Our current king, Jigme Khesar Namgyel Wangchuck had joined the dancers this morning,' says Ugyen. 'He often stops his car to personally help old ladies trying to cross the road. At times, he gets rugs laid on the pavement, sits down with the old ladies and offers them tea. He loves travelling within the country, meeting his people.'

Ambling down Norzin Lam 1, we watch more dancers rehearsing at the Clock Tower Square. The number '60' is being written with flowers on a signboard: the digit 6 fashioned into a dragon. Hand-crafted dragons painted in gold adorn the four sides of the Clock Tower.

We admire the architecture of a hotel near by. 'Everything in Bhutan is governed by Gross National Happiness (GNH),' says Ugyen. 'GNH has four pillars, and several domains under each. To sanction a project, the builder must seek the approval of the GNH body, which ensures that the pillars and domains have been adhered to.'

Sumita makes a significant contribution to GNH by buying a pair of overpriced wooden bowls from a handicrafts shop.

The Centenary Farmers' Market is a place where the locals get value for their ngultrums. The ground floor stalls are heaped with vegetables from Falakata, Bengal, while the first has vegetables from Bhutan.

Ugyen points out bottles of honey made from an unfamiliar insect, more expensive than the kind the bees make. Shops stack rice cakes that look like tiny pizza bread. 'These are crumbled into boiled millet to make wine,' explains the shopkeeper. In a corner heady with fragrance are sack loads of incense powder with exotic names: Sangzay Natsok, Tung-Kuy and Pangpoi.

Transparent packs of chillies—all shades of red, all equally fiery—occupy pride of place in most stalls.

'I am allergic to chillies, UD,' I tell Ugyen.

'My three-year-old son likes all his dishes with chillies,' he says.

When her son, Bhutan's third king, died of a stroke while visiting Namibia, Queen Phuntsho Choden Wangchuk completed the National Memorial Chorten he had commissioned. On our second day in Thimphu, the gold-spired chorten looks striking against a lapis lazuli sky.

'We will go round the chorten three times,' says Ugyen. Our circumambulation throws up vibrant images: old ladies in pink silk jackets sharing *domas*, senior lamas seated under golden yellow canopies around the courtyard, pigeons fluttering to a shower of grain.

A sprawling hall inside the chorten has gods of Vajrayana Buddhism, and extensive and intricate carved-wood panelling bathed in a golden light. Ugyen points out the statue of Gongti, who had saved Guru Padmasambhava from a fire. We meet Kurukulla, the goddess with the bow and arrow, again.

'Is she a counterpart of Cupid?' I ask Ugyen.

'She was once a very beautiful woman,' Ugyen narrates. 'Many men wanted to marry her and would keep bothering her. So she prayed to Shiva to make her ugly, but also to give her a little power in return. Shiva kept her wish. Kurukulla turned into an ugly woman, but now she had the power to make people fall in love. So, she is similar to Cupid, and the Hindu god Madana.'

But for the purists, most Buddhists accept the similarities in Buddhism and Hinduism, he says. 'We have a god similar to Kali,' continues Ugyen. 'Guru Padmasambhava is said to have arrived in Bhutan wearing a tiger skin around his waist and carrying a trident, much like Shiva. But in Bhutan, he is shown fully clothed. In different geographies, the gods look different, but quintessentially they are the same.'

It is a short drive and then a shorter hike to the Shakyamuni Buddha statue on a hilltop in Kuenselphodrang Nature Park. Cast in bronze and gilded, the 169-ft sculpture was sponsored by some 20 individuals from Singapore, Taiwan, Hong Kong, and China. 'It has been made by Aerosol Corporation of Nanking, China,' Ugyen says, 'and shipped to Bhutan via Calcutta Port Trust.'

Buddha has a serene, compassionate expression. The throne he sits on is a large meditation hall.

Across Bhutan, the serenity of Buddha is complemented by the madness of Lama Drukpa Kunley. One of the legends about the lama goes thus: Kunley had become very drunk at a dinner, when local villagers asked him to perform a miracle. 'First, bring me a cow and a goat to eat,' he said. Since this went against the Buddhist belief of non-violence, the villagers were confused. Nevertheless, they brought Kunley a roasted cow and a goat. Kunley ate up all the meat. Only the bones remained.

Kunley then took the head of the goat and attached it to the skeleton of the cow. He clapped his hands and ordered the carcass to heal itself. To the surprise of the villagers, the skeleton grew into an animal, ran to the meadow and began feeding.

'Imagination is the beginning of creation. You imagine what you desire, you will what you imagine and at last you create what you will': Takin, Motithang Takin Reserve, Thimphu

That was how the takin was born: a hairy, hoofed herbivore with hunched shoulders, a short, thick neck and a large, broad face with small ears, a bulbous nose and backward-facing horns.

We meet the strange animal at the Motithang Takin Reserve. The takins look like a cross between a sheep and a deer. A takin calf may even bellow like a moose. 'The ones you see here had wandered into our towns looking for food,' says Ugyen. 'They had become too used to humans for their own good, and so they were brought to this reserve.'

The friendly animals push their nose through the fence to grab a leafy bunch from Ugyen. An especially large version tries to taste my camera, too. The takins live happily in the reserve with antlered deer.

On the elevated path leading to the reserve, there is a colourful corner where an old lady sits weaving cotton and silk scarves. 'She is my grandmother,' says Jimmy, the youth standing by the loom. Folded scarves in all colours of the rainbow rise in neat columns around the old lady.

'Select one,' Sumita says, 'I will gift it to you.'

I would rather have them all.

It is much more than simple scarves at the Gagyel Lhundhrup Weaving Centre. Young girls sit strapped to the *pangthag*, the back-strap loom, weaving extremely intricate designs for *kiras*.

Art Yantra next door is a gallery of paintings 'with a difference', says Ugyen. And it is. S. Bishwa, the curator, is a painter himself. So is his son, S. Bishwa II, 26. The youth has a very refreshing approach. One of his paintings shows a night sky with the circular pathways of streaking stars as in time-lapse photography. Colourful prayer flags and the silhouette of a bare tree stand in the foreground.

S. Bishwa shows us a painting of the Tiger's Nest in the chiaroscuro style. It is haunting.

The paintings are expensive. S. Bishwa jokes about it: 'There are visitors who ask me, so much for one painting? I tell them, when we go to a doctor, he may charge us ₹ 1,000 and then just feel our pulse. We have to consider the years a painter spends studying and practising his art.'

By now, we are quite impressed by the art and architecture of Bhutan. Trashi Chhoe Dzong—'Fortress of the Glorious Religion'—merely enhances that admiration. Maple trees line the path on one side of the road leading to the *dzong* and roses, the other. Before entering, Ugyen takes a white, raw silk sash with fringes and wraps it around him, from his left shoulder to his right hip. 'To visit a *dzong* or a temple, or to appear before a high-level official, all men must wear this *kabney*,' he says.

It is close of business hours at the *dzong*. A group of young lamas laughing among themselves walks towards the exit. Our cameras and phones are passed through scanners, and we are allowed into a quiet courtyard, empty but for the occasional lama twirling a prayer wheel, the hardworking official last to leave the administrative section, and the uniformed security guard.

At the steps to the *dzong*'s assembly hall, Sumita takes off her branded sneakers. Both Ugyen and I notice at the same instant that the heel of one of them is threatening to break off.

'You will need to buy shoes,' Ugyen declares solemnly. 'These will not take you to the Tiger's Nest.'

A visit to Thimphu's market complex becomes mandatory. Sumita gets off the car and walks to the shoe-store, the wayward heel now making a funny flapping noise. She walks with élan, while Ugyen and I cringe behind her. Some pedestrians turn to look. Once she selects a new pair, Ugyen picks up the used sneakers delicately, carries them to a waste bin outside the store, drops them in. I almost hear his sigh of relief.

Our travel agents Sonam Dendup and Tashi Wangmo have invited us to dine with them at the Bhutan Aroma Restaurant. Ugyen and Tandin drop us at the venue.

Tashi and Sonam have left their cushy UNDP and banking jobs to follow their dream. It has taken them years to break even.

'We have ordered a special dish for you,' Sonam says. 'This is *sikam*, a preparation of pork that is offered to very important guests. You will not get this preparation in too many places in Bhutan.'

We do not eat pork, but given Sonam's enthusiasm, we do not have the heart to refuse. Sumita and I eat a piece each. Sonam polishes off most of the rest.

'Did you get to see our national sport?' Sonam asks.

'Yes, we are staying right opposite the archery ground.'

'Archery is a very superstitious game, you know,' he says. 'I tried it for some time. You may have to walk in a certain direction, believe in numerology. Include archers in your team who are a number nine.'

'Well, if you go by date of birth, I am a number nine,' I say.

'Number nine people always win, somehow,' Sonam replies.

'Would you like some *doma*?' Tashi asks after dinner. 'I can order some.'

Sumita and I would not mind, we say.

The restaurant staff gets the *pani, doma* and *tsuni*—betel leaf, areca nut and slaked lime—in a transparent zip pouch. Tashi folds her legs under her and goes about making the *khamto*, or the quid.

'You know, there was a BBC report about *doma* being a killer addiction in Nigeria,' Sonam tells us with a cheeky smile.

'But not in Bhutan, right?' retorts Tashi.

'We have too little population to make that kind of news, *nah*?' Sonam continues, 'A report like that on Bhutan will probably say only 1,00,000 people died, but that may mean all of Thimphu's population!'

We chew on the *doma-pani*, nevertheless. The raw areca nut makes Sumita flush. Sonam has a *doma-pani*, too. He tells us the legend behind this Bhutanese addiction.

'Before Buddhism came to Bhutan, people followed the Bon religion. No crops grew in Bhutan, not even potatoes—these were first brought to us by a British envoy. So, the inhabitants were carnivores. When Guru Padmasambhava came to Bhutan, he said, "Do not eat animals. Eat *doma-pani* instead. *Doma* or areca nut is like bones, *pani* or the betel leaf is like flesh, and when you chew these, your saliva will be red like blood." That way, the people felt they were eating animal flesh.'

Tashi and Sonam drop us at our hotel, and wish us a happy journey. Tashi also suggests a visit to the newly-opened Postal Museum at Thimphu. The next day, we pay a visit.

Before 1955, official letters would be delivered by long-distance runners, known as *garps*. A traditional poem called *lozey* narrates the story of Garp Lungi Khorlo. He is said to have run from Trongsa to Punakha—roughly 130 kilometres apart—before lunch, and run back to Trongsa the same afternoon! People believed that he may have acquired the power to ride the wind.

Was he a *lun-gom-pa*, then?

'Do you know how Garp Lungi Khorlo died?' Ugyen says. 'One day, he saw a demoness washing something in a river. When he went closer, he realised that she was actually washing his intestines. He managed to deliver his message that day, and then dropped dead.'

Bhutan introduced postage stamps in 1962. In 1969, it became a member of the Universal Postal Union (UPU), the body of the United Nations concerned with postal affairs.

Letters and stamps of Bhutan have been known for their uniqueness. In the early days, confidential letters would be known by different names: *meyig*, or fire letter, *chuyig*, or water letter, and *lungyig*, or wind letter: their text would be readable only when they were burnt, dipped in water, or exposed to wind currents.

On April 15, 1973, Bhutan issued the 'Phonograph Records self-adhesive set' of stamps. These could be played at 33RPM on any record player to offer the listener a flavour of Bhutanese music, language and history.

Probably the world's smallest vinyl records that can still be played with a stylus, these collectibles are available online.

At jaw-dropping prices.

While these audio stamps were created by a foreigner, Bhutan is known for its *zorig chusum*: 13 traditional arts and crafts. Unfortunately for us, the National Institute for Zorig Chusum is closed to mourn the death of a member.

Ugyen takes us to the National Library instead. We are drawn to:

An exquisite wooden 'bowl of friendship' with paintings by Gangadhar Maharana from Odisha.

A photograph of Her Majesty Ashi Kesang Choeden Wangchuk in pigtails, riding a horse to her wedding in Paro Dzong. An Oxford alumnus, she is the grandmother of the Fifth King.

One five feet by seven feet book called *Bhutan: A Visual Odyssey Across the Last Himalayan Kingdom*, which, at 133 pounds had made it to the Guinness World Records as the world's largest published book. A copy of this book is a part of the Book Arts Collections at the University of Washington.

Teams from MIT and Friendly Planet went on four extensive expeditions across Bhutan—they flew by helicopters, rode ponies, trekked with packhorses and yaks—and took over 40,000 photographs. The photos in the book are from those journeys.

The book we see in its glass showcase has been printed with a gallon of ink, on a roll of paper that was longer than a football field.

'Pages are turned once a month,' says Ugyen.

Author Michael Hawley, a scientist at the MIT, has said it is not a book to curl up with at bedtime, 'unless you plan to sleep on it'.

PUNAKHA

'How long will it take us to drive to Dochu La, UD? We need to start early, for the best mountain views.'

'We will start at nine,' Ugyen tells me. 'If you arrive early, there will be fog.'

Dochu La, a pass at 10,171 feet, offers a panoramic expanse of the snow-swathed Himalayan ranges. The Druk Wangyel Café at the pass even offers a buffet breakfast at dawn for those arriving to watch the day break over the Greater Himalayan ranges.

A signboard put up near the cafeteria prominently displays the names of peaks and their somewhat arguable heights: Masang Gang (23,484 ft), Tsenda Gang (22,834 ft), Teri Gang (23,163 ft), Jejekangphu Gang (23,484 ft), Kangphu Gang (23,524 ft), Zongophu Gang (23,163 ft), and finally Gangkhar Puensum, the highest peak in Bhutan at 24,596 feet.

All we see at 10:00 am are snow-white clouds that have risen from the valley and now frame the horizon.

From all our years spent watching daybreak over the Himalayas across states, the movement of winds, and the rising of clouds, we are certain there was a majestic view at dawn.

It is what we yearn for: a blessed view of the mass and majesty of the Himalayan ranges. It is what makes the freezing cold, the sleepless nights, the altitude, and our hardships, not to speak of the expenses, so worth it.

Ugyen will never understand.

On an oval-shaped slope, the golden conical roofs of the 108 Druk Wangyal Chortens gleam in the morning sunlight. Commissioned by the eldest Queen Mother, Her Majesty Ashi Dorji Wangmo Wangchuk, these chortens honour the lives lost in the Fourth King's successful battle to flush out Assamese militants from their camps in southern Bhutan.

Operation All Clear was the first operation ever conducted by the Royal Bhutan Army.

Pines on the adjoining hill are draped in prayer flags, and the wind takes up the prayer from them and whispers it among the leaves. But for the storm of frustration in my mind, it is a serene place. The visitors—and there are many—walk among the chortens talking in low tones and posing for photographs.

On the other side of the wide, smooth road, a paved uphill path and a flight of steps lead up to Druk Wangyal Lhakhang. This is probably the only monastery where the murals tell the story of Bhutan's past and present. We discover paintings of: the Fourth King with his four wives; the Fourth King again, armed and in Army fatigues leading his soldiers against the Assamese insurgents; a Druk Air plane; a lama wielding a laptop.

Behind the *lhakhang*, the glass covered-enclosure holding a powerful telescope is abandoned for the day. A lone hoopoe watches us from the brick-lined edge of the lawn, unafraid.

Ugyen suggests we have our tea break a half hour down the road to Punakha, at the Menchuna Restaurant. It has a large dining hall, the walls covered with *thangka*s, and an adjoining shop full of souvenirs with prohibitive prices.

We take some of the buttery cream crackers to the black and the buff dogs snoozing outdoors. Too lazy to help themselves, the dogs wait for us to crumble the biscuits into smaller chunks and feed them. A lot of finger licking and bushy tail wagging follow. Given a chance, the dogs are now eager to join us in the Hyundai Sante Fe.

The roads are being turned into two-lane highways, a painful process for drivers negotiating the bumps.

Tandin does not mind the bumps, he minds the dust.

Cypress, hemlock and fir rise from the roadside slopes. On the distant hills lie the Talo village, the Nalanda Monastic School, the Nepali-style chorten of the Sangchen Dorji Lhendrub Choling Nunnery.

Almost every village in Bhutan has electricity and a road leading to it.

'Would you like to listen to some Bhutanese music?' Ugyen asks.

'Yes, of course, UD. Please play some for us.'

Young, melodious voices of Singe Dorji and Dawa Norbu sing to us of love:

'I cannot think of anyone but you...'

'They are only 11 and 12 years old,' says Ugyen.

'Eleven-year-olds sing love songs in Bhutan? You really begin early!' says Sumita.

The next song has a beautiful guitar prelude. 'That is the *dranyen*,' says Ugyen.

My favourite is the song that goes:

Lamo rere gyetse so ya
Lha dhar la rere char so
Tshering le so
Ami labtsa gyelmo so ya...
Lha dhar la zheba jonsho...
Tshering le so...
Chhumo rere gyetse so ya...
Chhu dhar la rere
Char so tshering le so...
Ami tsomen gyelmo so ya...
Chhu dhar la zheba jonsho...
Tshering le so...

'This tune is haunting, UD! What do the lyrics mean?'

Ugyen, humming along: '*Every time, while crossing a mountain, plant a prayer flag/Be blessed with long life.... Every time, while crossing a river, plant a prayer flag/Be blessed with long life....*'

Our first view of Punakha has the Puna Tsang Chhu flowing among golden yellow fields far below the Metshina-Punakha road and towards the yellow-roofed Chimi Lhakhang perched on a distant hillock. In the foreground, a cluster of red-roofed houses stand at the edge of a road now crammed with parked cars.

A short, downward drive and we are at the porch of the Rinchenling Cafeteria, Sopsokha village.

Time for lunch.

Punakha, at 3,937 feet, is sunny, warm. Inside the cafeteria, the whirr of fan blades blends with the tinkling of cutlery and the low-toned conversation of guests helping themselves to the buffet spread. Glass windowpanes offer a view of the entire village. Just outside the dining hall, a curio counter is loaded with wooden phalluses, *thangka*s and maroon wooden masks of the *atsara* or the clown. I am drawn to the masks and deflected: they come with a Nu 2000 tag.

The 20-minute trail from Sopsokha to Chimi Lhakhang is through the fields of the tiny hamlets Yoaka and Pana, and up a hill, winding past:

A young farmer ploughing his land with a motor-driven, two-wheel cart that offers more smoke than power.

Neat round silos topped with slender, ramrod-stiff tufts.

Prayer wheels in chorten-shaped alcoves watched over by tall flags and dwarf bamboo stalks.

A flock of pigeons constantly practising flying and landing skills.

The sepia ruins of a roofless house with empty window frames—silhouettes of boughs a haunting pattern on its fractured walls.

Village houses with humongous phalluses painted on the walls. Some have eyes; others are too realistic for the average visitor's comfort: down to the hairy details and the semen spouting.

A welcome sign shaped like a phallus.

Shops named Fertility Handicraft and Phallus Handicrafts.

I hear an American gentleman walking ahead of us tell his companion: 'I don't even want to look at a penis any more.'

Bhutan's organic obsession traces its origin to the Tibetan mendicant and teacher Drukpa Kunley (born: 1455), fondly called the Divine Madman. A lover of wine, women and song, Kunley used ribald humour and shocking diatribes to shake up prudish Buddhist institutions and hypocritical religious leaders.

And yes, he used his 'flaming thunderbolt of wisdom' both to subdue demons and to bless virgins.

On the lawns of Chimi Lhakhang, a fertility temple frequented by childless women, a colossal bodhi tree offers the tired walkers shade. It has grown from a branch of the peepal at Bodh Gaya. Dochula Dom, the demoness killed by Drukpa Kunley at Dochu La, lies buried in a tomb near it.

'The spirit of the demoness was placed in another body,' Ugyen says, 'and she was directed never to harm anyone again, only protect. Now she, too, is worshipped at the same sanctum as Drukpa Kunley.'

Inside Chimi Lhakhang, the statue of Dochula Dom stands next to the main altar. She has been offered a lot of trinkets: hair clips, brooches, necklaces. Drukpa Kunley occupies the centre of the sanctum, with Sachi, his dog, the Zhabdrung, Shakyamuni and Chenrezig. There is also a statue of Kunley's cousin who built this *lhakhang* on the hill—'shaped like the breast of a woman' was how Drukpa Kunley saw it—in 1499.

A young lama offers us holy water from a pot with a spout. Then he takes an iron archery set and a wood-and-ivory phallus—the 'flaming thunderbolt'—and taps us smartly on the head.

Though we did not ask for it, he has just given us a *wang*: his blessing.

European tourists have begun to believe in and seek such fertility blessings. Childless couples have the option to pick up bamboo slivers suggesting names for their baby, though the choice is somewhat restricted: Chimi, or Kunley.

If I ever meet a Chimi Badcock or a Kunley Dwight, I will know the reason for his being.

The path down the hill and back to the car has long strings of tiny prayer flags tied to bamboo posts. These small rectangular flags come in five colours: blue, white, red, yellow and green, with one word from the prayer '*Om Mani Pad Me Hung*' inscribed on each flag.

Ugyen tells us about the realms of samsara the Buddhists believe in.

'The first realm,' he says, 'is heaven, where the gods live. The colour signifying it is white. The second is for the titans or the asuras, who are always fighting. The colour: blue. The third realm belongs to humans, and the colour denoting it is yellow. The Buddha born in this realm is golden, and this is why gold is a precious metal in our times. The fourth realm is for the animals, the colour is green. The fifth is for the pretas or the spirits, and this is Hell. The colour is black.

'Every time we chant *Om Mani Padme Hung*, the prayer frees one spirit from Hell.'

I read later that these small rectangles of colour tied to the same string are called *lung ta*, or 'wind horse' flags, while the long vertical ones on bamboo posts are *dar chor*: *dar*, in Tibetan means 'to increase longevity, fortune, health and wealth' for *cho*, 'all sentient beings'.

I find that the five colours stand for the five elements and Five Pure Lights: blue for the sky or space; white, the air/wind; red, for fire; green, for water; and yellow, the earth. It is a belief in traditional Tibetan medicine that health and harmony are attained through a balance of the five elements.

The six syllables Om Mani Padme Hung, mean that by following a path which blends method with wisdom, one can transform one's impure body, speech, and mind into the pure exalted body, speech, and mind of a Buddha. A huge prayer wheel and the Bhutanese national flag welcome us to Meri Puensum Resort, even as the sun sets over a deep teal Puna Tsang Chhu and the golden rice fields that embrace its curves.

Morning arrives lightly, draped in a diaphanous veil of mist. Dew drops from the pines and the wooden chairs on our veranda are

'May your trails be crooked, winding, lonesome, dangerous, leading to the most amazing view': Tourist near Khamsum Yulley Namgyal Chorten, Punakha

clammy to the touch. We idle a while on the hotel portico, writing a couple of emails. Then Ugyen and Tandin arrive.

'Today, we hike to the Khamsum Yulley Namgyal Chorten,' Ugyen tells us. 'Tandin will drive us to the hiking point first.'

In the car, Ugyen tells us of a boy from Gasa and a girl from Galam who had fallen in love: much in the manner of Romeo and Juliet. 'When the girl's father got to know of their affair, he thrashed his daughter to death. While she was being cremated, the boy came looking for her to that very spot. When he heard whose body it was, he dropped dead, and was cremated on the same funeral pyre.'

'When did this happen, UD?'

'One hundred years ago,' he says. Then, with perfect timing: 'This is the Galam village, and that house you see there is the house of the girl.'

It is empty, as fragmented as the couple's fate.

'There are plans to turn it into a lovers' museum,' says Ugyen.

Empty blue rafts, men lolling next to life-jackets, helmets and paddles spread out on plastic sheets lead us to a suspension bridge. On its other side, a narrow mud track lopes through yellow paddy fields, past a gurgling rivulet, ponies, cattle and friendly local mongrels and then climbs smartly up the length of an entire pine-covered hill, until every tourist on it is dropping off by the sides, apparently to take photographs, but actually for a breather.

'It is good that we are doing this trek at a relatively lower elevation,' says an elderly tourist to his lady companion, 'it is preparing us for the climb to Tiger's Nest.'

A Golden Buddha sits in meditation in the alcove at the top of the 100-feet tall, three-storeyed chorten. He holds a glass bowl, said to contain medicines, in his hand. 'This statue was being carried from Punakha Dzong to someplace else,' says Ugyen. 'When the bearers reached this point, the statue spoke up and said that it wished to remain here.'

I am not surprised. With all of Punakha Valley laid out below, and the snow ranges of Gasa framing the sky on a clear dawn, even a Buddha might feel an attachment to the place.

Thanks to Ugyen's timings, we will never see such a dawn, but that is a different matter altogether.

Sweaty tourists lean against the smaller white chortens bordering the green lawns. Under a shady banyan tree, a white Buddha statue gleams with a sliver of the winter sunlight. The dew-drenched grass feels cool and comforting to our bare feet.

Sumita has started to keep track of the number of times we have had to take off our footwear on this journey. With some reluctance, the tired soul puts on her sneakers and we begin the climb downhill.

The soul of his mother had called out to Ngagi Rinchen of Chittagong, then a part of India. He dreamed that his mother was trapped in a boulder 4.5 kilometres from Punakha. When he came to the place of his dream, he did find a huge boulder. But the old woman who owned the land refused to let him break the boulder. So Ngagi Rinchen worked for the lady for a while, to pay her for the favour. Finally, when he split the boulder open, a frog jumped out. He killed the frog and released his mother's spirit.

Dho Jhaga Lama Lhakhang, a small temple on our way to Punakha Dzong, marks the spot. *Dho* means a boulder, and *jhaga,* a land with many people: India.

'This is the boulder,' Ugyen points out.

A vertical crack runs through the huge mass.

I make Tandin pose next to the stone. His *gho* now folded clumsily along the waist of his jeans, he smiles widely for the camera.

It is a warm autumn day. Blue rafts are out on the Pho Chhu. Ugyen puts on his dark glasses and takes Sumita and me walking past the cremation ground. He walks regally, his hands held behind his back.

'If you spend the night here, you will be able to see the goddess of all cremation grounds in the world,' Ugyen tells me, 'Would you like to?'

I do not swallow the bait. 'The Khamsum Chorten has a painted image of her, right?' I reply. 'So I do know what she looks like.'

We loiter instead on the suspension bridge over the Pho Chhu—at 300 feet the longest suspension bridge in Bhutan—watching lamas wash their clothes in the river far below. Every bit of their apparel is a deep red, even the boxers.

The jacarandas on its lawns may not be in lilac bloom, but the 'Palace of Great Happiness' is seen at its best from a distance as it towers majestically at the confluence of Pho Chhu and Mo Chhu (*Pho*: male, *Mo*: female). This is the Pungthang Dechen Phodrang or the Punakha Dzong, the second *dzong* built in Bhutan, and the seat of government till the mid-50s.

We enter the *dzong* through steep, almost vertical wooden stairs. These were designed so that they could be pulled up if needed. The heavy wooden door at the head of the staircase is still closed at night.

Ugyen takes us to a high-ceilinged hall held up by ornate brass pillars. 'This is the first ceremonial lounge, the one opposite is

'It is good people who make good places': Driver Tandin and guide Ugyen Drukpa with Punakha Dzong as their backdrop

ceremonial lounge number two, and there is a third in Thimphu. Royal weddings and other ceremonies take place in these halls,' he says.

I know that in one of these halls, John Claude White had presented Ugyen Wangchuck, later the first king of Bhutan, with the Order of Knight Commander of the Indian Empire. That was in 1905. In 2011, the *dzong* hosted the wedding of the Fifth King Jigme Khesar Namgyel Wangchuck to Jetsun Pema.

In the *kuenrey* or the assembly hall, Ugyen points out the throne of Je Khenpo, the religious head of the state, and statues of the previous 69 Je Khenpos. Twelve episodes from Buddha's life play out across the walls. Statues of Guru Rinpoche, his consorts the Nepali and Tibetan princesses Yeshe and Mandarava, the Zhabdrung, past, present and future Buddhas and Sariputra look down upon the visitors. A foot-high jade statue of Buddha bejewelled with semi-precious stones sits on a window sill. It is a gift from Thailand.

There are 21 temples in the *dzong*, and administrative offices that function five days a week. They are currently closed for the Fourth King's birthday celebrations.

Steep wooden stairs lead up to the *utse,* the central tower of the *dzong*. Ugyen makes Sumita and me sit down at their base so he can take a photograph.

It is past 2:30 in the afternoon, and the light falling on our faces is gentle.

The rumbling within our stomachs is anything but.

'Would you like to taste typical Bhutanese food?' Ugyen had asked us in the morning. He had spoken to someone over the phone to order lunch.

At 3:00 pm Tandin finally drives us to Tashi Yarphel for lunch. Lhaden Denma the owner is a young lady elegant in a grey silk *kira.* She has studied at IIM, Delhi, stayed as a paying guest in Navi Mumbai with a very loving lady, travelled to Goa and Chandigarh for training, and to Howrah's West Bank Hospital for a surgery.

She feels a strange connect with Indians, she says. 'I have received a lot of love from Indians, in every Indian city. My mother says I am very lucky.'

Lhaden serves us a preparation of eggs, chillies and cheese, a chicken dish, boiled vegetables, and *ezzy:* a pickle that blends onions, tomatoes and chillies.

This is the best meal we have had in Bhutan so far. I make Ugyen promise to bring us back here for dinner.

It lives up to our expectations.

Morning finds us at the Sangchen Dorji Lhendrub Choling Nunnery. Young nuns—children, really—in red robes and shaven heads sit on the green lawn, their scriptures on little wooden stools before them, their backs to the sun. Teenage nuns run up the steps to the chorten that resembles Boudhanath of Nepal, their arms around one another's shoulders, laughing. At the sight of visitors, they freeze in their tracks a moment, bend their heads and walk past hurriedly, dragging their feet in rubber slippers. When they are past us, they laugh again.

Around the chorten, there are black statues of 84 Yogis or Mahasiddhas, including one of Nagarjuna from Hyderabad.

'There are only eight types of chortens,' says Ugyen, 'they depict eight actions of Buddha. This one stands for the act of teaching.'

In the sanctum, there are statues of the present Buddha, Guru Rinpoche, Bodhisattva Avalokiteśvara or Chenrezig with his 11 heads, 1,000 eyes and 1,000 hands. 'He could have been a Buddha,' says Ugyen, 'but he chose instead to help other sentient beings.'

'Is that Zangto Pelri at Bodhisattva's feet?' I ask him.

'Yes, that is the palace of Guru Rinpoche, on Mount Meru,' he replies, 'which we now know as Mount Kailash.'

Zangto Pelri, Ugyen narrates, is a translucent palace made by Vishwakarma. 'When Rinpoche asked Vishwakarma to build it, Vishwakarma said that he needed to be shown how. So Rinpoche put Vishwakarma to sleep for three hours.

'In each hour, Vishwakarma dreamed of each floor. When he woke up, he built the palace. The top floor was for the Red Buddha, who is beyond the Thousand Buddha clan. The middle floor is for Chendebji or Bodhisattva. The ground floor is for Guru Rinpoche: a hub of activity where preachers are assigned their roles on earth.'

'I have a question,' Sumita says.

'Yes, please ask,' Ugyen replies eagerly.

'Before we drive to Phobjhika, could we drop in at Tashi Yarphel for some tea?'

PHOBJHIKA

'Once upon a time,' begins Ugyen in his usual measured tone. Even though I do not remove my eyes from the viewfinder of my camera, I prick up my ears for yet another story.

With a guide like Ugyen around, the information overload on my pea-sized brain has been tremendous. When we came into Bhutan we knew of the one Buddha and his life. Within days, the number of Buddhas has gone up: first to eight, then to a thousand, then as many as there are grains of sand. We are still trying to catch up with their names, and figuring out the subtle differences between an emanation and an incarnation.

But this time, it is not a story about the Buddhas.

'Once upon a time,' says Ugyen, 'there was a snake and a boar. "Let us race to the Gangteng Monastery," said the snake, "and see which of us wins." "All right," said the boar, "but what does the winner get out of it?" "If I win, the people of Phobjhika will grow rice on their land," said the snake. "If *you* reach the monastery first, they will grow potatoes."

'Thanks to its natural gait, the snake had to meander along the way, and so the boar won the race. That is why potatoes are grown in the Phobjhika Valley. It is very difficult to grow rice here,' Ugyen continues. 'Those rivers that you see through your viewfinder are Nakay Chhu (black water) and Gay Chhu (white water), representing the snake and the boar,' he finishes with a flourishing sweep of his hand.

In the watered-down light of dusk, both the rivers are thin bands of silver streaking across a vast marshland. At 9,600 ft, Phobjhika in

Wangdue district is a bowl-contoured glacial valley on the western slopes of the Black Mountain Range. It borders the Jigme Singye Wangchuk National Park, home to muntjacs (barking deer), wild boars, sambars, Himalayan black bears, leopards and red foxes. Phobjhika is the largest of all wetlands in Bhutan.

And the most significant.

Significant, for every winter, this valley nestled in the Lesser Himalayas turns into the nesting grounds of the globally-endangered *Grus nigricollis*. Or, in the common tourist's language, black-necked cranes. The locals call them thrung thrung karmo.

Early November, the cranes migrate from the Qinghai-Tibet plateau and Siberia to Phobjhika, Gyetsa and Bomdeling in eastern Bhutan.

Juvenile cranes are brownish, the adults white. They do not destroy crops, and co-exist happily with cattle and other birds. The cranes choose their partners for life through a unique mating dance. Their arrival is considered a good omen, especially since each flock of cranes circles over the Gangteng Monastery before settling amid the marshlands. They circle the monastery once more before leaving the valley in March.

For their safety, all electric cables in Phobjhika are laid underground.

The Royal Society for Protection of Nature (RSPN) has a Black-Necked Crane Visitor Centre. This is our first halt at Phobjhika.

'November 6: the first batch of cranes has arrived!' says the note scrawled on a white board close to the entrance. The count at present is 41. More than 500 cranes had visited the year before.

Another board offers a crude sketch of the five shallow ponds that are a favourite with the birds. These also have hidden cameras around them. Inhabitants and visitors are meant to give a wide berth to these nesting areas.

A very wide berth, indeed.

On the Wings of a Prayer, an informative documentary by Dasho Paljor Dorji narrates how the cranes are a part of Bhutan's folklore and songs. The victory dance of Bhutanese archers mimics the dance of the cranes.

The centre's powerful telescopes magnify some 20 birds foraging right then on the marshlands. But the cranes are too far away, and it is impossible to make out their features in the constantly bobbing black-and-white bodies. They are polishing off fallen grain, tubers and insects like there is no tomorrow.

For the 4,700 residents of Phobjhika, however, 'tomorrow' is a big day. It is November 11, the day of the Black-Necked Crane Annual Festival.

Copies of the programme details have been left in our rooms at the Wangchuk Lodge: a two-storeyed wooden structure that overlooks the valley. I am drawn to an event: 'Launch of Commemorative Black-necked Crane and White-bellied Heron stamps by Dr Kinley Tenzin, Executive Director, Dr George Archibald, Co-Founder, International Crane Foundation (ICF, USA), RSPN and Chairperson, GPEMC.'

We do not plan to arrive at the monastery in time for the launch, but I make a mental note to pick up the first day covers from the post office in Thimphu on our return journey.

Night falls over the wide open valley. It is an extremely cold night, and we are really glad about the presence of the geyser, the electric blankets on the bed.

Just before dinner, we hear a loud bang. The light goes off, a lot of smoke suddenly seeps in through the gap under the door.

Sumita digs out our torch. I open the door and run out to the wooden corridor to check. Amid the dense smoke, there are more bursts, like fireworks, and they seem to be going off right under the wooden ladder that leads down to the ground floor.

It is, incidentally, our only exit.

I come back in, shut the door. Despite the biting cold, I throw open our first floor window, consider walking out onto the slated, sloping roof with Sumita. Decide against it: the ground is too far below.

For a long while, we wait in the room. No one comes up to check. When the smoke subsides, we hear voices. One of them is Ugyen's. I call out to him.

'The transformer burned down,' he says. 'There was a surge of electricity just before that, and it led to a short circuit. The entire meter box under the ladder is gutted.'

We go down to the dining hall and have a candle-lit dinner with: many diners; one large hall table; two small candles; a group of Europeans having their drink around the *bukhari*, the wood-stove fire. They have heard nothing, they are calm.

Ugyen and Tandin sit round the kitchen *bukhari* with the other drivers and guides and have their drink. They are calm, too.

Sumita and I decide to go to bed fully clothed: Himachali woollen socks, thermal wear, pullover, down jacket, woollen cap. The works. Sounds like we could survive Antarctica.

It is still a very cold, very dark night.

Dawn breaks with the shrill cry of the cranes, out before the sun. I carry my tripod and camera down the steep, precariously vertical ladder—it is a great balancing feat without the use of my hands—and reach the ground floor balcony behind the kitchen.

A Bhutanese lady with bobbed and dyed hair talks agitatedly with Ugyen: '...and I had such high blood pressure, and no one from the family around. Then someone suggested Artemisia. You know, I always thought it was good for skin rashes (*waves her palms around the nether zones*) and all. But lowering blood pressure? I had no idea... it worked!'

Ugyen sees me approach. 'Meet the owner of this lodge,' he says, pointing to the lady. 'She stays in Thimphu.'

'Aren't you so happy to see these birds?' the lady turns to me, 'Isn't this a different world altogether? I am a Bhutanese, but I had no idea how wonderful Phobjhika was!'

She has no idea. About a lot of things.

Fire safety and emergency exits, for instance.

True to its name, the 17th century Gangteng Sa-Ngag Choeling Monastery (*gang teng*: hill top) sits atop a hill at 9,840 feet, representing the Tibetan style of architecture. It is the largest Nyingmapa monastery in Bhutan, founded in 1613 by Gyalse Pema Thinley, the grandson of

Happy feet: Children dance as cranes, Gangtey Monastery, Phobjhika

tertön Pema Lingpa. A *tertön* is someone who has discovered hidden Buddhist treasures.

The cold and dimly lit interiors of the monastery hold seven large Buddha statues in a row on the altar, and eight more standing Buddhas along the side walls, four on either side.

One thousand little statues of Buddha sit in the lotus pose before the altar. A throne meant for the current His Highness Gangtey Trulku (ninth reincarnation of Pema Lingpa) occupies a prominent slot. The walls have intricate paintings of Kali and Tara, deities of Vajrayana Buddhism. There is one of the Buddha and the first five monks who were with him during his search for enlightenment.

Ugyen has a story, of course: 'One day, while Buddha and the five monks were all meditating, there was a very heavy shower. The monks ran away. They returned when the rain had stopped and found Buddha sitting on a lotus held by a coiled snake. That's very much like your Vishnu, isn't it?' he asks. As an afterthought, he adds that all religions borrow from one another. 'The Christian idea of confession was actually adopted from Buddhism,' says Ugyen.

On the monastery courtyard, locals have turned out in their best, and schoolchildren are taking part in a 'Balloon Blasting' competition. Every little boy has a balloon tied to each foot. They have to stomp on and burst everyone else's balloons; all the while keeping theirs untouched. The boy who manages to keep his balloons intact till the end, wins.

It is a pitched battle, with: a whole lot of high-pitched yells; merry interruptions from furry dogs; totally irrelevant instructions from the *atsaras* or clowns in red masks.

A series of dances follow. Adults as well as schoolchildren dance in colourful costumes and masks.

The most significant of these dances is the Black-necked Crane Dance—'Ngachey Thrung Thrung Detshu'. Children from Bayta Primary School have dressed up like cranes. Their dance steps imitate crane movements. If this is not the best way to teach conservation to the next generation, we do not know of a better one.

There is a short, untimely shower, but the show must go on. Fortified with handfuls of roasted rice sprinkled over hot butter tea, the Gangteng Shedra dancers begin the Drametse Nga Chham. *Shedra*—the Tibetan word for a place of teaching—refers to the educational programme in monasteries and nunneries.

The dancers wear yellow skirts and animal masks, and beat with bent drumsticks on what I think is the *nga chen* drum, all the while twirling and leaping into the air. They represent Guru Rinpoche's entourage.

The orchestra includes cymbals, trumpets and drums. There is the *bang nga*, a large cylindrical drum, the *lag nga*, a small, hand-held, circular, flat drum, and of course, the *nga chen*.

In 2005, UNESCO proclaimed Drametse Nga Chham as a masterpiece of the oral and intangible cultural heritage of humanity.

Someone has dropped an empty potato chips packet on the ground. An *atsara* insists that a European photographer pick it up. The gentleman smiles, does not oblige. 'Move to the back,' the *atsara* tells us tourists next, 'you are obstructing the view for the others.'

Bhutanese believe that *thong droe*, liberation through watching, is one of the six ways of liberation. If watching the masked dances will unfetter the people of Gangtey, we would rather not be in their way.

Ugyen suggests we take a lunch break.

Buffet lunch has been arranged for us at Hotel Ugyen Choling, a short walk from the monastery. In a small, crowded dining hall where many of the travel agents have brought their guests, we share a four-seater table with Stephan Barthelmess from Brussels and Laurence, his wife. Tashi and Sonam are their travel agents, too. A young guide accompanies the couple. Stephan is German, Laurence French-Belgian. We hit it off instantly.

Stephan has spent some time at the Ananda Spa in Uttarakhand. He has not got over the experience, yet. He takes out his mobile phone to show us a photograph: a bone-china dinner plate with a molecule of food on it. The low-fat, low-calorie molecule was a part of the spa's wellness cuisine.

'This is all they would give me for dinner,' he says, pouting.

'Come on, it did you good,' Laurence gives him an indulgent but disapproving look.

'It has been plated well, though,' I tell Stephan, laughing. 'Looks good, doesn't it?'

The Barthelmess couple returns to the monastery after lunch. Ugyen takes us on the Gangteng Nature Trail.

We walk past thickets of dwarf bamboo, the wood cabins of Semchubara village, and gurgling rivulets. Fallen pine needles with their smooth, round shapes lay an auburn, if slippery, carpet underfoot. The monotony of tall pines covered in a veil of lichen is broken by rhododendrons, birch, maple, fir and the occasional hemlock.

On the surrounding slopes, farmers grow potatoes and turnips. Potatoes are the region's primary cash crop and one of Bhutan's important exports to India, and the fields growing them offer a russet contrast to the rich green of the hills. A few cranes sit by the marshes in the distance, and a couple of Himalayan wagtails sun themselves on a makeshift wooden bridge.

The valley will be snowbound soon. In December and January, many of its residents and monks will shift to their winter homes in Wangdue Phodrang. The cranes will stay on, braving the cold blizzards to nest with their lifelong mates.

Even through my down jacket, the cold wind sends its long finger down my spine. We, too, are braving the cold. We have survived the serious fireworks from the electrical short-circuit, lived without the geyser, the room bulb, the electric kettle and the electric blankets for all of our 48 hours in the valley.

Are these 41 cranes, these black-and-white dots still bobbing up and down in the distant marshes and occasionally leaping gracefully in the air worth it?

As a photography enthusiast, I would probably say, no.

As a nature lover, it simply uplifts my soul to know that in a world exploding with humans, there is at least one valley where a few hundred birds can still dance with abandon.

BUMTHANG

It is a long and dusty 200-odd kilometres from Phobjhika to Bumthang, a seven-hour drive that we had wished to avoid.

'Why are we going to Bumthang, UD? Aren't we supposed to halt overnight at Trongsa, first?' Sumita asks Ugyen.

'Yes, you were to stay at Trongsa,' replies the ever-unperturbed Ugyen. 'We had your room booked at Yangkhil Resort. But a programme has been organised there. So they cannot accommodate you tonight. We are putting you up at Jakar Village Lodge in Bumthang. I have spoken to them, they have no problem.'

Such changes in itinerary are normal in Bhutan, adds Ugyen. 'One of our royals may wish to take a flight with his retinue, and a lot of tourists may have to be dropped from that flight. Sometimes, tourists will not even be informed in advance, for even the airlines may not know about the royal plan well enough in advance.'

That is food for thought. Could we be dropped from our return flight? I mull that a while, until Pele La jerks me out of my brooding.

For at Pele La (10,830 ft), we have our first ever sight of an entire snow-covered range of Bhutan. Mount Jomolhari, Jichu Drakye and Tserim Gang stand out against a deep azure sky.

Tandin parks the car. 'That's a hemlock,' he says, pointing to a giant tree. I go closer for a look. When I return to the team, Tandin is busy photographing Sumita and Ugyen against the pristine peaks.

Both Ugyen and Tandin are in love with my DSLR, though Ugyen hogs it most of the time.

We are now into central Bhutan.

From Pele La, large trees graciously give way to the dwarf bamboo, a favourite with yaks. We pass conifer forests, fenced farms and the clustered houses of Rukubji village. Rivers flow along the valley to our right: the Nikka Chhu, then the Nyala Chhu, and soon after they meet, we are at the Chendebji village.

The Chendebji Chorten or the Chorten Charo Kasho at the confluence is an excuse to get off the car, take a couple of shots and stretch a stiff leg.

The legend goes that Lama Shida from Tibet who built this chorten in the 19th century—on the remains of an evil spirit, of course—had been visiting Swayambhunath Stupa in Nepal. He liked the structure of Swayambhunath, and crafted a model of it on a carrot. But by the time he travelled to this spot in Bhutan, the carrot had dried up and shrunk in size. That is why the Chendebji Chorten happens to be much smaller than Swayambhunath.

Near the white walls of the chorten I discover a frisky, month-old pup with a short, thick rope knotted around his neck. 'We need to remove this rope,' says Ugyen, and picks up the puppy. The pup looks deep into Ugyen's eyes, and promptly places his paw on the guide's lips.

It is the first time I have seen Ugyen flinch.

The pup senses that such intimacy is not welcome, removes his paw, and looks apologetically at Ugyen. Ugyen recovers; smiles. That is when I take the pup into my arms.

I realise why Ugyen was flinching: it is the dirtiest, most stinky pup I have ever met, and that is saying something, for I have met hundreds. I guess it even smells of amniotic fluid.

And then, quite without notice, he decides to lick my lips.

When Sumita cradles him—it is very brave of her to do so—she makes sure he does not face her. After we have put him down, he runs to a little village girl who has appeared out of nowhere, and tails her devotedly. Going by the volume of dust on her bare limbs, the petite mistress does not believe in baths: for herself, or her pet.

'Love is a four-legged word': Guide Ugyen Drukpa meets a stray pup

Dust from the freshly gouged mountain sides fills the air on our journey, and it is so much the worse if we happen to have another car or truck ahead. The roads are being widened. Trees have been lopped off from the slopes.

Mountain bikers do not seem to mind the dust, doggedly pedalling on their way. I notice: exposed limbs a sunburnt, frightening pink; the back of a biker's tee saying 'Mid-Air Crisis' and 'Newscastle Mountain Bike Club'; a pair of biker shorts with 'Tradewind Cycling Team' and 'Hawaii' printed down the side of a leg.

Ugyen watches me take their photographs. 'These bikers will probably go all the way to eastern Bhutan,' he says.

He points to the distant mountain ranges on our right, 'Those are the Black Mountains. Those have not been explored; no one knows what is up there. There may be snow leopards. Years ago, when the roads had not been built, some of the animals would come down the mountain. Not any more.'

This is no place for snow leopards, or the *yeti*. Mini-trucks stuffed with rafts overtake us, raising a film of dust that covers our windshield. A lone waterfall softens the landscape. We pass the Mangde Chhu valley, then Tsangkha village.

'Everyone at Tsangkha sings beautifully,' says Ugyen. 'It is believed that Goddess Saraswati has blessed this village.' He points to a local source of water: 'If you drink that water, you should be able to sing too.'

Since there are hardly any stops on our way, music plays on in the car. It is at times Bhutanese, at others, Bollywood. Ugyen prefers Bollywood songs that are soft and lilting, much like those in his own language. 'This is Shantanu,' he says, 'in a duet with Shreya Ghoshal.'

Ugyen is happy to sing along. So is Tandin, when he relaxes on a relatively easy stretch.

Just before Trongsa, an array of green-roofed buildings appears on the mountain range on the other side of the valley. 'That is the University of Language and Cultural Sciences,' says Ugyen. He points to a speck of white atop a high mountain: 'That is where we are going, that is the Yotong La.'

It seems far above us, the end of the world.

We stop at Trongsa for lunch; have a roadside view of the Trongsa Dzong and its watchtower.

Yotong La (11,155 ft) is marked by: a chorten at the centre of the road; numerous prayer flags; two large banners with photos of the Fourth King and of the Fifth King with his queen; a signboard with a crude map that says 'Welcome to Bumthang Dzongkhag'. When we step out of the car, I discover another signboard that reads 'Thank You No Time to Joke with AIDS'.

No time for punctuations, too?

We have left the dusty road behind, but dense, fast-moving clouds are enveloping the pass. The temperature drops sharply, painfully. I am dying to return to the insulated confines of our car, but Ugyen urges Sumita and me to pose with the kings' life-sized images while he photographs us.

An hour later, tall pines part to reveal the Kiki La (9,383 ft), with a chorten that serves as a roundabout. There are no signboards with the name. Pine needles have turned the sides of the road into a soft fawn carpet, continuing to drop slowly, soundlessly, from the trees.

'This is where I was born,' Ugyen says suddenly.

'*Here*? On this pass?'

'Yes. I haven't shared this story with Tandin even. During the time of the third king, roads were being constructed from Samdrup Jongkhar to Bumthang. My father was sent to monitor the work. They had all camped at this spot for the night. My mother gave birth to me in the camp.'

Ugyen looks pensive in the dying light of the day. I make him stand near the nameless chorten, and take his photo.

Signboards of Jakar Village Lodge start appearing on tree trunks. Night falls by the time we check in at the lodge.

Young, pretty waitresses serving us breakfast the next morning ask about our plans for the day. When we mention Mebar Tsho, they have fear fleeting across their faces.

'Please be very careful,' they say, 'there has been an accident.'

At Punakha, Lhaden warned us about visiting Mebar Tsho, the Burning Lake. 'Just recently, there has been a mishap,' she said. 'A tourist fell into the lake. His guide too has gone missing, his body has not been found yet.'

'Yes, we know about that incident,' I tell the girls.

'There is a slope next to the Tang Chhu,' they continue, 'please be very careful while you take photos.'

They have noticed me photograph the Jakar Dzong that we see partially from the hotel lawns, the yellow-billed chough in a tree loaded with pink berries, even the broccoli and the lettuce patches in the kitchen garden.

'Thank you for your concern,' I reassure them, 'we will be very careful.'

It is a wonderful 10.5 km drive to Mebar Tsho in the Tang Valley, through avenues of golden-leaved weeping willows and pink fields that have thrown up a good crop of barley and now offer fodder to lazy cows. Chir pines replace the willows, and a magpie cackles in their shade. Wooden crates on a field nurture beehives in them.

A short downhill walk from the car park takes us to Mebar Tsho. Numerous *tsha tshas* fill the stone ledges by the steep dirt track. The frothy green waters of Tang Chhu flows under a wooden bridge, and when it comes out on the other side, it is a deep black pool.

Nothing stirs, not even the wind.

We walk under the canopy of a million prayer flags, over the rickety wooden bridge, and reach a boulder directly above the placid pool. It holds no reflections.

Guru Rinpoche had left many of his teachings, or *terma* hidden in Bhutan. Pema Lingpa, a saint from the 15th century, followed a vision and found a chest of such treasures in this pool.

The *terma* he found instructed Pema Lingpa to dive in again. This time, a lot of people gathered to watch. But the sceptical *penlop*, the district administrator, accused him of deception. An enraged Pema Lingpa took a lighted lamp and declared that if he were a genuine *tertön* or treasure-seeker, he would return from the depths of the pool with more treasures and the lamp still burning. If not, he would perish in the lake.

People waited a long while by the shore, but the saint did not surface. Just as they were about to leave, Pema Lingpa emerged with a statue, a chest of treasures, and the burning lamp. Mebar Tsho came to be called the Burning Lake.

Bhutanese believe enlightened beings can see the temple that stands below the waters. All we see in the clear pool are layers of boulders smoothened into strange, wavy shapes.

A couple of Himalayan blue magpies flies overhead. Tandin takes us from Tang to Chokhor Valley, a drive that has pleasant interruptions: a Himalayan wagtail watching us from an electric wire over the road; local people planting hazelnut seedlings on their fields; red chillies drying on cane winnowing trays on the rooftops of houses and on the bonnet of a parked blue car.

'Dew falls on the chillies at night, right, UD? Don't they rot?'

'Nothing happens to chillies,' Ugyen replies, 'even the wind does not blow them away. Gods do not like chillies.'

We get off by the shores of the Chamkhar Chhu, and walk along it to the runway of the future airport at Bumthang.

A black redstart suns itself on a weeping willow, and the bristly red sweet briar grows in hedges by the blue-green river. We cross the bridge over it to pay a visit to the 9th century Khenchogsum Temple and its sprawling modern annexe.

A lady farmer has put out a low wooden bench full of handicrafts in the middle of a meadow by the road to Kurjey Lhakhang. Two round, silver brooches near each shoulder hold her *kira* in place, and a *baelo*—the round cane hat—shades her head and eyes from the sun.

On an impulse, Sumita and I pose with her for a photograph. As Ugyen composes the shot, the lady puts her arms around our waists, pulls us in tighter.

Kurjey Lhakhang is an impressive block of tall buildings at the centre of a sprawling lawn. More women sell their wares near the gate, its brick-red and white pillars supporting a two-tiered pagoda-style arch.

Just inside the grounds, Ugyen pauses near a large white chorten with a golden pinnacle.

'Let me tell you the story of Kurjey Lhakhang,' begins Ugyen.

'Sindhu Raja or Sendha Gyab was a prince from Kapilavastu, and a descendant of King Shuddhodhana. Sindhu Raja was banished by his younger brother, so he travelled to Bumthang with 84 wives, 300 followers, horses and buffaloes. Bumthang at that point had very few inhabitants, and because of the Raja's large contingent, they thought he was God or at least a great king. So they accepted him as their king. He built palaces for his queens, and an iron castle. The castle came to be known as Chakhar—*cha*: iron, *khar*: palace.

'Sindhu Raja got into a fight with Naochhe (Big Nose), a rival king. Naochhe killed Sindhu Raja's son and 16 of his attendants. Raja was so distraught that he defiled the home of Shelging Kharpo, the chief deity of Bumthang. Shelging Kharpo was very angry. He stole Sindhu Raja's life force.

'This was 746 AD. Sindhu Raja was close to death. He invited the tantric master Guru Padmasambhava or Rinpoche to Bumthang to cure him. The Guru came to Bumthang and meditated. He left a *jey*, an imprint, of his *kur* or body in the rock. Kurjey Lhakhang was built around that rock.'

'Was Sindhu Raja cured?' we ask Ugyen.

'When the Guru arrived,' he continues, 'Shelging Kharpo hid in a cave. To draw him out, Guru Rinpoche made eight of his manifestations dance on this field. Every local god came to watch, but Shelging Kharpo stayed hidden.'

'Then?'

'The Guru then turned his consort into five princesses, each holding a golden pitcher. The sunlight fell on the pitchers and made them gleam. Curious, Kharpo changed himself into a snow lion and came out to watch. Guru Rinpoche transformed himself into Garuda and grabbed the lion. He told Kharpo to behave himself and restore Sindhu Raja's life force.

'Shelging Kharpo agreed to become a protective god of the Buddhist pantheon. As a mark of their agreement, the Guru planted his staff in the ground at this spot. That cypress tree you see has grown from the Guru's staff.'

'So what happened to the iron castle made by Sindhu Raja?' I ask Ugyen.

'It does not exist,' he replies. 'The king might have dismantled and taken all the parts back with him when he returned to Nepal with Guru Rinpoche. No one lived to tell the tale. It is said that Sindhu Raja and his brother were reconciled, and they lived in Kapilavastu in harmony ever after.'

Below the eaves of Guru Lhakhang—the oldest of the three temples in the complex—are the figures of a snow lion and a *jachung* or Garuda above it, legends frozen in time. Wind chimes ring out from the upper floor balcony, and prayer flags flutter.

From the porch of Kurjey Lhakhang, we see the golden roof of the Tamshing Lhakhang on the other bank of the river. Established in 1501 by Pema Lingpa, and formally called Tamshing Lhendup Chholing—'Temple of the Good Message'—it is said to be the most important Nyingma monastery in Bhutan.

Pema Lingpa built the monastery himself, with the help of *khandromas*—female spirits poetically called sky-walkers—who sculpted many of the statues.

Guru Rinpoche is seated in the inner sanctum, with Jampa or Maitreya, the Buddha of the Future, and Shakyamuni. The Guru looks upward, as if following the flight of the sky walkers. He does not wear shoes. A small statue of Pema Lingpa sits in a glass case in front of the chapel.

The upper floor is actually a narrow balcony that runs along all four sides of the assembly hall, and not much below its ceiling. 'Pema Lingpa was a short man,' says Ugyen, 'he built the balcony to match his height.'

Someone hastens past us in the almost pitch dark passage around the assembly hall. Something jangles. The next time he passes, we are able to make out the heavy cloak of chain around his body. This is said to have been fashioned by Pema Lingpa himself. It is auspicious to hoist it on one's shoulders and go around the path or the *kora* three times. The cloak weighs 25 kgs, so it is no wonder that the man is rushing to complete his *kora* and burn off his *karma*.

We are but granted this one life, the *karma* of our past forgotten, and our future unknown. Inside Jampey Lhakhang, three stone steps represent the three ages. The first signifies the past. This was the age of the historical Buddha, or Shakyamuni. The step has sunk into the ground. The second step stands for the present, and is at the level of the floor. The top step represents the future.

'When the middle step that stands for the present age sinks to the ground,' says Ugyen, 'gods will become like humans, and the world as we know it now will come to an end.'

The temple was built in 659 AD by the Tibetan king Songtsen Gampo, on the same day as Kyichu Lhakhang of Paro. They were part of the 108 temples built across the Himalayas to subdue a demoness. Jampey Lhakhang is believed to pin down her left knee. A computer printout hung from one of the pillars in the sanctum shows the body of the demoness, and the locations of the temples, though most of them do not exist any more.

It has been a long day. Sumita and I sink into the deep couches by the glowing fireplace in Jakar Village Lodge's dining hall, waiting for dinner. Ugyen finds us there.

'There is a surprise for you,' he announces, 'you have guests for dinner.'

It is Stephan and Laurence Barthelmess.

We have not met them since Phobjhika, and it is good to share our stories. 'You know, I managed some close-up shots of the black-necked cranes,' Stephan says.

'Really, *how*? Did your guide let you get near them?'

'Of *course* not. There was this field below the road, and some of the cranes had come a little closer. I got off the car, and slid down the slope. Got a couple of good photos. I will email them to you.'

Both Laurence and Stephan are a little unhappy with their trip schedules. 'It is always nine o'clock, never earlier,' says Laurence.

Don't we know that?

'And then they talk about this Gross National Happiness... how can an entire nation be happy?' asks Stephan, 'Don't you think there's something that they don't want us to see?'

There is something that I do see: It is close to 10:00 pm, much later than bedtime on the hills, and while the waitresses still stand at attention, their smiles are a tad frozen, and their eyelids heavy with sleep. We bid the Barthelmess couple a very good night.

Outside the dining hall, the owner of the lodge waits to wind up, too. 'This is such a beautiful place,' Sumita tells him, 'it must feel so great to live here!'

'The younger generation does not quite feel that way,' he replies ruefully. 'They wish to get away to the big cities, even out of the country. I wish they would go, too: only when they have lived a while out there would they learn to appreciate this place.'

Just out of curiosity, I would later look up the results of Bhutan's GNH survey for the year. This is how the Bhutanese saw themselves:

'Deeply Happy: 8.4%
'Extensively Happy: 35%
'Narrowly Happy: 47.9%
'Unhappy: 8.8%'

TRONGSA

Resplendant rugs hang from horizontal poles outside the Thokmed Yeshey Handicraft and Yathra Production Centre at Chumey. On our way from Bumthang to Trongsa, we stop by.

In the Bumthang region, strips of hand-spun wool are hand-woven with specific geometric patterns and a border. Called *yathra*, these strips are joined to make a *charkep*, a blanket, or a *toego*, the short jacket worn over a *kira*.

We seem to have stepped into a stocking just visited by Father Christmas. The red, velvet-papered walls of the centre are chock-full of bags, jackets, shawls, carpets, and caps. Shelves brim over with trinkets, Garuda masks, mouse pads, trumpets, and striking knee-length shoes to be worn by kings and government officials.

'Take a look around,' Ugyen tells us in low tones, 'if you like something we can go to the shop we have just passed. The same item will cost you much less there.'

That is good advice. I do like a woollen cap, and we walk across to the Sonam Lhaden Tshongkhang next door—to an unexpected welcome.

Near the *thrue tha*, the horizontal frame loom on the porch, a little bundle of joy clinging to her mother's back like a baby koala blows us a loud flying kiss. She is Pema: rosy-cheeked, honey-tempered, just a few months old. It is hard to take our eyes off her. Pema enjoys the attention, blowing us nineteen to the dozen slobbery kisses, and punctuating them with her smiles.

Pema and I have a 'who-can-blow-the-most-kisses' game. I lose, summarily. I buy a woollen cap similar to the one at Yathra Production Centre. The Fidel Castro style headgear would later lend colour to a cloud-dulled Trongsa.

Tandin drives us onward, past: flaming red Japanese barberry bushes rising from the slopes; sunny glades ringed in by chir pines; the surprise burst of prayer flags over a tiny, almost unseen rivulet; the Chumey Institute of Civil Engineering; a small field of mustard flowers like a yellow scarf fallen by the roadside.

'This is where Trongsa town begins,' says Ugyen, pointing to two rows of houses along the highway. 'Trongsa city,' he corrects himself with a smile. After we walk past six or seven houses, he says, 'and this is where it ends.'

It is indeed that small a town, but with two highpoints overlooking the Mangde Chhu: Ta Dzong, and Trongsa Dzong.

Ta Dzong the watchtower is now a museum built in collaboration with an Austrian team. There are 11 galleries in all, and as usual, photography is not allowed.

Sumita and I are impressed by the collection: the Mont Blanc Miguel de Cervantes #4810 pen used to sign the Indo-Bhutan peace treaty in 2007; a royal amulet containing medicines or relics; ivory flasks; masks representing eight manifestations of Guru Rinpoche; five Tathagatas; a *lhakhang* dedicated to Gesar of Ling; a temple dedicated to Maitreya Buddha; 108 volumes of Kanjur text written on pages of daphne bark held between wooden covers; a wooden dagger crafted by Pema Lingpa; the *chag kar* and *trimi,* containers for betel leaf, areca nut and lime.

The 2011 earthquake has damaged the walls of the museum. It has also damaged portions of the Trongsa Dzong.

'The earthquake had caused even more damage in eastern Bhutan,' says Ugyen, 'the present king had rushed there. The home of an old childless couple had been the most damaged. The king cooked dinner for them, and slept with them that night, in the remains of their house.'

'We shape our buildings; thereafter they shape us': Trongsa Dzong

The king had slept very well, says Ugyen, but the old man—worried that a pillar or a wall may come down on the king any minute—had stayed awake through the night.

At lunch in the watchtower cafeteria, we meet Laurence and Stephan Barthelmess again. Laurence looks shattered. She has just heard of a series of bomb blasts in Paris, and a gunfire outburst at the Bataclan nightclub and concert hall near Paris' Place de la République. At least 130 people are dead. The gunmen were from ISIS.

On the grounds of Trongsa Dzong, armed men stand near two cherry trees in full bloom. Arrows fly by the minute, followed by applause.

In 1541, Ngagi Wangchuk, a monk from the Drukpa Kagyupa religious school, and the great-grandfather of Zhabdrung Ngawang Namgyal, had arrived at Trongsa from Ralung in Tibet. In 1543, he had built a small meditation room at Yuling.

'One night,' Ugyen narrates dramatically, 'Ngagi Wangchuk had seen a light burning in the middle of a forest. When the monk had gone to investigate the source, Palden Lhamo had given him the vision of a fortress, and Ngagi Wangchuk had built the Trongsa Dzong to control east and west Bhutan.'

Trongsa Dzong—or the Chhoekhor Raptentse Dzong, meaning 'Fortress on the Tip of a Conch'—was later extended by Chhogyel Mingyur Tenpa, the first governor of Trongsa. The trail connecting eastern and western Bhutan passed directly through the fortress, and the *penlop* of Trongsa had complete control over all trade between the two zones, and naturally, the tax revenues.

'All our kings have to first serve as the *penlop* of Trongsa before they ascend the royal throne,' says Ugyen.

Stephan's guide has told the Barthelmess couple that some of the arrows shot from the Ta Dzong during wars had hit the huge cypress tree on the grounds of Trongsa Dzong.

'UD, is it true that some of the metal arrowheads may still be found in the tree trunk? The other guide has said that if you do find one, it is lucky to wear it as a charm round your neck.'

'I know of no such story,' Ugyen replies with a stiff upper lip.

TAKTSANG

Clumps of dull green weed float in a bed of water. This is no river I am looking at, but one of the food trays on the buffet table.

It is breakfast time at the Bhutan Mandala Resort, Paro.

'What is this green stuff?' I ask the lone waitress.

'*Churu jaju*,' she says brightly.

'And what's *churu jaju*?'

I can almost hear her mind whirring.

'It is... it is... (*light of brilliance in her eyes*) seaweed!'

The only other steel tray has fried rice. Looks cheesy. There are some bananas on a dinner plate.

'Do you have anything else for breakfast today?'

The smile fades from her face. 'No....'

'Simple things, something you don't have to cook? Bread, butter?'

By this time, another waitress has joined her from the kitchen.

'Y-yes, bread, butter possible.'

I push our luck: 'Maybe two omelettes?'

'Y-yes. Please wait at table. We get.'

Today, our penultimate day in Paro, we will trek 3,000 feet uphill to Taktsang Palphug Monastery, or the Tiger's Nest, 10 kilometres north of the town.

Legend goes that the fiery Dorje Drolo, one of the eight manifestations of Guru Rinpoche, flew to a cave high up on a mountain on the back of a tigress. The flying tigress was a form assumed by Yeshe Tsogyal, the Guru's consort.

A flying tigress. I am reminded of this conversation between Tigger and Roo in *The House at Pooh Corner:*

> *'And as they went, Tigger told Roo (who wanted to know) all about the things that Tiggers could do.*
>
> *' "Can they fly?" asked Roo.*
>
> *'"Yes," said Tigger, "they're very good flyers, Tiggers are. Stornry good flyers." '*

Guru Rinpoche meditated in the cave for three years, three months, three weeks, three days and three hours to subdue eight types of evil spirits. He then converted the Bhutanese to Buddhism.

In 1692, Paro *penlop* Gyalse Tenzin Rabgye built the first monastery around the holy cave. It is said that when the monastery was first built, it was anchored to the cliff by the hairs of *khandromas*, female celestial beings. A severe fire devastated the *lhakhang* in 1998, and it had to be reconstructed.

Tandin drives us to the base of the Taktsang mountain range. He takes a photo of Sumita, Ugyen and me. In the photo, the Tiger's Nest is but a white speck high up on the towering mountain.

Tandin wishes us luck. He is going to stay behind with the car, wait for our return.

This is the starting point of the trek: under a row of tall pines, horses and mules waiting to be hired swish their tails and flick their ears at flies; women set up little benches covered with red cloth and bring out ethnic jewellery from fat sacks; an old man sells trekking poles made of white, unpolished oak.

'I could do with a pole,' says Sumita. Ugyen buys her one, for Nu 50.

Ten minutes into the gradient, I am short of breath. That is normal: even a short flight of stairs at sea level makes me breathless, always has since childhood.

Sumita is slowing down, too. That is quite unusual. Ugyen is unsympathetic. 'You should not start halting already; we have a long way to go. Walk slower if you wish, but keep walking.'

Each step on the trek is a foot high, made of a long log placed on a row of stone slabs broken from use, the log and the slabs layered in dry, cream-coloured mud. Over us is a canopy of pines that keep the sun out, and the ascent is still gradual.

After a half hour of climbing, Sumita pauses again. 'I am feeling dizzy,' she says.

'Maybe we should let her sit down for a while, UD,' I tell Ugyen, 'she is not the kind to complain without reason.'

Before he can reply, Sumita closes her eyes, crumples. I rush in to break her fall, and we both go down in a tangle of limbs and down jackets by the outer edge of the uphill track.

In the long moments that follow, I have intense aural, visual and tactile clarity: my right forearm around Sumita registers her pulsating diaphragm; my right shoulder knows the entire weight of her head; I cannot see Sumita's face, but I watch Ugyen standing before her, his eyes locked on hers; I feel the jagged edge of a boulder thrusting itself against my left waist—I am pinned to it.

I have no thought, just the words of a familiar prayer going over and over in my mind.

A tourist rides by on a horse. 'She isn't feeling well? Put her on a horse,' he says, disappearing round a bend above us in a flurry of dust.

Ugyen still watches Sumita's face. Then he takes out his mobile phone from the pouch of his *gho* to call up Tandin. 'I think you need to climb up,' he says. 'We may have to carry Sumita down to the car.'

This, then, is the end of our trek.

We wait for Tandin. Sumita stirs, sits up. 'I think I feel better,' she declares.

'What do you wish to do? Shall we return?' Ugyen asks her.

'I think I will give it another shot,' Sumita tells him. She then turns to me: 'I am carrying the Diamox tablets. Do you think I can take one?'

It is a miracle she has the acetazolamide pills with her. We have had one dose last night, and that was meant to suffice against altitude sickness. 'I saw the strip of tablets lying on our room table this morning,' she would tell me later, 'and thought I may as well put them in my bag.'

Sumita takes a Diamox. I have one, too, for good measure.

'Let us set a smaller target,' I say, 'do just a third of the trek and reach the cafeteria. I know it offers a good view of Taktsang.'

We keep climbing. Ugyen plucks some Himalayan strawberries—Bentham's cornel—from a tree growing by the uphill path. With a skin like the lychee, though softer, the fruits are covered with dust.

'Never mind the dust,' Ugyen says, 'these are good for acclimatisation. Eat up.'

We eat up. The pulp is soft and creamy like an over-ripe banana and full of tiny seeds. It has a bitter tang.

An elderly couple is climbing down.

'Did you go all the way up?' I ask.

'No,' replies the gentleman. 'We were both getting a slight headache, so we have decided to return.'

It gets hotter as the day progresses, and when we finally reach the arch leading to the cafeteria, two hours into the trek, both of Ugyen's arms are loaded with our down jackets and Sumita's sling bag.

He still manages to look formal.

There are many Europeans at the cafeteria compound. A stocky man with a grey beard sits under a lawn umbrella gazing up at the sunlight cascading off the golden roofs of Taktsang. 'I have always been a smoker,' he says, 'this tiger cannot go up there.'

'Now that we are here, we should try climbing some more,' says Sumita.

'Let's have lunch then,' suggests Ugyen.

'We would rather not, UD,' we tell him, 'best to climb light.'

We buy mineral water, refill our bottles and continue.

An hour and a half later, we are on the peak of the mountain we have been climbing. It is a location that offers: a stone bench for two; a direct view of the maroon-and-gold Taktsang Lhakhang perched precariously on a crag of the mountain opposite; the prospect of climbing down 300-odd stone steps and then climbing up 400-odd more to reach the monastery's portals.

A team of men from the south of India stands at the head of the steps. They do not have a guide, and Ugyen is glad to have them as his audience. He plucks off some leaves from a small shrub growing on the slope. 'This is Artemisia,' he tells them, 'lowers blood pressure.'

While we chat, a lady walks up to me with a question: 'What's your camera model, if I may ask? It's a Nikon, right?'

I answer in the affirmative.

'Please may I borrow your battery for a while?' she pleads. 'Mine has just died. Imagine coming all the way up here and then not being able to take a photograph of the monastery!'

'I would hate to be in your place,' I say. Lend her my battery and wait till she has taken quite a few shots.

'Would you also like me to take one of yours with the monastery as the backdrop?' I ask her.

'Oh no, I am happy with what I got, thank you,' she says, leaving as suddenly as she had turned up.

The steps are steep, brutally so. Ugyen says he has counted all of them once, and they are no less than 1,200. We start walking down.

In a little niche at a turn, a tea-shack offers butter tea and roasted rice. 'It is free,' says Ugyen. 'But it will be good for them if you leave a little donation.'

The donation is gratefully accepted.

We have not eaten for hours. Our stomachs accept the tea and the roasted rice with gratitude.

The stairs wind down to a narrow bridge over the waters of a gushing 196-ft waterfall and then it is up and up again till the monastery porch.

A peek through the gate, and our hearts sink. More steps.

The camera and the tripod are deposited at a security point. We take off our caps and sneakers and enter the sanctum that harbours Dorje Drolo's cave.

The cave has a door, and this is closed. 'It is opened once a year for the general public,' says Ugyen, 'usually around mid-July.'

'Where tireless striving stretches its arms toward perfection':
Taktsang or the Tiger's Nest

A statue of Dorje Drolo stands at the altar of the small room. A genial lama sits before it. He smiles at the three tired souls, and pours saffron-laced holy water into our hands. We drink some of it from our cupped hand, and wipe our palms on our heads. The monk rummages through the offerings at the altar, finds two persimmon fruits. Sumita and I give Ugyen one, and keep the other for sharing later.

In a long and narrow hall, a solitary monk sits on the floor chanting a prayer. On the raised altar that occupies all of one side, Buddha Tshepamey, Dorje Drolo and Dorje Phurba Yab Yum are resplendent in gold.

Despite the stiff, swollen and completely un-cooperating knees, we are happy to squat on the floor for a while, in the august company. Though we do not understand any of the sacred words—over years of constant utterance, they have rolled into one lone, seamless, fluid sound—the chant is strangely calming.

A slow, painful walk through the other temples reveals:

A large chorten that holds the bones of Langchen Pelgyi Sengay, a student of Guru Rinpoche.

An image of Dorje Phagmo or Mother Earth who had appeared before Sengay to bless him. Sengay had drawn the first image on a rock, but over hundreds of years, the sketch has been redrawn many a time.

A triangular cavity marking the spot where Guru Rinpoche thrust his *phurba*, the ritual dagger, while he subdued the demons.

A statue of Guru Rinpoche made by Panchadeva, a Nepali sculptor.

'Now that you are here, let me tell you something,' Ugyen says. 'Only those who were connected with Guru Rinpoche in the 8th century can reach Taktsang. So, you both must have known him, too. He put you through a test, but you have arrived.'

I think of Rainer Maria Rilke's lines:

'God speaks to each of us as he makes us,
then walks with us silently out of the night.
'These are the words we dimly hear:
'You, sent out beyond your recall,
go to the limits of your longing.
Embody me...
'Let everything happen to you: beauty and terror.
Just keep going. No feeling is final.
'Don't let yourself lose me...'

'About 15 trekkers did not reach the monastery today,' Ugyen tells us sombrely.

'What is *your* record, UD?' Sumita asks him, 'Has anyone travelling with you failed to reach the monastery in the past?'

'None,' he says, simply.

The return journey up and down the rock-hewn steps is excruciating. We reach the highest point of the trek once more. In the warm late afternoon light, Taktsang is aglow.

The light wind drying our sweaty T-shirts is chilly. A dog accompanies us all the way down the mountain, pausing just once for a photograph. He poses with full concentration—one ear cocked, the other flat across his forehead—refusing to look at us while Ugyen focuses the camera.

We have many pauses, turning to look at the sun-bathed Taktsang receding further and further away. And then we are back at the fruit-laden Himalayan strawberry tree.

Ugyen behaves like a schoolboy suddenly, heaving his large frame up the tree to collect a *gho*-full of fruits.

This is a side of Ugyen we have not seen before.

'For my younger son,' he says, blushing at our surprise. 'I will see him tomorrow, at Thimphu.'

I am at the end of my tether. My legs behave as if they belong to a rag doll. I notice that the tips of my sneakers are turning inward, threatening to overlap.

Sumita manages to match her pace with Ugyen's. While I bring up the rear, a black-faced laughing thrush shuffles among the bushes on the slope.

When we reach the car park, most of the temporary shopkeepers have left with their wares. Tandin waits patiently, anxiously, for us. He is immensely relieved to see us still walking.

The drive to the hotel is a silent one. Ugyen, older than me, is tired too. But the day is not over yet.

'Five minutes to pick up a change of clothes,' Ugyen tells us even as we arrive at Bhutan Mandala Resort, 'and then we all go for the traditional bath.'

'Er, UD, we are not very keen on going out again... couldn't we just rest?'

'Trust me, you will feel much better,' Ugyen says.

Word has been sent of our arrival. At the home of Paro's administrator, the baths are ready.

In a dimly lit room, tin tubs placed perpendicularly against dark holes in the wall hold very hot water. Large stones are kept in a coal oven until they are red hot, and then immersed in the water to keep it warm. We do not see or feel the stones, for the far end of the tub has a wooden barricade. The water is opaque with gritty mineral particles, the ones meant to heal our aching bodies.

'Shout out when the water starts getting cold,' Ugyen has told us, 'they will hear you and replace the stones.'

After us, Ugyen and Tandin have their turn at the bath while we start on a home-cooked dinner served by the administrator's family.

They join us a half hour later, and generously help themselves to home-brewed rice wine. For the first time in this unforgettable trip, *driglam namzha* takes a backseat as four friends share a meal.

'UD, how did you decide that I would not be able to do the trek?' Sumita asks.

'You were rolling your eyes,' replies Ugyen. 'I think you lost consciousness for a while there, but in the end, you were the stronger person.'

I have no issues with that.

The early morning return flight from Paro to Kolkata is a grand finale to our trip, with the clearest possible view of the Himalayas. For a long while, Mt Jomolhari, Jichu Drakye and Tserim Kang—distant but majestic—keep us company.

ARUNACHAL PRADESH

BHALUKPONG

'Why do you want to go to Arunachal Pradesh? My husband's colleague was sent there on work, and he faced a lot of trouble... there is so much of insurgency... anything can happen any time...'

That, from a concerned cousin.

'Do not try to combine two circuits in Arunachal Pradesh. For two ladies travelling on their own, it is best to stick to the Bhalukpong-Bomdila-Dirang-Tawang circuit.'

That, from a fellow male traveller on the Trip Advisor forum.

After all our journeys along the Himalayas in Jammu and Kashmir, Himachal Pradesh, Uttarakhand, Nepal, Sikkim, Bengal and Bhutan—no relative or friend had tried to scare us off any of these—it is a little surprising to sense such fear in a relative's voice and such caution in a stranger's. We do shelve the Ziro circuit for the time being: not from fear, but purely because of the extremely long and arduous car drives that combining two circuits would necessitate.

Hitesh picks us up from Guwahati airport, and will drive us through our trip in Arunachal. He is Assamese and speaks with the slight lisp I have often found in my friends from the north-eastern states.

Pp 386-387: '..the new soft-fallen mask / Of snow upon the mountains and the moors': Nameless lake on the way to Sangetsar, Tawang

Facing page: 'There is nothing in the world so irresistibly contagious as laughter and good humor': Monpa girls on the steps of Dirang Dzong

Assam roads are good. The over-200-km drive to Bhalukpong on this November morning, a breeze.

About 20 kilometres before Bhalukpong, we notice a man in fatigues and a helmet by the tree-lined avenue. Rifle in hand, he stands with his feet apart, his back to the freshly-laid asphalt, facing the canopied forest. At a fleeting glance, he seems to be watering a tree while he waits for transport. But Hitesh says he is on duty. Half a kilometre ahead, there is another of his kind, this time on the other side of the road. Also facing the trees, his rifle raised.

Then another. And another. They dot both sides of the road at regular intervals.

Though under control, the threat of insurgency is still very real in these parts, says Hitesh. The soldiers are on guard every day. When the shift changes, an Army truck comes along to pick them up and drop the next batch.

There are no other cars on the road, and for a brief while the mind runs riot with the prospect of an ambush. But we are past the forested stretch, and no insurgent heads pop up from the fields of abundant crop. The late afternoon sun tints everything with a gentle light no HDR software can master.

Soon, we arrive at Assam Tourism Development Corporation's Prashanti Cottages: safe, if a jot tired.

The day has not ended yet, and Hitesh is willing, so we offload the luggage and drive back to the road that has forked off into the forest. We find a forest office bungalow, and a handful of employees about to leave for the day.

'Do you conduct wildlife safaris?' I ask one of them.

'Pakhui Wildlife Sanctuary is on the other shore of Kameng River,' he replies. 'You need a boat to ferry you across. There is no wild life this side of Kameng.'

'But I have heard that you offer elephant rides,' I persist.

'Used to. The service has been discontinued: too few tourists. We have just three elephants left now. They are reserved for forest officials.'

We ask them about the Bhalukpong Fort, built around the 10th century by King Bhaluka. The Archeological Survey of India, Guwahati Circle, says that the fort is associated with first the Salasthamba rulers of mid-7th century, then the Palas who ruled Assam between the 10th and 12th centuries.

The ruins of the fort—brick structures and remnants of ring wells—should be somewhere on the banks of the Kameng River, or Jia Bhoreli as it is called in Assam. Not just the ruins, the remains of Bana, the grandson of King Bhaluka, are also said to be preserved at the spot.

The men seem to hear about the fort for the first time: 'Haven't seen any such fort or its ruins around here.'

Daylight is falling, and there is no time for a boat ride. Back at the hotel, we release Hitesh for the day and trot off to the local market.

Some of the quaint town of Bhalukpong is within Assam, the rest in Arunachal Pradesh. Pillars on either side of the road connected by an overhead arch shaped like buffalo horns define the state borders. At the Inner Line Permit (ILP) check post on the Arunachal side, soldiers casually inspect the tourist permits but carefully sift through the vehicle's papers for an opportunity to line their pockets.

The inspection does not extend to pedestrians—tourists or otherwise. So we walk into Arunachal Pradesh, buy a bunch of bananas, visit a tiny temple. Walk back to Assam, and return to our cottage.

We are in for an unpleasant surprise. Through a half open window, insects—a whole host of them in all shapes, wings and trembling tentacles—have invaded both our sitting room and the bedroom. Thousands are still drumming on the glass panes, waiting to get in.

It is impossible to keep the tube lights on, they fascinate the insects. Sumita and I spend the rest of the evening under the large mosquito net, with just the glow from a flickering television screen diffusing the darkness. Soon, most of that screen is a mobile mass of tiny wings.

By dawn, the invaders are all dead, from natural causes. The bodies are swept together into little heaps, then taken away. 'Never leave any window open at dusk,' the old sweeper warns.

Ours is the last in a wide arc of cottages around a lawn, and the nearest to the river. To our right, the forest is not half a kilometre away. Just beyond our balcony, a wicket gate leads to an embankment that drops sharply to a flat, grassy land. A winding strip of road through the head-high grass leads to the placid, green waters of Kameng.

Somewhere along this steep embankment is a shortcut to the river. I am about to consider clambering down, when I notice men, women and children squatting on their haunches amid the tall grass.

More than half of India's rural population defecate in the open.

That route to the river is not an option. It helps that the hotel grounds are a happy place, with an explosion of colours:

Flamboyant orange canna.

Haughty maroon cockscomb.

Yellow Mexican oleander.

Pink, soft-bristled rain-tree flowers wet with the morning dew.

Among the green, moist grass of the well-tended lawn dozes a pup. Starting vertically from his forehead, exactly half of his face is white, and the other black.

'I brought him from Bomdila,' says the chef-cum-waiter at the two-storeyed, thatched-roof restaurant that also serves up a great view of the river and the blue hills beyond. Right now that view is smudged with soft white clouds.

'I call the pup Bolu. He may be just a couple of months old, but a great watchdog.'

'Watchdog? Why, he can barely keep his eyes open,' I interject.

'Oh, he sleeps all day. We have a security guard who does his rounds of the cottages all night. Bolu keeps him company throughout.'

Hitesh turns up with the car after breakfast, and we drive a few kilometres to Tipi Orchidarium. This is not the best time to visit: most orchids bloom in spring. But the sprawling orchidarium does not fully disappoint. *Dendrobium nobile*, the purple-white national flower of Sikkim, is in bloom, and so are the *Dracaena fragrans* and the *Acampe ochracea*, while the pitcher plant waits to trap its first insect of the day.

For the uninitiated, photographs of orchids with name tags adorn an entire room. In another room opposite the glasshouse, a friendly gentleman is at his desk, willing to answer questions about the orchids. But he, too, has not heard of King Bhaluka's fort. 'There is a black rice factory nearby,' he offers, 'you could visit that instead.'

He means the glutinous, short grain rice that comes in three shades: red, brown and black. There is a Nepali legend about its origin. Among the common people of ancient China it was known as forbidden rice: because of its high nutritional value, only the emperor and the nobles could eat it.

The nutty-flavoured rice is a favourite with people across northeast India. We have had the red variety many a time, and I have so far failed to acquire a taste for it.

A more appealing prospect is to sit by the green, gurgling Kameng River we meet on our drive, the white pebbles and boulders on its shore smooth as eggshells. A cool wind blows inland, crinkling the water into gentle ripples at our feet.

Bhalukpong, ruled by the Aka tribe, was most probably named after King Bhaluka. But a soldier we meet at the border check post has a different story to tell.

'*Poong*, in the local language, means a pond,' he says. '*Bhalu*, or bear, would come to drink water from it. So this place was named Bhalukpong.'

He shows us the miniature pond in a grassy compound right opposite the check post. 'Aka Holy Spring Water Pool,' says the signboard at the gated entrance. Fish swim in the star-shaped pool of water.

If we wished to, we could go angling, or rafting downriver. Or climb the monkey ladder—a tall mesh of fat ropes—on the hotel lawns. But then, 'why should life all labour be?' We, the last generation of lotus eaters, take advantage of the absence of children and occupy the swings, swaying gently while we watch a butterfly flex its wings on a nearby bush. The sun's rays filter through the insect-riddled leaves of a peepal tree: 'The wound is the place where the Light enters you...'

Very late that night, we hear the watchman's whistle close to our cottage. His torch flashes once in the dark, and then he switches it off and walks quickly, but quietly, past our balcony. Bolu, glued to his heels, is quiet, too.

For behind our cottage, where the forest begins, a lone elephant is visiting.

DIRANG

From the large concrete buffalo horns atop the entry gate to Arunachal Pradesh, Dirang is five hours and a whole world away. On the road again, we pass by a waterfall. The road and the river glide along in slow, meandering curves. Pockmarked oranges hang casually from a roadside tree. Grey-blue clouds loom over the blue Eastern Himalayan ranges.

Dirang (4,910 ft) in the falling November light is a beautiful watercolour: ordered silhouettes of fir and deodar rising from broad mountain ranges covered in multi-coloured vegetation.

It is a painting carelessly smudged by clumps of wet, grey clouds.

Hotel Pemaling sits on a slope by the Chariduar-Tawang road. There is no electricity. The watery light of day barely comes in through the open balcony door of our room. It is cold. Not the dry, crisp chill we so love on the mountains, more like a wet finger running down the spine.

The generator will be switched on at 5:00 pm, says the notice behind the door. It is a half past five. The room-service bell does not work without electricity, so I walk downstairs in search of staff. Find a youth sitting on a stool outside the reception.

'Why don't you switch the generator on?' I ask him in Hindi.

I can see he understands the language, but something about me brings a smirk on his face, and keeps it there. He makes no attempt to rise.

Back at the reception, I find a slightly older youth stepping in for the absent hotel manager. I request him to switch on the generator. He calls out to the first youth, who walks in, still smirking.

'A light wind swept over the corn, and all nature laughed in the sunshine':
Corn cobs at Zemithang Village

'Have I said anything funny?' I ask the reception guy in English, 'Why is this boy smirking?'

'*Kyun has raha hai re tu? Bus aise hi*?' he asks the boy. The question wipes the smirk off his face.

The generator is turned on.

The sun does not appear the next morning. Dirang River winds its way through a mist-burdened town. The only bright colour in this landscape is the yellow tarpaulin on goods trucks lumbering down the rough road. A private car follows the trucks. A small boy looks up at me through its window, waves. I wave back. He is overjoyed.

Driver Hitesh takes us to a kiwi orchard that belongs to a local minister. We have permission to enter, provided we keep our hands off the fruits. Covered with soft brown bristles, hundreds of kiwis hang from vines loping along a low wire mesh that stretches across the field. They share space with sweet lime trees heavy with unripe fruit and blood-red tomatoes glistening with dew.

The road to the apple orchards in Zimthung village winds uphill past a cherry tree all ablush with pink flowers. But we are late. Every single apple has been plucked from the trees and must now be travelling in crates to large Indian cities. There is no dearth of the colour red, though. Porches and roofs of Zimthung's houses have little carpets of red chillies drying in the sunlight—when it gets past the consistent cloud banks, that is. The backyards have tall bamboo frames loaded with golden corn cobs.

Tapering black chillies hang like inverted witches' hats from creepers near a stone hut. On a bare patch outside it sits an old lady in: a red-and-white woollen cap; black slacks pulled up to her knees; and a hooded tee that reads 'California Berkeley', but was most probably made in China. Her legs are stretched out in front of her. The ground between her plump, bare feet is filled with golden corn cobs. She separates the corn from the cobs while two grimy little children, a girl and a boy, watch her idly.

'Some of this corn will be packaged and sent to the cities,' the old lady says. 'We will use the rest to make beer for ourselves.'

The girl is shy at first, but offers us a wide, beautiful smile as she poses for a photo: her eyes turn into narrow slits; her chapped lips are ready to burst at the seams. The boy, a snub-nosed toddler, decides to hold on to his frown.

In a Van Gogh landscape, red fields stretch for miles around us. We stop a villager and ask him about the produce. He plucks out something the size of a coriander seed from one of the red-leafed plants, and peels off its sheath carefully to reveal a cream-coloured core.

'This is the portion we eat,' he says, 'try some.'

It has a nutty taste.

The sun comes out for a second through an azure gap in the clouds. Tall strands of kans grass (*Saccharum spontaneum*) catch the light, the dull-white flowers waving in the breeze turn gold.

In November 2010, and in December 2011, the Zemithang region beyond Tawang had seen some exotic visitors from China: the migratory black-necked crane or *Grus nigricollis*. Some black-necked

'Rainclouds dragged down the sky': At Dirang

cranes had also spent the winter of 2013 amid the dense forests and rivers of Sangti Valley, 12 kilometres away from Dirang. Since this was another November, we could have a sighting.

At Sangti, the road cuts right through the tribal village. Multi-coloured Buddhist prayer flags flutter overhead, and the wooden balconies of two-storeyed village homes are bursting with loads of golden corn.

The valley lies below, blocks of green and matte gold fields dotted with somnolent cattle. But there are no black-necked cranes—locals call them tung tung ka uk—strutting among them this year.

Hitesh pops his head out at a villager driving his tractor and asks about the black-necked cranes.

'Oh, *those* cranes? Aren't here yet,' says the tractor-driver, with a somewhat sheepish smile. 'They will probably fly in later, why won't they? Sometime soon, I guess.'

After the tractor has trundled away, Hitesh blurts out the tragic reason behind the sheepish smile: six cranes had arrived the previous winter, and the locals killed and ate some of them. 'They eat anything that swims, walks or flies,' he says.

He thinks for a moment, then adds solemnly: 'except maybe helicopters.'

The sky seems darker suddenly. As we retrace the road to Dirang, a boy watches us from the first floor balcony of his home. He has lazily draped his upper body over the wooden railing, and his eyes are deep, dark slits.

He looks feline.

Kalchakra's 500-year-old Buddhist monastery, a bright red-yellow structure that sits a little way above the village, is deserted. Through the locked collapsible gate, it is possible to peer at the sanctum and the painted Buddha on the wall.

An old lady watches us from her balcony nearby. 'The lamas have gone to the *dzong*,' she calls out. 'They have a festival there.'

She means the Dirang Dzong, a four-storeyed stone-and-wood fortress built in the 17th century. The Monpa tribe was then under a monastic rule, and this fortress was the centre of all administrative activities. This was also a stronghold where the entire village population could take refuge in times of war.

War is a distant memory as we climb up the steep steps to the carved-wood threshold of the *dzong*. Two little girls are coming down the steps. They break into shy smiles and hold hands for a photo, doubling over with laughter once it is done.

There seems to be an entire village inside the *dzong*. Little houses surround an open patio that is a beehive of activity this morning. Mahayana Buddhist Monpas are celebrating an annual festival.

Veteran monks welcome us into a small sanctum, where young lamas play long, slender brass trumpets: their round red cheeks tight with air. We sit down on the floor next to them. Now, their eyes are round, too.

The porch has benches along the wall, filled with Monpa men. At the centre of the porch, masked youth dance intermittently, and the children have a ball. Women squat on the wooden stairs of their homes and watch with indulgent smiles.

Behind the anonymity of the masks, the youths pose jauntily for a photograph, and then it is time for the children to pose. They huddle together, some flashing a victory sign, some a gap-toothed smile.

With the shutter going off, the children surge towards us, cheering, jostling; laughing their heads off. It is the most beautiful sound I have heard.

TAWANG

Half-way into our trip to Arunachal, the dullness of the day fails to surprise. The mountain tops are crowned with lowering grey clouds as we bid adieu to Dirang and set out for Tawang.

Four kilometres into the drive, we are looking at a minor mudslide from the slopes to our left. A bright-green hydraulic excavator crawls on the slope at a precarious angle, slowly lifting and sorting the rust-brown clumps of clay with its claw. Somehow, it reminds me of a praying mantis.

This is where we get off the road and take the winding staircase down to the hot spring.

'Water with medicinal values...' says a signboard placed by the Arunachal Government, 'Have a refreshing ba....' The rest of the text is obscured by a callously slapped on 'missing person' poster. Quite useless, that: the photograph portion has been peeled off deliberately.

In a small concrete hut, a prayer wheel turns ceaselessly with the gushing spring. Water comes out of the hut through a pipe: it is warm to the touch.

Before it merges with Dirang River, the hot spring also flows into two open-air baths built into an adjacent cemented dais. One of them is unoccupied. Gentle bubbles pop in the sulphur-rich water. In the other, a local man in black shorts lies spread-eagled, his arms around his two small sons. Three heads bob above the warm, clear water, the half-submerged necks creating odd, flamingo angles with the fluid surface while the owners fix their indifferent gaze upon us.

We are the ones embarrassed. We step back, out of their sight. The Dirang River flows below the hill, and the valley on its other shore is bright with a maroon crop. Even as we watch, a truck drives across the gentle stream.

At the Nyukmadong War Memorial, tall prayer flags and deep green conifers silently watch over a white-and-gold chorten. Not a leaf stirs, not a bird calls. This is the battleground where the 62 Infantry Brigade died fighting Chinese forces on November 18, 1962.

Visibility gets progressively worse. It is down to 20 feet as we reach the colourful gateway of Se La, a pass at 13,700 ft, and the entry-point to Tawang.

There is just one teashop, which offers to serve up a bowl of noodles and some hot coffee. The shop interior is warm; the kitchen warmer, thanks to the stove alight at its centre. Young men sit around the stove—motley crowd of drivers and tourists—and warm the cockles of their heart with readily available beer.

Buying the noodle-and-coffee brunch at the shop allows us access to the shop's small, padlocked Indian toilet. Within, the water in the bucket is completely frozen, and threatens to pop out in the shape of its container.

The dun-coloured grass on its shores barely marks out the boundaries of Sela Lake, named Paradise Lake for its beauty. The rest is a bowl of mist, beyond which rises the dark-brown hump of a hill.

It could also be Nessie.

The monstrosity of war also creates a hotbed for heroes. The Chinese invasion of Arunachal Pradesh in the winter of 1962 witnessed the bravery of Rifleman Jaswant Singh Rawat, of the 4th Battalion of Garhwal Rifles Infantry Regiment.

His battalion had been instructed to fall back from the Indian Army post of Nuranang—21 kilometres from Se La, and at an altitude of 10,000 feet. But Jaswant Singh, helped by Lance Naik Trilok Singh Negi, and Rifleman Gopal Singh Gusain, snatched a medium machine gun mounted by the Chinese and held on to his post for 72 hours.

He killed 300 Chinese soldiers.

History blends with legend as locals speak of Sela and Nura, two girls who helped carry the ammunition as Jaswant Singh moved from bunker to bunker so the Chinese would not know they were fighting a lone soldier.

Rawat was severely injured by enemy bullets, captured and hanged by the Chinese. Sela and Nura committed suicide. The enraged enemy cut off Rawat's head and carried it back with them. After the ceasefire, the Chinese commander acknowledged Rawat's heroism, and returned the head, along with a brass bust of the soldier.

Jaswant Singh Rawat was awarded the Maha Vir Chakra after his death. Rifleman Gopal Singh Gusain and Lance Naik Trilok Singh Negi were awarded the Vir Chakra, the latter posthumously.

The bust gifted by the Chinese stands at the core of the war memorial on the battle venue, now named Jaswantgarh. The rifleman's personal belongings share the space.

The war memorial is a sombre place. The pillars and plaques are painted to resemble Indian Army fatigues. Slightly damp walls hold a visual history: crude maps that show the position of the Chinese and Indian armies in the battle that had spread across Thagla, Bomdila, and Namka Chhu.

A truckload of soldiers arrive, and the young men jostle one another at the local shop-cum-canteen that stores Army fatigues and souvenirs. We order some tea and samosas. A furry dog licks at the little stream of milky tea spilled near a bin. Since there are no biscuits at the canteen, I buy a samosa for the dog and place it near him. He sniffs at it and looks up at me expectantly. I do not know what he wants. A soldier has been watching me. When he catches my eye, he motions to me to break the samosa into small portions. I do it. The dog starts eating.

In Arunachal, most names have a ring to them: Bhalukpong, Dirang, Tawang. Gakyi Khang Zhang, the name of our hotel in Tawang, has a ring to it, too. *Gakyi khang zhang*: the zone of ultimate comfort, in Tibetan.

'All Heaven and Earth/Flowered white obliterate.../Snow...unceasing snow':
Gateway near Sela Lake, Tawang

BRO

'The sorrows of your changing face': Nun at Ani Gompa of Tawang

'Ultimate comfort' in a remote, high-altitude town—Tawang is at 10,000 feet—comes in the shape of: a flat-screen television, a room heater that actually works, drinking water served boiling hot in a flask, and a Boy Friday named Chhotu at the tourists' beck-and-call.

Power supply is intermittent, though, and the evening is interspersed by moments of complete darkness. During one such moment, we discover that the concentric circles printed on the cover of our blanket are fluorescent. Later, when I am in bed for the night and there is a flash of light in my left eye, I attribute it to visual retention of the fluorescent image.

It is the first warning of macular degeneration.

At dawn, the room window frames the red-and-gold Gaden Namgyal Lhatse or Tawang Monastery perched atop a distant hill. A significant seat of Mahayana Buddhism, this Gelukpa monastery was founded in the 17th century by Merak Lama Lodre Gyatso, considered a contemporary of the fifth Dalai Lama.

It is India's largest monastery, Asia's second largest, and administers 17 *gompas*.

The view from the monastery is no less than the view of the monastery. The entire Tawang Chhu Valley spreads out before us with its layered, complex growth, tin-roofed one-storey houses cheek-a-jowl with multi-storeyed hotels and tall columns of unfinished structures. At the farthest point in the valley, close to the horizon fast filling with rain clouds is an unfinished story: a huge, copper statue of the Buddha being built bit by painstaking bit. A sliver of sunlight escapes through the clouds. The copper gleams.

The Buddha in Tawang Monastery's assembly hall is golden, true to the legend that this Shakya prince was born with limbs that shone like the sun. The statue is an impressive 28 feet tall. His right palm is in the *bhumisparsha* mudra: touching the earth. Just before his enlightenment, the ascetic prince had touched the ground with his slender fingers and invoked the earth goddess to witness his transformation into the Buddha. The earth shook in response, and the demons tormenting him fled.

The statue bears the customary bump on the top of the head known as *ushnisha*: it signifies wisdom, spirituality and enlightenment.

Right across the porch is the monastery museum, with its plethora of antiques. Dha Zhu, a 17th century tiny bow-and-arrow set made of shining metal draws attention. Gyalwa Tsangyang Gyatso used to play with this as a boy. He was the sixth Dalai Lama, perhaps the most controversial of them all.

The monastery library is what we visit last. Its polished wooden racks hold a delightful array of well-labelled tomes. I find:

Three fat volumes of *The Jatakas*.

An English translation of *Caraka Samhita*.

Jawaharlal Nehru's *Glimpses of World History*.

Books by the current Dalai Lama.

Books on Tenzing Norgay.

Enid Blyton's *Mister Meddle's Muddles*.

When it comes to locating the Thukje Chueling Nunnery or Ani Gompa, directions from teashops are totally muddling. After quite a few twists and turns, we come upon the cluster of yellow-roofed cottages piled on a hillock nine kilometres away from Tawang town. It is home to some 45 Anis, as Buddhist nuns are locally called.

A smart drizzle pursues us as we walk the maze of narrow lanes between cottages to reach the monastery porch. Inside, the nuns are at their daily prayer. They sit in two rows, facing one another. Their heads are neatly shaved. Red bands go round their fair foreheads, and are tucked behind the ear. Each has a prayer book—a handful of unbound rectangular leaves in red or yellow satin wraps—open over a low, wooden stool. The red bands slip occasionally over their eyes as they chant aloud: the nuns do not tuck them back in place.

At a break in the prayer session, butter tea is served, in polished wooden bowls that have ornate silver lids. We are offered tea too: in prosaic, ceramic mugs.

The nuns surround us, curious about our lives.

'You have a family back home, husband, children..?'

'No, we are single, too,' Sumita says.

They stare at us with a glance that is disbelieving at first, then a silent question: but you had the option..?

> *'...their eyes betray the sadness that even they don't know they carry in their soul.'*

The rain has stopped. We say goodbye. The nuns resume their prayers.

Under a sunset-flushed sky, we reach the Tawang War Memorial. The 40-ft Namgyal Chorten was built in memory of the 2420 soldiers who had died in the Sino-Indian War of 1962.

There is still some time for the light-and-sound show organised by the Indian Army to begin, enough for a quick look at the little handicrafts store. Picking up a turquoise-coloured bust of Tara Devi, I ask the young soldier manning the sales counter where he is from.

'Kerala,' he says.

'I have a quite a few friends in your state. We are from Bengal.'

'I do not know anyone from Bengal,' he replies with a smile.

It has begun to drizzle. Dim yellow streetlights fight to dispel the ambient darkness. Three tall soldiers lead us to a small, covered enclosure at the back of the memorial. A batch of Gujarati tourists is seated already: all of them past middle age.

The 45-minute show offers an overview of Tawang and an emotional narration of the war and its heroes. The video is good, and the narrative enhanced by Lata Mangeshkar's songs. It is difficult not to get goosebumps.

As the presentation ends and lights come on again, the Gujarati tourists raise their fists in the air and chorus '*Bharat Mata ki jai*!'

While leaving, an old gentleman stumbles on the steps, falls in a heap. I extend a hand, but he struggles to his feet on his own.

His body language: inspired.

'Cannons are locks and keys of an empire,' says the red sign by the road to Pankang Teng Tso, or PTSO lake. An Army goods truck is parked behind the sign. On the mountain slopes lining the road, a lone man who could be a soldier on duty plods through the snow. The lake is a 17-km drive from Tawang.

Pankang Teng Tso could have been named after the pankang trees. Till 1914, the Tibetan Government used to collect pankang logs from the area. In summer, rhododendrons bloom around the water, and brightly-plumaged birds flit over them.

A lone brahminy shelduck now swims across the water that mirrors the frost-covered firs. It is a photo-worthy scene, and I urge Hitesh to drive closer to the trees. The car halts near a boulder with

'PTSO 12,946 Ft' written on it. But the clouds have reached the trees before me, completely shrouding their limbs in grey.

Plan B: I make Sumita pose next to the boulder. Even as I raise my camera for the shot, I sense eyes drilling into my back. Do I also hear the click of heels and rifles coming into position?

There is no mistaking the fear in Hitesh's urgent whisper: 'Ma'am, this is not a tourist zone. Please get into the car and I'll take you to the lake.'

'Hurry up,' hisses my model through half-closed lips, 'we're being watched.'

I still take the shot, making sure not to include the Army bunkers that I have just noticed in my composition. Turn on my heels slowly.

A huddle of soldiers is still eyeing us three, but their stance has now relaxed. Fussing under his breath at my stubbornness, Hitesh reverses the car, and parks it next to the lake.

Stunted rhododendron trees stand by the PTSO, their branches and leaves heavy with snow. A string of multi-hued prayer flags hung across them adds brightness to a rugged landscape. A lone snow-covered peak looms beyond the rolling green hillocks popping frost-covered rows of Christmas fir.

It is time to drive to the other lake: Sangetsar.

But this is where Hitesh has his foot firmly on the brake.

'Nobody told me you wanted to visit Sangetsar. It is far, the road is difficult. It is not part of the travel package.'

No amount of persuasion and insistence that my deal with his agency did include a visit to the Sangetsar Lake can change his mind. We return to the hotel in a huff.

A phone call to his car rental agency the next morning and a promise to pay a few thousand rupees more—since we need to retrace our tracks somewhat—help.

This time, we drive past the PTSO and over a mud road edged by hills that are at times covered by snow, at others a patchwork quilt of yellow grass, red-leaved low shrubs and green rhododendron bushes. The colours change gradually, until all the hills are russet, brown and

Magnificent desolation: Sangetsar Lake, Tawang

black. And among the towering russet, brown and black hills nestles the Teesri Udasi Guru Nanak Dev Ji Gurudwara Sahib.

Guru Nanak's travels in four directions are known as *udasis*. On his third *udasi,* he visited Tibet twice. He went to Manasarovar and Mount Kailash in 1514, returned to India and travelled again through Nepal, Bhutan, and Tawang in Arunachal Pradesh to Lhasa. Images of Guru Nanak Dev are said to have been preserved in monasteries around Manasarovar.

Buddhist lamas know Guru Nanak as Guru Rinpoche of Amritsar, says the signboard on the road to the Gurudwara Sahib. In their welcome address for Pandit Jawaharlal Nehru in the 50s, the Chinese are believed to have mentioned that to acknowledge the great respect shown to Guru Nanak by their people, the city of Nanking had been named after him.

It is a steep, uphill climb to the gurudwara, so we pay our respects at the base of the mountain and drive on.

Ringed in by tall mountains, Sangetsar Lake is visible from the road much before we can drive down to its shores. Sangetsar, pronounced Sho-Nga-Tseir by locals, was once a grazing ground of Shok-Tsen village. An earthquake in 1971 turned the fields into a lake. All the trees died. Their frost-blackened trunks and boughs rise from the still waters: silhouettes of ballet dancers frozen in time. Brahminy shelducks swim past the slender trunks, occasionally flipping into the ripples for food.

In the late 90s, parts of the Bollywood movie *Koyla* starring Shah Rukh Khan and Madhuri Dixit were shot in Tawang. After a song sequence with Madhuri Dixit at Sangetsar, locals now refer to it as Madhuri Lake.

A yak grazes on the shore. Prayer flags flutter. The anglers' log hut is vacant. We are at an altitude of 12,000 feet and more. It is cold, extremely so.

As I compose a photo with Sumita and Sangetsar, I notice some old Gujarati ladies walking behind her on the cemented path that encircles the lake. I motion to them that they do not need to hurry—I can wait till they are out of the frame. They take my gesture to mean an invitation to join the shoot. Before I know it, all four of them have lined up behind Sumita, trying to keep their smiles from freezing in the harsh cold wind.

The photograph has all of them in it.

Returning to Tawang, we halt a while at the snow-covered Khukhuri View Point (14,615 ft) at the Y-junction, one arm of which leads to Bum La, on the Indo-China border. The road is slushy from partially melted snow, and the tips of our shoes get wet. A couple of minutes later, the water on them has turned to a crusty layer of ice.

Even with the necessary permit, a visit to Bum La in this kind of weather would be uncertain. Without a permit, we can only look for the pass among the distant snow-covered peaks in the bleak horizon.

The Nuranang Waterfalls on our return journey from Tawang is said to have been named after Nura, one of the girls who had helped Jaswant Singh hold the Chinese at bay in the war of 1962.

In a surge of white spray, the falls meet the calm onyx-green Kameng River. The hydro-electric plant next to it is a necessity. That does not prevent it from being an eyesore.

This was where Amrish Puri 'threw' Shah Rukh Khan off the cliff during the shooting of *Koyla*.

It is a good thing the cascading waters have not been renamed Shah Rukh Falls.

Hitesh suddenly speaks of a young couple who had come to Tawang with their little boy. Not heeding the altitude, and the impact it could have on an unacclimatised body, the boy and his mother had played badminton all morning. By afternoon, she fell ill, and by evening, she was no more.

Se La has seen more snowfall since we passed it three days ago, and the Welcome to West Kameng arch with its bevy of prayer flags is a jumble of colour among the snow-laden hills on either side. Even as I pause to take a photo, a black, furry dog comes and positions himself in the middle of my composition.

I let him be.

BOMDILA

It has rained in Bomdila.

On the terrace next to our hotel room, the round plastic tables and the chairs hold puddles of water. This dusk, the sky has been washed clean of rainclouds: all that remains of them are wispy strands of orange candy floss that change pattern with the nippy wind.

On the gentle brown slopes of a mountain now bathed in the magical orange twilight, Bomdila is a random cluster of houses, roads pencilled among them in a zigzag fashion, and bright yellow-roofed monasteries at three different levels.

The sky is a brilliant azure the next morning—a rarity throughout our Arunachal sojourn—tempting us to drive some distance towards Tawang again, in the hope of sighting Gorichen. At 22,500 feet, it is the highest peak seen from Arunachal Pradesh and the source of River Kameng.

But white, cottony clouds have settled above the tops of green ranges, just where the snow-covered massif should be. We drive on, not wishing to give up the chase, and reach 5th mile.

Dawa Hotel, a small eatery by the road, is a good stop for tea. Pot-loads of yellow orchids sit on the roof. As we sun ourselves by the car, hotel owner Sonam Chiring strikes up a conversation. His family has been here for generations.

We tell him about our quest for Gorichen.

'Yes, some days you get to see it,' Chiring says. Adding, with some awe in his voice: 'It is always covered in snow. We believe that the day the snow melts from Gorichen would be the day we meet our doom.'

The talk veers to the dirt roads. On our way to Bomdila the previous day, we passed a dangerously mist-covered stretch, and it did not help that the road was bad too.

'Our car had crossed President Pranab Mukherjee's convoy travelling towards Tawang,' I tell Chiring.

'In a few days, Prime Minister Modi is also expected to visit Arunachal Pradesh,' he says. 'The Indian Government plans to extend the railways all the way up to Tawang. Let them build proper roads, first, and then talk about railways.'

Tea arrives in little red bone-china cups, ornate gold-and-green dragons on them. But by then I have wandered off a bit and made friends with Mala, a local girl going to fetch water in a shocking pink plastic canister.

Mala shows me her house on the slope just opposite Dawa Hotel, a one-storey structure with a tin roof, cheek-by jowl with two others. Red blankets dry on her fence, next to golden marigold bushes.

Mala poses readily for a photograph, then takes a look at it on the camera's LCD.

'I look quite good, don't I?'

That she does. She has full lips, carefully tended, and her fair cheeks are flushed pink with the warm sun. The broad vermilion mark on her forehead and the red glass beads around her neck match a bright red salwar.

Gorichen eludes, but Bomdila's hills are resplendent with autumn leaves in all shades of red, gold, yellow and orange. The mood is festive at Mon-Bomdila, where the Gentse Gaden Rabgyel Ling Monastery or the Upper Gompa is holding the 8th Annual Events of Drubchod Chenmo cum Bomdila Torgya.

We are halted at the temporary arch declaring the festivities by a young, uniformed soldier. Sumita is carrying my folded tripod in its black bag, and this could be mistaken for a rifle. At my insistence—it lends colour to my photos—and much to her embarrassment, she is also wearing the rainbow-hued woollen cap bought in Kurseong. It has three rainbow-hued plaits hanging from it.

I cannot think of a single reason why someone in this slightly ridiculous headgear should arouse suspicion.

Whatever the trigger—speaking metaphorically, of course—the tripod is taken out of its bag and its purpose explained. The soldier lets us pass.

On a large stretch of land before the impressive monastery, local men and women sit on carpets. In the centre, a batch of very young schoolboys in blue shirts and red pullovers squat patiently, whispering into one another's ears. On the monastery porch, their contemporaries aspiring for lamahood do the same. Only, their heads are shaved, and they wear maroon robes.

The monastery is said to have been started by the 12th reincarnation of Tsona Gontse Rimpoche in 1965-66. It is a replica of Tsona Gontse Monastery at Tsona in South Tibet, established in the 15th century.

A golden Buddha statue occupies the sanctum. White scarves are offered to the chief lamas on the porch, and the chants begin.

There is a little fair, too. Outside the monastery, wares for everyday use with a predominance of woollens are displayed on cheap plastic sheets spread over the ground. Serious buyers inspect the goods and check out prices.

Textiles, *thangka*s, driftwood sculptures, woven cane baskets, embroidered woollen prayer mats and wooden furniture are on sale at the ethnographic museum as well. The price of the crudely crafted wood-and-metal tobacco pipe I collect there seems a little high, but I am sold on its quaintness.

ZIRO

For a good half hour, NH 52 seems to straddle the border of Arunachal Pradesh and Assam. On our left, the shop signboards say 'Banderdewa, Arunachal'. On our right: 'Banderdewa, Assam'. The shops and the people look alike, but for one detail—the people who walk on our left are slit-eyed.

Kimin is where we are officially let into Arunachal a second time—two years after the first—our inner line permit and our driver's papers checked at a tiny post manned by two men in uniform. The papers are all in order. But driver Trailokya still comes back fuming under his breath.

Is something wrong?

'They are so used to bribes from drivers whose papers are not in order, that now they ask every driver to pay them ₹ 100 anyway.'

Traffic rules, obviously, are not for the locals. At least three cars zoom past ours at break-neck pace: with no number plates. They are loaded with families. Moon-faced children paste their snub noses on the window panes.

We pass the villages of Cher and Potin. Cher: a row of banana trees lining our route, its houses unseen. Potin: spread along the wide and winding Ranga Nadi—copper coloured at sunset—flowing far below.

An hour later, we seem well and truly lost. The roads do not have streetlights, let alone signage. If lumpy stretches of red mud, often slushy in places and puddle-riddled in others could be called roads, that is.

Our car's headlights are abruptly blocked by a huge black shape, and a smaller black one. The mithun lowers her head to look at the car: her eyes red-veined, menacing.

The mithun—*Bos frontalis*—often called 'the cattle of the mountains' and 'ship of the highland', is said to be a descendent of the wild Indian gaur or bison. These animals prefer cold and mild climates, and thrive on forest leaves, shrubs and grass. An adult mithun might weigh between 400 and 600 kilograms.

The one confronting our Innova is closer to the 600-kg mark.

This cross between a cow and a yak is reared under 'free-range conditions', that is, it is allowed to graze in the open. It is a gentle species.

But tonight, this is an aggressive mother defending her calf. Trailokya slows down for an instant, and then picks up speed. Frightened by the headlights, the calf runs squealing to the other side of the road, separated from the mother, temporarily blinded.

We finally find our hotel. Our room is spacious, on the first floor of a two-storeyed building some distance away from the main reception and dining block.

There is a phone in the room.

'Do we dial 9 for room service?' we ask the guy who has carried our luggage in.

'Sorry, Ma'am, intercom not working,' he says.

'Is there a bell to call the staff?'

'Bell not working, Ma'am. You can tell me what you need now.'

Dinner ordered in haste, he leaves. Quite soon, we discover many other 'needs'. There are slits over the window frames, and the light in the room is inviting insects.

I refuse to have another Bhalukpong on our hands. We always carry some electrician's tape, a multi-purpose knife and old newspapers. I drag the only chair available to all the windows and the skylights, and, standing on it on my toes, stuff the slits with newspaper, secure the newspaper with tape.

Morning brings relief from blankets heavy with the odour of sweat from the room's earlier inhabitants. It also brings bad news. The water from the taps is so black with sediments it seems to have flowed directly over a coal mine. It is totally unusable.

'You see, this is the water from streams that flow over the hills,' the Manager explains to us. He speaks slowly, patiently, for he is speaking to women, and does not expect either intelligence or experience of mountain-living. 'It is *natural* water, we do not treat it. And it has also been raining, you know, so the streams bring in some mud...'

For the next three days, we go without a bath. Use mineral water to brush our teeth and wash what must be washed.

The first day is well spent. We visit a natural Shivalinga inside Kardo forest, a 20-ft high phallic boulder in an open ground ringed by hills, and drive on to Hapoli, the new township of Ziro.

Hapoli has a busy market: ladies sell fresh bamboo shoots; a gentleman from the Nyishi tribe proudly displays his machete and his headgear made from hornbill beaks and feathers; disembodied pig heads sit on butchers' shelves with their eyes wide open—death must have come as a big surprise.

Mudang Tago of Mudang Tage village is our Apa Tani guide. He meets us at the hotel the next day, and suggests that we begin with Hong village, 'it used to be known as the second largest village in Asia,' he says, 'but I am not sure of that now'.

At Hong, most houses are deserted. The women have all gone to work among the paddy fields. We do find one old woman on her porch though, busy scraping at the joints of a long, slender bamboo stalk.

'She will use it to clean the water channels that connect paddy fields,' says Tago.

'She has the traditional nose-studs,' I whisper. 'Please ask her if she will let herself be photographed, talk to us a little.'

Tago asks dutifully, and gets a volley of what we suspect are admonitions in fluent Apa Tani. But the lady does let us into her one-room home.

A cat crouches next to the dying log fire over which sits a jet black kettle. Above the fire is a two-tiered wooden platform suspended from the low wooden ceiling. The first tier holds shafts of wood, kept dry by the fire. On the second tier, a cane mat holds a spread of paddy, also kept dry by the fire. A little distance away from the second tier, though at the same level, is a third hanging rung. This is for storing pork. The smoke rising from the fire will keep the flies away.

Two is company: Old Apa Tani lady and her cat

A narrow wooden ladder leads up to a loft. In there, right above the fire, rice beer ferments in its heat. That one fire is also the source of warmth for the family sleeping around it.

The lady of the house has followed us into the room, muttering under her breath.

Is she still angry at the intrusion? What is she saying?

Tago listens, interprets: she hasn't had time to clean up, the house is dirty. And now she has guests.

The lady takes a small broom, furiously sweeps the floor, picks up a wooden floor plank and summarily shoves the dust under her house. The plank is put back in place.

I am still pleading for a photo, but I must pay for it.

'These photographers will go sell my photos everywhere, everyone asks for a photo...'

'Who will buy your photos, *anné*? You aren't even pretty...'

'Pay me ₹ 100, only then.'

'Fifty, okay?'

'Okay.'

She now settles on the low wooden stool I hand her, from her own stock of three. She squats, recovers her mood. Her cat sits with her.

'Who did the tattoo on your face, *anné*?'

'My mother.'

Local history says that Apa Tani women used to be so beautiful that they would often be abducted by men from the Nyishi tribe. So, when an Apa Tani girl was between 7 and 10 years old, her mother would pierce her nostrils and put in flat, circular nose studs. She would make a mix of rice water, ashes of burnt grass and coal, and smear this paste vertically across her daughter's forehead, nose and chin. Then the mother would pin her child down, and with a bunch of thorns hammer numerous tiny holes over the smeared area. Some more paste would be applied over the wounds.

The tattoo thus made would last a lifetime. The blue-black nose studs would be replaced with larger and larger versions until the nostrils were flared and the nose became drum-shaped. It would be a transition from beauty to ugliness, from danger to safety.

'Anné, didn't that hurt?'

Yes, it sure did. But she can now laugh at it. I show her the photos I have just taken. Enlarge them a bit on the DSLR's screen. She admires her photos, breaks into happy laughter. She seems years younger, prettier when she does that. Instead of the 50 rupees Tago had bargained for, I hand her a 100 rupee note. She gives us a wide, gap-toothed smile and rushes out with us. Her friends and her paddy fields are waiting.

The slight commotion has attracted the attention of a gentleman passing by the house. He carries a machete in a sheath slung from his shoulder, and an old-fashioned umbrella in his right hand. Even as we nod a greeting, he points to a mirror slung across his paunch. The glass is ordinary, a little hazy even, but the mirror frame is not.

It is the jaw of an animal, the teeth still attached, the canines blunted by death.

'Leopard,' he beams.

The *lapang*, a wide platform originally made of wooden planks, still occupies a prime spot in the village, though it might now be made of concrete. Each clan has a *lapang*. This is where the *gaonbura*s, as village elders are known, gather: for a festival, a sacrifice, or to resolve a conflict. The *babo*s, long bamboo poles standing next to the *lapang* and along the narrow village streets are a symbol of fertility. They also served as trapeze poles for village youth showing off their skill. There would be regular acrobatic contests during festivals.

'So, if we came here during the Myoko festival in March or Dree festival in July, we would have seen the boys swinging from ropes and performing stunts?'

'That does not happen now,' Tago says. 'Earlier, the father of every house would put up as many *babo*s in front of his porch as the number of boys he had. Even that is not done any more.'

'Why is that?'

'Well, folks think all this a waste of time.'

Not all traditional practices have been done away with. We are walking past a *nago,* a thin plaited pole with two bows at the top and a small circular fence at its base. This is where a shaman or a priest prays for the peace of the village.

'Priests can identify the problem a villager faces. Say, the spirit of a tiger is harming the village,' Tago explains. 'The priest will sit at the base of the *nago,* hold a chicken by the neck and utter prayers. The chicken keeps squawking and the priest goes on chanting. After a while, the chicken falls silent. That is when the priest knows that the spirit of the tiger has accepted the offering. The chicken is then buried under a stone inside this circle.'

The *ropihko,* a house-like framework of bamboo and the branches of a certain long-leafed plant is where heads of a monkey, hen or pig may be buried, again for peace. This structure is also believed to protect the village from evil, as well as any individual who chose to get inside it.

Walking briskly past us is a lady with face tattoo, but no nose studs. I smile at her and tap my own nostrils questioningly. She understands, replies with a yanking gesture followed by a tinkling laugh. She has pulled out her nose studs and thrown them away.

Despite her grey hair and wrinkles, she still looks pretty.

I point to my camera, smile: a photo, please?

'I am ugly,' she ends our dumb charade rather abruptly by rattling off in Apa Tani, and runs away.

Many of the older Apa Tani women have discarded the ugly nose studs. The younger women have not had their nostrils pierced. The Nyishi men are no longer a threat, and inter-tribe marriages, acceptable. But if a boy marries a girl from a lower caste, she will never have the right to dress in traditional attire and circle the *lapang* with the others during a festival. She will also not be allowed to smear flour on the head of the sacrificed mithun along with her husband.

The village may be deserted, but Kago Yamang seems to be doing brisk business at her small all-purpose store. A father carrying his infant son strapped onto his back buys lollipops for him and his elder child, a shy, fair girl. She refuses to look at my camera and clutches her father's hand tighter. But when I take a photo of her brother and show it to her, she breaks into a huge smile. I click her now, and the smile is wider. Only then we notice that she, too, is carrying something: slung across her chest with a little shawl is a pup, barely days old.

Kago Yamang has been patiently putting up with an unexpected photo shoot, and the least we can do is buy some toffees from her.

'Where are you from?' asks one of Kago Yamang's customers.

He is pleased to know we are Bengalis.

'I have been to Kolkata. You Bengalis cook fish very well. You have so many recipes, we can't cook all that. You mostly speak Bengali and English, don't you?'

'Yes, and a smattering of Hindi too,' I reply. 'But my stock of Hindi words is exhausted as soon as I am. And that is usually by 4:00 pm on any tour day.'

He is still laughing his head off as we continue our walk.

Tago offers to show us something unique: an 'egg garden'.

'We will need to take a walk. The road is slushy. Okay with you?'

'Why not? Let's do it,' I say.

The 'road', we discover, is a cappuccino-coloured muck track. At every step, our boots sink an inch into it, come up with a smacking sound. But we plod on. Halfway down the route, there is a low bamboo barricade right across the path. We need to get to the other side of the track via two low ladders placed as two sloping arms of a triangle.

The first ladder is made of four narrow slivers of wood nailed to a plank, at 12-inch intervals.

By now, our shoes have doubled in size with their huge additional soles of mud, and only their tips fit on the rungs. We still manage to climb to the top. The steps of the other ladder are made of green bamboo poles. They are smooth, slippery.

Sumita and I wobble on different rungs while Tago waits ahead. Just then, someone right behind us breaks into a peal of laughter. We are in no position to turn and look, but have sufficient ego left to scramble

'Faith is a knowledge within the heart, beyond the reach of proof': Egg Garden, Ziro

hastily down to the other side, managing to land on our feet. Just about.

It is an old lady who joins us, nimbly climbing down the same rungs we were on a second ago. She has a loaded wicker basket suspended from her head, and a long umbrella in her hand. Her basket is so heavy that she cannot keep her head straight, yet she looks up at us with twinkling eyes. We laugh with her at our recent feat, even as a happy mongrel jumps around us in the muck, and splashes some of it on to our trousers.

And thus we reach Myoko Agyang, or the egg garden. It is a small patch of land where strange altars have been made with sticks and wicker, and adorned with feathers and numerous egg shells broken into neat halves.

'A brother or a cousin builds these altars to pray for a sibling who is away,' says Tago. Eggs are broken as offerings. It is a quiet, peaceful spot, the silence broken by unseen birds, and the occasional mooing of cows grazing on nameless shrubs among the altars.

Back on the village road, we try to scrape off the heavy, sticky muck clinging to our soles. These have meanwhile gathered a couple of small pine cones, and numerous pine needles. Scraping is a difficult task, and the soles of Sumita's Nike threaten to fall off. We do not look forward to getting in the car with all this muck, but there is no way we can get rid of it.

When we sight our Innova, Sumita and I try to walk nonchalantly. It would have helped if we could whistle. Just when we are in Trailokya's line of vision, Tago hastily scrapes his boots on the pebbled road.

Trailokya looks at Tago's boots. The driver cannot believe his eyes. He tilts his head to look at ours, and straightens up stiffly in his seat. With a lot of effort, he retains a poker face. We slink into the car like naughty school kids.

At one end of Hari village is Hari Rantu, one of the oldest and most sacred groves of the entire plateau. Tall trees—they measure roughly over 100-120 feet and have matching 5-7 metre girths—line a green, quiet forest of pine and bamboo. Rantu Pussa, or the 'sacred trees' are named Pumin Pubyan, Yalyo-Yabo, Soki-Soli, and Sai-Taje, after the Apa Tani women who had planted them centuries ago.

A cone-like structure made of bamboo poles rises on the hillock just beyond the trees. That structure marks a woman's grave, says Tago. There are different markers for men and babies. Surrounded by rows of slender green bamboo stalks and lulled by a gentle wind rustling among the leaves, it is a serene resting place.

It wasn't always this serene. 'This is the path that the Apa Tani women would take on the way to the paddy fields. And this is where they would often be abducted by the Nyishi men,' narrates Tago. 'So the men from the Apa Tani tribe would hide on these hillocks and lie in wait for the Nyishis. They would fight to save their women, and all the blood spilled here over the years has made the soil red.'

Bright red dots stand out among the audience at the silver jubilee celebrations of Hija village. The *gaonburas* or village elders have turned up in the red coats given to them by the Arunachal Government, and are keenly watching young girls dance onstage.

The girls are in red-and-black mini skirts; the music is the Apa Tani version of Pop.

Elsewhere, on the porch of his house in Billa or Bula village, a shaman or priest sits weaving a basket from flat, green strips of cane. His wife squats by him in a woollen cap and a shawl of indeterminate hues. These have, like the couple before us, never had a wash.

At our request, the shaman agrees to tell us about the origins of his tribe. This is a difficult conversation: the priest speaks in Miji Migung,

The bridge across forever: The old Shaman of Billa village tries to pass on his wisdom to the next generation

the poetic language of the chants. Most of this is lost on the 25-year-old Tago, who can only speak the Apa Tani dialect. But the priest is patient, and Tago crouches close to him, his ears cocked like a pup's.

'In the beginning,' says the priest, continuing to tease the cane strands in and out of the weave with his inch-long nails black with dirt, 'there was Abo Tani (*abo* or *abu*: father, *tani*: human), the ancestor of the Apa Tanis as well as the entire human race. He could have been of any shape: water, or any other form. He was then transformed into a human being.'

Even as I listen to the semi-coherent but steady flow of Miji Migung from the priest, and its halting, poorly translated English version from Tago, I wonder how this old, illiterate man's knowledge about the origin of life comes so close to the scientific version of single-celled prokaryotic organisms.

'There was also the Danyi, the sun, which was born from Kollolodu, a single burst of ray,' the priest continues. Once again, his lore comes close to scientific data. The sun, as we know it, came from a supernova explosion. Supernovae explosions release cosmic rays that travel through space. It is impossible to believe that he or any of his teachers—priests from the same village—would have even heard about supernovae and cosmic rays.

But the story is not over yet, and I strain to gather the threads of the tale he is weaving.

'One day, an evil force called Burupucha trapped Abo Tani into a log of wood. Abo Tani had to pray to Danyi, the sun, to save him. He pledged to worship Danyi and offer him mithuns and other sacrifices in return. So Danyi turned his heat on the log of wood, burned it down, and set Abo Tani free. That is why, the Apa Tanis worship Danyi, the sun, as their God. We also worship Piilo, the Moon, who is a smaller version of the sun, as our Goddess.'

In the Roman Empire, the feast of Sol Invictus (Unconquered Sun) on December 25 was celebrated with great joy, and this date was later adopted by the Christians as the birthday of Christ. In what seems a re-run of history, sun-worshipping Apa Tanis are witnessing their younger generations shifting to Christianity. Church steeples dot the villagescapes. As a counter measure, white flags bearing a red sun flutter from tin-roofed bamboo-and-wood huts. Quite a few Danyi-Piilo temples have come up, with Sunday services.

Mudang Eliyu at the Danyi Piilo Meder Nello or the Sun and Moon Temple in Hong has just conducted the Sunday service. Sumita, our driver, guide and I were a part of the small congregation.

We seem to have drawn a lot of attention away from the religious hymns. A gentleman in a hat who claimed to be the Chief Advisor of the temple committee has taken our photographs with his mobile phone, asked us thrice where we came from, and has patted Sumita's back more than once in a totally uncalled for familiarity. Fortunately, he has left after the service, and we now have the opportunity to talk to Eliyu.

'Youngsters are turning away from the Apa Tani tradition of animal sacrifice,' says Eliyu. 'They are reacting to violence, the taking of another's life to protect one's own. So we are trying to bring about changes in our modes of worship. But we should not do anything radical, or we will have our priests up in arms. That would not work.'

Mudang Eliyu's first task is to know about every ritual and understand the reasons behind it. The absence of an Apa Tani script has made this task difficult. 'We are conducting workshops with the shamans and writing down everything in Roman script. Videos are being filmed. We are also trying to steer folks away from negativity by discouraging the practice of black magic.'

Eliyu has been accused of leaning towards Hinduism, for he lights a lamp before the image of the sun, rings a bell while he reads out the hymns. 'But the sound of the bell is a call to all the homeless spirits. That is not just a Hindu ritual.'

He is pinning his hopes on Ziro being accepted as a UNESCO World Heritage Site. 'Then we would have to follow certain policies to retain our culture. When you went around the villages, you did not see even one traditional home. Our traditional homes were built of straw. Then came bamboo, then timber, then tin. Now we are using concrete,' Eliyu continues. 'What we don't realise is that straw homes were safe from earthquakes, concrete homes aren't. And we live in an earthquake-prone zone!'

The lack of funds and necessary infrastructure, manpower and computers are issues too.

'The youth are all going away to work in Itanagar and other Indian cities. They do not wish to stay back and learn about their rich culture and history,' Eliyu says. He has taken up a humongous task, and is afraid there will be no one to carry on with it after him.

'But you simply must involve youngsters in your work,' Sumita tells him. 'Could you not take the help of the local guides like Tago, teach them their history and tradition so that they become invaluable for researchers and serious travellers? They will earn more as experts, and you will be able to pass on your knowledge to the next generation.'

The idea appeals to Tago, and Eliyu is visibly excited at this new thought. They decide to meet up later for a discussion, and Eliyu thanks us for our encouragement.

Elsewhere in Ziro, there are others trying to preserve and promote tradition. In Siiro village, Mrs Kago Kampu runs a successful homestay, and the reputation of her traditionally-cooked bamboo chicken has spread to Kolkata. Even though we aren't staying with her, we have managed to invite ourselves to dinner.

'It is a simple recipe,' says Mrs Kago. 'Boneless chicken is blended with egg yolk, and stuffed inside the hollow of a bamboo stalk. The bamboo stalks are then placed in a ring around a log fire, and rotated occasionally till the stuffing is cooked.'

But first, we have the appetiser: goblets of home-made rice beer accompanied by tiny bits of *tapiyo*, the local salt. The latter is so rich in iodine that none of the locals has ever had goitre.

Kago Kampu narrates how she has mobilised the village women to grow their own vegetables and sell these directly at the Hapoli market.

'We used to buy tomatoes from the plains, at ₹ 100 per kilogram. It was believed that tomatoes would not grow at this altitude,' Mrs Kago says. 'I told the village women that we should try growing them when it was considered off-season on the plains, for then it would be the right season for them up here.'

The timing worked. 'Tomatoes are now sold here at ₹ 25 a kg,' adds Mrs Kago.

The first time round, the village women were shy to take their produce to the market and sell them on the streets.

'There were nine women. I went with them,' says Mrs Kago. 'My brother found me at the market selling vegetables, and he said, 'Wait till you get home, you'll hear from me.' But I went ahead with my task. Now we have 875 women selling their products.'

We express our concern about the cutting down of trees—we have seen entire hills taken over for terraced Kiwi orchards—and the concretisation of houses. 'The Apa Tanis do not engage in terraced cultivation. It is the Nyishis who do that,' remonstrates Mr Kago, a civil engineer.

'Apa Tani villages follow a pattern,' Mr Kago explains. 'First, there is the *lapang*, at the core. Surrounding it are the village homes. Around these are the granaries, and beyond the granaries are the paddy fields. Beyond them, you have the forested hills. Those are the property of the entire community. Any one individual cannot cut down trees.

'There must be development in Arunachal too, just as there has been in other states in India,' he continues. 'We have a population density of 13 people per square kilometre and a huge forest cover in the state. But that does not mean we will be able to send any extra oxygen to the plains, does it?'

He is talking about climate justice.

Mr Kago is justly proud of the widespread paddy cultivation. 'Ours is not a riverine terrain. There is just this one Kile River, and that is hardly a river. Yet, we manage to harvest rainwater, and our rice fields are kept waterlogged. Fish is cultivated in the same fields, and they grow fast. The fish eat insects that would have otherwise damaged the crop.'

'You can spread your soul over a paddy field': At Ziro

Like an impressionist's painting, rice fields stretch for miles on either side of the roads through Ziro. From 4:00 am, women are at work, painstakingly planting each bright green sapling by hand. The water comes up to their calves, and their hands are caked with mud. Finely woven cane baskets slung from their heads with long straps carry their essentials for the day. An umbrella, usually the long-handled one, is a must have.

Fish the size of newborn tadpoles wriggle in the stagnant water in the fields. Many more are grown in a cluster of large ponds at the Tarin Fish Farm. The farm is a beautiful, serene place, with tall trees and verdant green grass lining the ponds.

The workers carry sack loads of gymnosperm twigs from one pond to another. They are eager to show us their load. Each green twig shines with small pearl droplets. These are fish eggs, the men tell us. With long sweeps of their muscled, sun-tanned arms, they throw these twigs into the waters. Each pond is connected to the next through channels, and fish can swim easily between ponds.

'What type of fish are you cultivating?' Sumita asks.

'*Koma kapey*,' the men reply.

'Sounds like an Apa Tani name,' I tell Sumita. 'Do try and remember that. We will ask someone the English name later.'

Sumita gives herself cues: 'You drink coffee to come out of a coma. There, now I shall remember *koma kapey*.'

Later, Mr Kago is the one we ask. He has a good laugh: 'But they *did* give you the English name. It is the common carp!'

EPILOGUE

It has been a love affair straddling 10 long years and many peaks. And the mind tends to forget: the first orchid we saw on the jagged bark of a tree, our first waterfall, the thrilled sighting of the first, unfamiliar pug mark. In the autumn of our lives, forgetfulness is seasonable.

Yet, even as I close my eyes to look within, I see the *lung ta,* Buddhist prayer flags fluttering in the icy cold wind. Five bright colours that break the starkness of the snow-laden ranges: blue, white, red, green, yellow. Each colour holds a word: Om, Mani, Pad, Me, Hung. I know what the hymn says: I bow to the jewel in the lotus.

We know the significance of the colours, the realms in the cycle of death and rebirth. I am no Buddhist, and I cannot envision my soul's visit to those realms. I am not sure I am a Hindu either, enamoured though I am by the idea of a handsome, trident-bearing God dancing on Mount Kailash, the snow blown like spray from his feet. Religion, to me, is as private as grief. Sumita, for her part, has always been a pagan. Awed by the force of thunder; overwhelmed by the might of an earthquake.

There, on the Himalayan ranges, we both have lived a religion. We have learned that a peak is elusive, yet one must always believe in its presence behind the clouds. Yearn for and climb towards that vision. We have seen how the fir survives the onslaught of snow by

---

Facing page: 'So consider carefully, what prevents you from living the way you want to live your life?': Prayer flags at Khardung La

accepting the load with lowered branches, while the pine resists the snow and breaks. We have watched the mighty waterfall stagnate in a pool and the gentle stream move on to meet its ocean. And we have heard the warbler in the shadow of the falcon's wing fill its present with song.

We have not discovered a new place, one that lay hidden among the mountains. Covered in aeons and aeons of snow, silent and beautiful. We have discovered a new place, one that lay hidden in us. Covered in the detritus of social norms; the dos and don'ts from our upbringing; the never-ending pursuit of goals. There, in that secret, silent glen, we have learned to listen to our souls, and be free.

Sumita and I are quite different from one another, very much the proverbial chalk and cheese. Travelling together, we have grown somewhat similar. Like her, I am now able to let go. Instead of chasing a bird that proves too swift for me to photograph, I sit back with her and trace the bird's flight with my eyes alone. Like me, she is learning to hold on to names: of birds, and peaks, and little villages by the roadsides. As each day passes, we are both able to live more simply. To believe more in the impermanence of life. And thus, to appreciate our today.

When a Buddhist dies, the family selects a crag to plant a row of *dar chor*, vertical white flags on tall bamboo poles. The richer the man, the more the flags. High up on the mountain, the white flags flutter against an azure sky, and the prayer written on them is cradled by the wind and carried across the somnolent valleys.

With time, the dead is forgotten, the riches are spent, and the tattered flags are heavy with grey dust. All that remains, and will forever remain, is a snow-blown massif that reaches out to an unbelievably blue sky.